RECOVERING ETHICAL LIFE

Jürgen Habermas and the future of critical theory

J.M. Bernstein

London and New York

First published 1995
by Routledge
11 New Fetter Lane, London EC4P 4EE

Simultaneously published in the USA and Canada
by Routledge
29 West 35th Street, New York, NY 10001

© 1995 J.M. Bernstein

Typeset in Baskerville
by Pat and Anne Murphy, Highcliffe-on-Sea, Dorset
Printed and bound in Great Britain by
T.J. Press (Padstow) Ltd, Padstow, Cornwall

British Library Cataloguing in Publication Data
A catalogue record for this book is available from
the British Library.

Library of Congress Cataloging-in-Publication Data
Bernstein, J. M.
Recovering ethical life. Jürgen Habermas and the future of
critical theory/J. M. Bernstein.
p.   cm.
Includes bibliographical references and index.
1. Habermas, Jürgen.   2. Habermas, Jürgen – Ethics.
3. Critical theory.   4. Ethics, Modern – 20th Century.
I. Title.
B3258.H324B37   1994   193–dc 20
94-12152 CIP

ISBN 0–415–06194–6 (hbk)
ISBN 0–415–11783–6 (pbk)

For Gillian Rose – for everything

'Yet the absence of imagination had itself to be imagined.'

CONTENTS

ACKNOWLEDGEMENTS

Acknowledgement is made to journals and publishers for permission to use material that originally appeared in a different setting. Chapter 2 as 'Habermas' in Zbigniew Pelczynski and John Gray (eds), *Conceptions of Political Liberty*, The Athlone Press. Chapter 5 as 'The politics of fulfilment and transfiguration', *Radical Philosophy* 47 (Autumn 1987). Chapter 6 as 'The causality of fate: modernity and modernism in Habermas', *Praxis International* 8(4) (January 1989). Chapter 7 as 'Praxis and aporia', *Revue européenne des sciences sociales* XXVII(86) (1989).

ABBREVIATIONS

Unless otherwise noted at the beginning of a chapter, references in the body of the text are as follows:

HABERMAS

JA   *Justification and Application: Remarks on Discourse Ethics*, translated by Ciaran P. Cronin (Cambridge: Polity Press, 1983).

KHI   *Knowledge and Human Interests*, translated by Jeremy J. Shapiro (London: Heinemann, 1992).

MCCA   *Moral Consciousness and Communicative Action*, translated by Christian Lenhardt and Shierry Weber Nicholsen (Cambridge, MA: The MIT Press, 1990).

PDM   *The Philosophical Discourse of Modernity*, translated by Frederick Lawrence (Cambridge: Polity Press, 1987).

PT   *Postmetaphysical Thinking: Philosophical Essays*, translated by William Mark Hohengarten (Cambridge: Polity Press, 1992).

R   'A Reply', in Axel Honneth and Hans Joas (eds), *Communicative Action* (Cambridge: Polity Press, 1991).

TCA, I   *The Theory of Communicative Action, Volume One: Reason and the Rationalization of Society*, translated by Thomas McCarthy (London: Heinemann, 1984).

TCA, II   *The Theory of Communicative Action, Volume Two: The Critique of Functionalist Reason*, translated by Thomas McCarthy (Cambridge: Polity Press, 1987).

TP   *Theory and Practice*, translated by John Viertel (Boston, MA: Beacon Press, 1973).

ADORNO

AT   *Aesthetic Theory*, translated by C. Lenhardt (London: Routledge and Kegan Paul, 1984).

ND   *Negative Dialectics*, translated by E.B. Ashton (London: Routledge and Kegan Paul, 1973).

CASTORIADIS

IIS   *The Imaginary Institution of Society*, translated by K. Blamey (Cambridge: Polity Press, 1987).

ROUSSEAU

DOI   *Discourse on the Origin of Inequality*, translated by G.D.H. Cole (London: Dent, 1990).

E   *Emile*, translated by Allan Bloom (New York: Basic Books, 1979).

SC   *The Social Contract*, Everyman's University Library, translated by G.D.H. Cole (London: Dent, 1990).

INTRODUCTION

Too regularly, the Anglo-American reception of Jürgen Habermas's thought has been skewed in the wrong direction. He is regarded, understandably, as a spokesman for a version of Kantian moral thought, with his notion(s) of the ideal speech situation or the unlimited communication community or the ideal communication community, titles I treat as more or less equivalent, as directly replacing Kant's conception of the categorical imperative in its universal law formulation. While this is not wrong, indeed Habermas himself conceives of his theory in these terms, it does abstract from the philosophical impulse orienting Habermas's linguistic and communicative turn. Throughout his career Habermas has regarded Hegel's theory of recognition as a continuation of Kantian moral theory in intersubjective terms; hence, salvaging the Hegelian critique of Kant has been as central to Habermas as has been his defence of deontological proceduralism. So, on the very first page of *Justification and Application: Remarks on Discourse Ethics* (1933; the German original: 1991) we find him saying:

> Whereas the communitarians appropriate the Hegelian legacy in the form of an Aristotelian ethics of the good and abandon the universalism of rational natural law, discourse ethics takes its orientation for an inter-subjective interpretation of the categorial imperative from Hegel's theory of recognition but without incurring the cost of a historical *dissolution* of morality in ethical life. Like Hegel it insists, though in a Kantian spirit, on the internal relation between justice and solidarity. It attempts to show that the meaning of the basic principle of morality can be expli-cated in terms of the content of the unavoidable presuppositions of an argumentative practice that can be pursued only in common with others.

The details of his theory of communicative action apart, the spirit and theoretical orientation of Habermas's project are ones I would unconditionally endorse, namely, to read Hegel's conception of mutual recognition as a realization of the intentions theoretically rigidified in the categorical impera-tive that avoids, or attempts to avoid, a dissolution into relativistic historicism.

1

This is how I understood Habermas's programme when I first read him over twenty years ago, and it has been the spur that has led me to continue tracking the development of his thought since then.

In part, at least, the essays collected in this volume attempt to measure Habermas's achievement against the standard implied by those terms of reference. And while my final judgment is that Habermas's theory is indeed too Kantian, too formal and procedural, because the theory's ambitions are philosophically sensitized by the demands of the Hegelian critique of Kant, it consistently raises what appear to me as the most salient and urgent philosophical questions. What gives Habermas's theory even more depth, and this is the second way in which his Anglo-American philosophical reception has been skewed, is that he locates his account of communicative rationality in the context of developing a critical theory of society. As is argued in the first and last chapters of this study, critical theory is best understood as attempting a theoretical synthesis of Marx's and radical liberalism's concern for the problem of justice (and so domination and exploitation) with continental philosophy's concern for the problem of meaning (and so the problem of nihilism). Achieving such a synthesis is a difficult matter, but, I would argue, it is the only one which in fact takes seriously the problems that emerge *directly* from a philosophically unbiased consideration of either of the two limbs composing it. Measured against the standard projected by this conception of critical theory, Habermas's liberal Marxism looks to have too abruptly dismissed the claims of Adorno's romantic Marxism.

Although written for separate occasions and for specific purposes, these essays do range over almost the whole of Habermas's philosophical career. Chapter 2 attempts a summary of the main outlines of Habermas's theory – with special attention being paid to the connection between his theory of the public sphere and his philosophical defence of the ideal speech situation – as it was prior to the publication of *The Theory of Communicative Action* (1984; German original: 1981). Readers already conversant with the broad outlines of Habermas's theory can safely bypass this chapter. In the third chapter I take up the idea of a science of self-reflection as it emerges from the Freud sections of *Knowledge and Human Interests* (1972; German original: 1968) – a book I still believe to be Habermas's best. Chapter 4 looks at a central moment in *The Theory of Communicative Action*, namely, Habermas's account of the 'linguistification of the sacred', which rehearses and defends the project of giving moral theory a linguistic turn through a consideration of Durkheim's idea of the sacred origins of morality. In broad terms, I there defend Durkheim against Habermas's critique while criticizing his use of George Herbert Mead's account of the 'I' and the 'me'. For reasons apparent in the essay itself, throughout that piece I frame and contrast Habermas's claims with those of Rousseau. A study review of Seyla Benhabib's *Critique, Norm, and Utopia*, forming Chapter 5, offers me the opportunity of more adequately framing Habermas's project with respect to Hegel and Adorno, while beginning a more detailed evaluation of his discourse ethics. The final two chapters both originated as engagements with *The Philosophical Discourse of Modernity* (1987; German original: 1985), in particular Habermas's critiques of Foucault and Adorno (Chapter 6), and Cornelius Castoriadis (Chapter 7), although Chapter 7 also evaluates the addition of a discourse of application to discourse ethics as elaborated in *Justification and Application*. I intend to take up the problems raised by Habermas's recent *Faktizität und Geltung* ('Factiticity and Validity') in a future study relating specifically to problems in political philosophy.

Except for Chapter 2, all these pieces have been rewritten for this volume, some so extensively as to make the original all but invisible, firstly, in order to provide fuller coverage of the philosophical aspects of Habermas's programme, and secondly, in order to make some of my 'darker' claims more generally accessible. Nonetheless, because each chapter originally did appear as a separate essay, and because my critical line on Habermas has remained fairly constant, some repetition proved unavoidable.

Despite their textual basis, all these essays are more thematic or problem oriented, argumentative, than exegetical in character; while the book as a whole eventually comes to the claim that the future of critical theory will require both a return to Adorno and a fuller vindication of Hegel's causality of fate doctrine – the version of Hegel's theory of recognition which expresses it in terms of the dialectic of moral life. A few words about these themes, arguments and claims is hence in order.

Chapter 1 originated as my introduction to six volumes of essays on the Frankfurt School I edited for Routledge's Critical Assessments series; hence its odd attempt to come to a view about the very idea of a critical theory of society without, as it were, favouring any particular version. After delineating the formal features of such a theory – a cultural Marxism harmonized with a non-instrumental conception of reason and cognition – I put forward two arguments: first, that the now very standard complaint that critical theory is too philosophical and lacks an adequate conception of the unity of theory and practice fails because it presupposes a contemplative philosophy of history which squanders what I call, following Seyla Benhabib's lead, the transfiguring character of human activity. This entails that what was really voiced in the original complaint was a call for more theory, a blueprint for emancipatory activity. And second, that the requirement for a non-instrumental conception of cognition and reason, under conditions of late capitalism, can only be satisfied if that theory is answerable to, and hence possesses the conceptual resources for reversing, Weber's diagnosis of rationalization as engendering a loss of meaning and value – the problem of nihilism. Habermas's programme, however faulty in detail, does match my formal model.

'Liberty and the ideal speech situation' originally appeared in a volume of essays, designed for undergraduates, in which different conceptions of liberty were each addressed in terms of Isaiah Berlin's distinction between positive and negative liberty. This essay ends with an unresolved consideration of the hermeneutical critique of the ideal speech situation: how can a norm be action-guiding if not a component of the immanent self-understanding and form of life of those for whom it is said to be a norm? 'Self-knowledge as praxis' was written at the same time and is more sceptical; it picks up and develops Habermas's criticism of the hermeneutic claim to universality and his consequent elaboration of a 'depth hermeneutics', combining inter-pretation and explanation, that was briefly sketched in the previous essay. My fundamental claim in this essay is that Habermas's analysis of the restrictions on theory confirmation for self-reflective sciences, sciences having the features of a depth hermeneutics, in fact leads him toward just the sort of trans-figurative conception of knowing and doing mentioned in Chapter 1. Thus part of the animus of this essay derives from the attempt to show that the text-book distinction between creation and discovery, which I claim underlies the less significant debate between idealism and realism, is misbegotten: making and finding are not different activities, but ideal endpoints along a continuum. When self-knowledge is the object of inquiry, the creative aspect of the endeavour involves not merely the creation of a new theoretical framework, but the realization of that framework in individual lives. This directly throws, doubt on any idea about universalist accounts of human development, that is attempts to separate the logic from the dynamics of developmental sequences.

Habermas's attempt to differentiate moral reason, as stipulated by com-municative reason, from ethical identity is precisely intended to keep the logically formal and the dynamically transfigurative analytically separate; that duality thus forms the target of Chapter 4. The argument has four parts. First, I contend that Habermas rushes past the central point of Durkheim's social theory of morality: it is explicitly designed as a critique of Kantian formalism. Durkheim's contention is that there cannot be a (philosophical or theoretical) deduction of morality because moral rules that are only logically binding, which is all a pure theory can show, are not moral rules at all. Second, Habermas's appropriation of Mead for the purposes of a theory of ethical identity fails because validity there becomes equivalent to authenticity, but that notion of authenticity turns on a conflation with the requirement that self-identity be autonomous or self-determined. Habermas's idea of our ethically being 'unique and irreplaceable' must hence give way before the ideal of leading an autonomous life, where the idea of autonomy is itself an uncondi-tionally moral one. Third, autonomous lives are for us necessarily the lives of citizens of a democratic polity, a self-conception that is at once moral and ethical. These three arguments are linked together by a general contention that social integration is a cognitive and not a volitional achievement; that the shift from cognitive to will-based accounts traces the historical evolution of nihilism; and hence that any theory of morality that conceives of the problem of morality as a problem of social cooperation in fact operates with a nihilistic

4

premise. It follows from these claims together with the third argument that belief in value pluralism must be both incompatible with the moral, and hence, assuming moral norms exist, illusory. My fourth argument is diagnostic; I suggest that both the idealizations that give the idea of an unlimited communication community its critical edge and Habermas's claim concerning the trisection of reason into separate spheres of truth, moral norms and the aesthetic-expressive *can* be reconstructed from the logical demands deriving from the development of modern natural science as the study of a subject-independent, natural world. If the rest of the argument works, then we should interpret Habermas in this way. I offer further support for this argument in the final chapter.

In Chapter 5 I first enthusiastically track Seyla Benhabib's reconstruction and Hegelian critique of Habermas, which in a sense repeats the line of argumentation of the previous chapter in another idiom and from a slightly different angle. Now a constant theme in the literature on Habermas, and something I return to in most of these essays, is that his theory of communicative rationality and discourse ethics, while unconvincing as a general moral theory, does provide a useful model for political democracy. Benhabib construes this as a direct implication of Habermas's appropriation from Mead of the idea of the generalized other. Following the lead of Carol Gilligan's *In a Different Voice* (itself a critique of the scheme of moral development elaborated by Lawrence Kohlberg and appropriated by Habermas), Benhabib suggests that the perspective of the generalized other be supplemented or complemented with a conception of the concrete other, hence a conception of moral awareness that is attentive to others in their uniqueness that permits a response to them not in terms of deontological moral principles but through concern, care, friendship, love and so on. This, Benhabib suggests, allows a return of the weighty comprehension of particularity that was the hallmark of Adorno's critical theory. So long as this return is just a matter of complementarity, then it falls short of Adorno's worries about the antagonism between the universal (the generalized other and the logically formal) and the particular (the concrete other and the dynamically historical) in modernity. Adorno thought that cultural rationalization had eliminated the possibility of making rationally supportable validity claims, to use Habermas's terms, about concrete particulars under conditions of modernity. It was this that led him to aesthetics: a discourse about a practice dedicated to the production and validation of claims lodging with intransigently particular items (paintings, poems, etc.). Hence, the revision of critical theory suggested by Benhabib, consonant with the claims of Chapters 3 and 4, can only be carried through by a reconsideration of the conceptions of rationality and cognition implied by Adorno's theory.

I begin this task lightly in Chapter 6. There I suggest that Habermas's misreading of Foucault and Adorno derives from the trisection of reason that keeps the universal (truth and moral norms) and the particular (aesthetic-expressive discourse as evinced in modernist art) apart. One tempting way, for me at least, to read this separation, which Hegel would see as the separation of phenomenology from logic, is in terms of Kant's distinction between determinate, subsumptive judgment and reflective judgment. The problem of judgment ties together both a familiar Hegelian criticism of Habermas discussed in the previous chapter, namely, how can the meaning of moral norms be determined apart from their application? (application being the work of reflective judging), with Adorno's attention to particulars. With some sense of how determinate judgments (Habermasian validity claims) require reflective judgings in hand, I claim that there is in fact an aporetic entwinement between the positions of Habermas and Foucault: Habermas offering us a morality of determinate judgments that refuses or is incapable of reflectively judging the objects of moral norms, and Foucault offering us texts focused on vulnerable and injurable human bodies in reflective judgings that imply but refuse the moment of subsumption and determinacy. Foucault writes books that are to be judged, like art works, while Habermas offers a discursive theory lacking concrete embodiment. This provides evidence for both the existence of the trisection of reason and its theoretical untenability. Needless to say, my entwinement of Habermas and Foucault is a speculative and aporetic version of the failed synthesis of generalized and concrete other surveyed in the previous chapter.

My conclusion from all this is that cultural rationalization has produced a *diremption* of universal and particular, generalized other and concrete other, the moral and the ethical, determinate and reflective judging, self and society. The notion of diremption (*die Entzweiung*) implies the now wholly unfashionable idea that the diremped items belong together as components of what can only be called an ethical totality. Clearly, no direct evidence for such a totality is possible; all we have to go on are its fragments and the way in which our experience of them *as* fragments, as components torn from some larger but indefinite whole, point to or reveal or presuppositionally imply that totality. One seeks to overcome diremption in seeking reconciliation.

The pattern of transgression leading to diremption, suffering through or because of diremption and seeking reconciliation would be a mere theoretical figure in this context were it not for two facts. Firstly, this pattern, the pattern of the causality of fate, has been at the centre of Habermas's philosophy from at least the time of his essay 'Labour and interaction', where he first traces the Hegelian critique of Kant. As I attempt to demonstrate in Chapter 3, it is really this pattern, the dialectic of ethical life, that governs Habermas's reading of Freud and, by extension, underlies the dynamic structure of self-reflective sciences. Secondly, in Chapter 6 I argue that Habermas's defence of discourse ethics, that is, his use of performative contradiction, as well as the theory itself, deploys exactly this conception of the dialectic of ethical life; hence communicative ethics generally can be conceived of as the attempt to restore the logic of the causality of fate at the level of language and communication.

6

This is the *ethical claim* of discourse ethics. Discovering this structure at the heart of Habermas's conception of communicative rationality has explained to me, if no one else, why despite its too-Kantian look it continues to exert a claim and an appeal. As I attempt to show, that appeal, and by extension the strengths and weaknesses of Habermas's argumentative defence of discourse ethics using performative self-contradiction, depends upon its being an instance of the dialectic of ethical life; but as only an instantiation which attempts to put communicative reason in the place of ethical life, not only is it open to obvious logical objections, but it covers over and disfigures its own ground of possibility. What is even more startling is that Habermas seems to be acknowledging this fact in his various statements to the effect that moral theories are only effective in rebutting other moral theories.

Could discourse ethics really be an intentional *mis*representation of the dialectic of ethical life designed for moral sceptics? It would be absurd to accuse Habermas of theoretical hypocrisy of this order. Far more plausible is the belief that throughout his career Habermas has been torn between allegiance to the full ethico-ontological doctrine of the causality of fate and the conception of the dialectic of ethical life it presents on the one hand, and a sense of both the inadequacy of the cultural means available for presenting such an account and the existence of a sceptical audience on the other. Defeating the actual and theoretical sceptics in his own culture is achieved by giving the dialectic of ethical life a Kantian and quasi-transcendental twist in a manner compatible with the original doctrine remaining untouched. If this is the hermeneutical key, as it were, to the unfolding of Habermas's theory, and I know of no competing account that would explain his curious, late disclaimers about the status of his theory, then these essays begin to offer back to Habermas's theory the ethical ontology from which it derives.

If in Chapter 6 I am seeking to illuminate how a bias of formal universalism disfigures the logic of reflective judgment oriented to concrete particularity, in Chapter 7 I seek to show how it disfigures a transfigurative conception of language itself. Hence my target here is the relation between communicative reason and the notion of disclosive truth, the linguistic equivalent of transfigurative praxis discussed earlier, as the latter notion appears in Castoriadis and in Charles Taylor in his debate with Habermas. My central contention is that language must be conceived of as possessing two axes: an orientation to communication (the dimension of validity) and an orientation to truth disclosure (the dimension of meaning). Habermas accuses his opponents of reducing communication to a moment of disclosure, but, I argue, it is he who attempts to make disclosure a moment of communicative interaction, and that in a way he must do this if communicative reason is going to be constitutive of communicative interaction and hence rationally binding. If, on the other hand, language does have two axes, then necessarily the claims for discourse ethics lapse. I complete this run of argument by attempting to show how the new notion of discourses of application, read against the grain, drives out rather than supplements the discourse-ethical moment of justification for moral norms, so rounding off, so to speak, my defence of the role of reflective judgment begun in the previous chapter.

Each of the final five chapters has at its centre an attempt to mediate or reconcile particular conceptual dualisms: creation and discovery in Chapter 3; ethical identity and moral reason in Chapter 4; concrete and generalized other in Chapter 5; reflective and determinate judgment in Chapter 6; and communicative interaction and world disclosure, or validity and meaning, in Chapter 7. Arguably, it is the last duality, between meaning and validity, that is explanatorialy most basic. In vindicating the equiprimordiality of validity and meaning, I thereby vindicate the mediations attempted in the previous chapters.

Properly speaking, philosophy belongs to discourses oriented toward disclosure rather than communication; what Habermas has provided us with is a powerful and complex interpretation of modernity. However flawed his theory, it seems to me more philosophically innovative and reflective than any comparable project produced in the past twenty-five years. If my critique of Habermas, which remains internal to the paradigm of critical theory, is anything like correct than its future will depend upon taking more seriously Hegel's causality of fate doctrine and Adorno's comprehension of the problem of universal and particular. One can find traces of each of those ambitions being pursued in Axel Honneth's *Kampf um Anerkennung* ('Struggles for Recognition'; an English translation is forthcoming) and Albrecht Wellmer's *The Persistence of Modernity* respectively. A phenomenology of modern theory that works *within* the dialectic of ethical life rather than being about it is to be found in Gillian Rose's exuberant and demanding *The Broken Middle*.

Originally I had intended this book to be a collection of essays on both Habermas and Adorno. However, the reader (William Outhwaite, it transpired) of the original manuscript noted that all my Habermas essays, irrespective of explicit topic, had a slant toward problems in practical philosophy; I noted that this was not explicitly the case for any of my Adorno essays. As a consequence, I decided to write a reconstructive essay on Adorno's moral philosophy in order to round off the book; once this essay had reached somewhere between 50 and 60,000 words, the idea of a single volume collapsed. The Adorno study will appear separately under the title *The Ethics of Non-identity: Modernity and Moral Theory in the Thought of T. W. Adorno*. A more sustained account of the causality of fate is in progress.

Acknowledgements here are easy. Seyla Benhabib has had a hand in three of the essays: her own thought provided the occasion for Chapter 5; she invited me to write the piece that appears here as Chapter 6 for a special issue of *Praxis International*, and she offered numerous suggestions on a very early draft of Chapter 3. My colleague Peter Dews has patiently listened to my thoughts on Habermas, critically evaluated them, and informed me of the latest twist in the theory with which I would need to engage.

I owe another kind of debt to the late Deborah Fitzmaurice. Our life together offered no boundaries between love, friendship and philosophy. In it the eros of thought and the cognitions of passion entwined as easily as our vulnerable, injurable bodies. For learning that from her, I shall be eternally grateful. Daily in our too few years together we argued over the question of autonomy; that Debbie's important researches on autonomy will now remain incomplete is a loss for us all. My borrowings from her work at the end of Chapter 4 are an impoverished acknowledgement of it and my debt to it and her. A fuller expression will follow.

My son Daniel's tolerance and patience with my frequent mental absences have now reached heroic proportions. His youthful enthusiasms and generosity of spirit continually reveal to me the depths and promises of everyday life.

I began reading Adorno almost exactly twenty years ago. That his thought has become so important for me, however, dates, according to my note on the title page, from 22 September 1978 when Gillian Rose gave me a copy of her *The Melancholy Science* over a meal in her flat in London. Gillian, this one, here and now, and for all the reasons you know, must be for you.

Wivenhoe
New Year's Day, 1994

1

CRITICAL THEORY – THE VERY IDEA
Reflections on nihilism and domination

The name 'critical theory' was not used to define the theoretical programme promoted by the *Institut für Sozialforschung* (Institute for Social Research), originally set up in Frankfurt-am-Main in 1923, until 1937 in an article appearing in the Institute's journal, the *Zeitschrift für Sozialforschung*, by its second director, Max Horkheimer. In his article 'Traditional and critical theory', Horkheimer attempts to elaborate how the interdisciplinary research programme of the Institute is to be distinguished from the 'traditional' paradigm of scientific knowing as a theoretical representation of a wholly independent object domain – the paradigm then dominant in both the sciences and philosophy.[1] According to traditional theory, scientific knowledge involves the subsumption of given facts under a conceptually formulated scheme; this scheme can either be a hypothesis that is experimentally tested against the facts or a correlation of the facts themselves. Overturning this paradigm requires denying that theory, the conceptual scheme, and fact, the world of objects, are fundamentally distinct existences belonging to forever diverse universes of discourse: 'The facts which our senses present to us are preformed in two ways: through the historical character of the object perceived and through the historical character of the perceiving organ.'[2] Horkheimer regards the socio-historical preformation of subject and object as the consequence of social labour: the synthesizing, cooperative activity of all labouring subjects.

Even this minimal statement of the purpose of Horkheimer's article provides us with some hints as to the meaning of the term 'critical theory'. It is not just more or better knowledge of the world that critical theory seeks, rather it portends a different form of knowing, a different sense of what human knowing is and does. Hence, at its most fundamental level, critical theory requires an engagement with central problems in epistemology and the philosophy of science. However, its treatment of this question, displacing the synthetic activities of the knower by social labour, immediately displaces the purity of the philosophical issue and submits it to historical accounting and reflection. Hence, a critical theory of society is one in which philosophical reflection and social scientific knowing are joined. This assumes that the most fundamental categories which shape human existence are themselves subject

to social and historical formation and determination. Conversely, if fundamental categories of human existence are historically formed, then representational construals of social science, directing themselves solely at social facts,
structures and patterns, inevitably suppress the self-reflective dimension of
both its object and its activity. The idea of joining a historically informed
philosophy with a reflectively self-aware and self-implicating social science was
meant to engender a body of knowledge that was both critical and practical,
both about society and immanently action-guiding.

All the leading critical theorists deny subject–object dualism as an ontological premise for all theory, and search for an alternative to the traditional
representational conception of knowledge that follows upon it; all equally cast
doubt on the rigid duality between philosophy (which, at least in modernity, is
a coded term for the knowing subject) and social science (representing the
object known), and thus intrigue an account of their entwinement or mutuality or interdependency; in denying, at least, the hegemonic legitimacy of
traditional theory, all are concerned to demonstrate how theory can be critical
and, more tenuously, emancipatory and practical. Underwriting and driving
these abstract characterizations of critical theory lies a shared concern for
social justice, and a belief that contemporary industrialized societies all suffer
from pervasive injustice. Characterizing the source(s) and mechanisms
reproducing this injustice is more difficult: in the first instance, Horkheimer
views this question in classically Marxist terms as a matter of domination and
exploitation; yet, even before the focus on class struggle began to wane,
critical theory drew upon conceptions of modern societies that figured them as
alienating, rationalized and reified. If we regard these last items as interrelated, then we might say that critical theorists typically fuse a concern for
justice with a concern for 'meaning', or, said otherwise, following on from an
understanding of the young Marx or the Marx of *Capital* conjoined with
Nietzsche (mediated through Weber), they perceive a connection between the
problem of domination and the problem of nihilism, where the terms
'domination' and 'nihilism' themselves recall the dual provenance of critical
theory in social science and philosophy. These broad concerns and orientations certainly do not define *a* critical theory of society, but then neither would
any alternative accounting, say one that highlighted the themes of materialism
(construed either in Marxist terms, or as an antidote to philosophical idealism,
or as referring to the significance of suffering and happiness as ground issues,
or as designating the priority of the object over the knowing subject, etc.) or
the attempt to integrate psychoanalysis into social theory.

Critical theory is not *a* theory of society or *a* wholly homogeneous school of
thinkers or *a* method. Critical theory, rather, is a tradition of social thought
that, in part at least, takes its cue from its opposition to the wrongs and ills of
modern societies on the one hand, and the forms of theorizing that simply go
along with or seek to legitimate those societies on the other hand. The oppositional movement of critical theory is refined as it engages with its philosophical

11

(Kant, Hegel and Nietzsche) and social scientific (Marx, Weber and Freud) sources, finding and transforming a tradition of thought for itself, and then, at a later stage, self-consciously transformatively reworking its own history.[3] Critical theory makes the reflective self-understanding of the theorist a central moment in theory; considering critical theory a contested tradition of social thought underwrites and furthers this continuously reflective dimension of its activity. Tradition, as here conceived, is inseparable from critical and self-critical elaboration; in forwarding a tradition, its guiding ideas and concerns are historically re-counted and theoretically analysed. Through the continuous interplay of historical and critical reflection a tradition is sustained. Throughout his career, Jürgen Habermas has sought to develop his own brand of critical theory in just this way, consistently engaging with the history of modern philosophy, modern social theory, and the first generation of critical theory itself.[4] My essays on Habermas proceed in this same fashion, guided by the belief that his critical engagements with, above all, the philosophies of Hegel and the leading exponent of first-generation critical theory, T.W. Adorno, however timely, however necessary if critical theory was to survive in changed political and cultural situation, are not decisive. A return to those sources seems to me to be now necessary and philosophically justifiable. But a return to those sources cannot be done directly, without, that is, going through their displacement by Habermas, and even more important, making that return necessary through a reading of Habermas's version of critical theory. That latter ambition defines the explicit aim of this volume.

In saying this, there is a large presupposition, namely, that the tradition of critical theory itself possesses a theoretical depth that makes its project deserving of continuing reconstruction, which is itself to claim that there is more in the project and tradition of critical theory than what can be extracted from the inevitably flawed character of any one of its explicit elaborations. Traditions, of course, are more than their component parts; but making a claim for a tradition of thought without supporting some explicit version of it must seem a peculiar undertaking. Nonetheless, such a risky venture is worth doing both for its own sake, as a form of self-clarification, and because it will provide a 'frame' of sorts for or a theoretical horizon within which my dialogue with Habermas can be placed. Persisting with a discussion of Horkheimer for a moment, I want to attempt *formally* to outline the requirements that a critical theory of society should satisfy, hoping to indicate thereby the scope of its project, and then link that formal set of criteria to the more substantive entwinement of the problem of domination and the problem of nihilism, hence demonstrating how critical theory's formal structure and substantive aims mesh and support one another. Along the way, I attempt to clarify critically what has been a constant sore point for critical theory, namely its apparent failure adequately to link theory and practice, and I signal some of the dominant themes to be interrogated in the essays that follow.

12

CRITIQUE AND PRAXIS

There is a familiar Marxist flavour to the argumentative strategy of Horkheimer's 'Traditional and critical theory'.

> But the critical theory of society is, in its totality, the unfolding of a single existential judgment. To put it in broad terms, the theory says that the basic form of the historically given commodity economy on which modern history rests contains in itself the internal and external tensions of the modern era; it generates these tensions over and over again in an increasingly heightened form; and after a period of progress, development of human powers, and emancipation for the individual, after an enormous extension of human control over nature, it finally hinders further development and drives humanity into a new barbarism.[5]

At first glance, it is difficult to distinguish the theoretical assumptions at work here from the account of the 'fettering' of the forces of production by the relations of production in the Preface to Marx's *A Contribution to the Critique of Political Economy* (1859). This line of thought, reading domination wholly in terms of class domination, which is itself construed in economic terms, gains further support when Horkheimer claims that 'the theoretician and his specific object are seen as forming a dynamic unity with the oppressed class', which entails that 'his presentation of societal contradictions is not merely an expression of the concrete historical situation but also a force within it to stimulate change . . .'[6] From these and like lines, we might conclude that 'critical theory' is but another term for Marxist materialism: 'critical' theory is the 'critique' of political economy.

Against Horkheimer's scheme a range of questions arise to which it would be all but impossible for it to provide answers. Why should we believe that all forms of domination are grounded in economic and class domination? Even if we concede that relief from economic domination provides a necessary condition for the joint overcoming of bureaucratic, sexual, racial and religious forms of domination, why should changes in the relations of production be conceived as providing the sufficient conditions for overcoming these latter since they each contain a specificity that is definitionally extra-economic? How, without returning to the suspect Lukácsian idea that identification with the cause of the proletariat provides the theoretician with an epistemologically privileged position, are we to conceive of the 'dynamic unity' between theoretician and the oppressed class? How is the specialist knowledge achieved by the theoretician to be transformed into action-guiding norms?

While Horkheimer's early writings contain no answers to questions like these, they nonetheless do contain internal tensions that reveal a more complex theoretical vision. One set of tensions relates to the role assigned to philosophy within the programme. Consider, first, the following:

13

The fruitfulness of knowledge indeed plays a role in its claim to truth, but the fruitfulness in question is to be understood as intrinsic to the science and not as usefulness for ulterior purposes. The test of the truth of a judgment is something different from the test of its importance for human life.[7]

Why, one might naturally ask, should a Marxist wish to distinguish truth from 'importance to human life' since it is, at least in part, traditional theory's conception of the indifference of truth to its 'importance to human life' that forms a central plank in critical theory's critique of it? In hearing what Horkheimer is saying here, one must hear in his criticism of pragmatism the Kantian, 'critical' distinction between *Verstand* (understanding) and *Vernunft* (reason).

For Kant the understanding provides us with causal knowledge of the world; this is the very same subsumptive knowledge that Horkheimer identifies as 'traditional'. The sort of knowledge delivered by the understanding is instrumentally useful, providing the means for human control over nature that permits us to satisfy our wants and needs. Hence, it is the understanding that secures knowledge that possesses 'importance to human life'. Central to the Kantian project is deciphering a form of reasoning different from this, a form that concerns the whole of human life rather than contingent 'parts', and that informs us about ends as well as means, hence challenging the hegemony of the understanding's instrumental knowing which both classical empiricism and rationalism embraced as the whole of reason. Reason, as opposed to the understanding, is assigned both tasks: it is holistic, seeking the unconditioned, and normative, specifying the ends of human action.

Kant hence inverts our usual comprehension of theoretical knowing: pure, representational cognition, with its correspondence theory of truth, is in fact not 'pure' but subjective and instrumental, bound to the project of mastery over nature within and without; while only a reason relieved of the task of control can attain to unconditioned or disinterested truth. Our natural outlook, inherited from Descartes and Hobbes, is that the end-indifference of scientific knowing mirrors nature's own indifference to human ends; hence human ends can only be of subjective significance, while causal knowing is objective. This judgment, Kant avers, suppresses the fact that causal reasoning is still reasoning, hence reflective of the immersion of the human subject in the natural world, and hence bound to a necessary, which is to say non-optional, anthropologically grounded interest in the natural world. Causal reasoning itself is blind to its own conditioning, and as a consequence all the more subjective, lacking as it does a reflective self-comprehension. To reflectively comprehend causal reasoning involves revealing its conditioning and specifying its role in relation to human reasoning as a whole. But these reflective accomplishments are themselves unavailable to the understanding. Practical cognition is thereby objective in a way that scientific knowing is not

14

and cannot be. Making good in materialist terms this Kantian inversion of the relation between theoretical and practical reason, which is to say, giving Kant's Copernican turn a materialist twist by replacing the transcendental unity of apperception by collective social labour, hence forms an essential ingredient in the contrast between traditional and critical theory since unless the Kantian inversion is accomplished theory remains caught in the toils of unreflective objectivism and metaphysical realism.

Horkheimer's distinguishing of traditional and critical theory is as much inspired by and beholden to Kant's 'critical' separation of understanding from reason as it is by the 'critique' of political economy. Indeed, it is not a mistake to regard Horkheimer's original idea as just the entwining of these two notions of 'critique'. Although construed from the Hegelian perspective in which Kantian reason is falsely tied to the demands and subjective outlook of the understanding, reason has an analogous role in Herbert Marcuse's complementary essay 'Philosophy and critical theory': 'Reason is the fundamental category of philosophical thought, the only one by means of which it has bound itself to human destiny.'[8] Of course, Horkheimer makes the Kantian transition from part to whole, conditioned to unconditioned and means to ends through immersion of science's instrumental knowing in the historically productive social labour of the species: society, figured as socially cooperative human labouring, is the transcendental subject and so the source of the powers of reason.[9] This way of accomplishing the materialist appropriation of the Copernican turn, derived from the Marxist reading of Hegel, is clearly inadequate since the cognitive dimension of social labour is not obviously or unproblematically formally different from causal reasoning. On the contrary, one very natural way of reading the cognitive dimension of social labour is to see its primitive forms as directly adumbrating the abstractive achievements of modern science. Hence, insofar as it is the paradigm of social labour that forms the unity of Kantian understanding and reason for Horkheimer, then the movement from understanding to reason, from subjective to objective reason, is reversed back into the understanding through the very gesture by means of which the priority of reason was to be established.

The second tension in Horkheimer's early writings relates to the role of culture.[10] In his inaugural lecture, 'The state of contemporary social philosophy and the tasks of an institute for social research', Horkheimer begins specifying how it is that multidisciplinary research can relate to the basic questions of social philosophy.

It is not a fashionable question, but one which presents an actualized version of some of the most ancient and important philosophical problems: the question of the connection between the economic life of society, the psychological development of its individuals and the changes within specific areas of culture to which belong not only the intellectual legacy of the sciences, art and religion, but also law, customs, fashion, public opinion, sports, entertainments, lifestyles, and so on. The intention to study these three processes presents merely an updated version by way of contemporary methodologies and the present state of our knowledge, of the ancient question as to the relation of particular existence and universal reason, of the real and the ideal, of life and spirit – adapted to a new problematic.[11]

Horkheimer's scheme for research depends upon relating three distinct domains of social life: the economic, the psychological, and culture. Even if we accept the dubious separation of the economy from its legal social form (private 'ownership' over the means of production) on the grounds that we can analytically distinguish power relations from their normative legitimation, Horkheimer urges the domain of culture as both functionally and normatively significant: culture mediates between the economic structure of society and the psyche of the individual who must reproduce it, *and*, moreover, takes up the burden of explicating the normative content of the philosophical ideas of human fulfilment – competing conceptions of reason, meaning, the good for man, and the like – as *practices* that interpretively install the meaning of social labour within a wider system of accounting for the individuals concerned. Because a functional conception of culture as securing adequate socialization of the psyche for the purposes of social reproduction – including the all-important task of normalizing libidinal renunciation – could find a role for itself even within a traditional theory of society, only the latter conception in which culture is understood as the social locus of non-functional ideas connects multidisciplinary research to the 'ancient' questions of social philosophy as to the relation between life and spirit. Conversely, without the relocation of reason and spirit in culture, Horkheimer could not accomplish his materialist critique of idealism. Horkheimer's hopes for a critical theory thus involves the simultaneous Marxist radicalization of social science and, through a double-accented conception of culture, making those same social sciences 'capable of bearing the burden of the strong theoretical demands in which the intentions of great philosophy were to live on'.[12] Clearly, without a non-functional conception of culture critical theory would collapse back into traditional theory.

Again, despite the indication of seeking in culture a new home for classically conceived ideas of reason and the good, giving them a materialist twist and making them accessible to 'scientific', i.e. critical, investigation, Horkheimer's unequivocal support for the paradigm of social labour together with the philosophy of history it enjoins undermines his critical gesture in the course of its performance. As Axel Honneth has clearly demonstrated, the option of perceiving in culture the filter through which collective norms of action are fixed 'in the group specific interpretations of "law" and "morality" and that are symbolically represented in the habitualized forms of "fashion" and "life-style," ' which would give to culture an action-theoretic orientation, is passed

16

over by Horkheimer in favour of 'the socializing function of formative institutions, the institutions of culture'.[13]

Horkheimer's attempts to forge an alternative to the instrumental reasoning of the understanding and to find within culture a materialist locale for that reason remain fateful for the tradition of critical theory. While the former goal binds critical theory into an ongoing debate with 'great philosophy', the latter goal keeps that debate within the ambit of a materialist problematic that would locate the potentialities for radical social transformation within the unfolding dynamic interactions of individuals in existing societies, thus making a (non-functionalist) 'cultural Maxism' the true successor to both classical Marxism and traditional sociology. The philosophical and sociological ambitions of critical theory are separately both demanding and compelling; add to those ambitions the requirement that they be harmonized, and the full extent and scope of what is involved in a critical theory of society begin to come into view.

My suggestion is hence that these three demands – for a non-instrumental conception of cognition and reason, for a cultural Marxism, and for an internal connection between those two items – are individually necessary and jointly sufficient for a critical theory of society. Of course, a theoretical tradition is as free to re-describe its goals as it is to propose different means of satisfying an agreed-upon end. The point of considering the thesis that a critical theory of society would need to satisfy these three distinct demands is to acknowledge the weight each demand might possess independently of the other two, a fact tacitly operative in the debates over and within critical theory. For example, on my reading of Horkheimer's original idea, his theory of social labour might permit him to satisfy the second and third requirements but not the first. It was only against the background of his failure to contrive a plausible non-instrumentalist conception of reason compatible with materialism that led us to query whether, in fact, he had satisfied the requirement of propounding a materialist theory of culture. Looking at the matter this way reveals that the debate over the role of culture is not strictly between an action-theoretic concept of culture and a functionalist concept, since one might easily construe the functionalist concept as requiring an action-theoretic moment without that addition entailing any new cognitive forms. Only the separate demand for cognition beyond instrumentality pushes critical theory toward a cultural materialism distinctly different from both the Lukácsian and neo-functionalist variety.

More generally, it is easy to perceive that these are three distinct demands since there are ways in which each of the first two requirements can be satisfied without the other being satisfied. So, for example, a general hermeneutical theory of meaning could provide for a non-instrumental account of cognition while denying a materialist theory of culture. And a sophisticated form of neo-functionalism might reasonably consider itself as providing a form of cultural materialism without that implying any form of

17

cognition beyond the empirical and instrumental. It may be logically possible for these three requirements to be met by a theory that is conservative rather than critical. Which is to concede that critical theory's substantive commitment to social justice cannot be deduced from its formal structure. Nonetheless, critical theory's dual origin in philosophy and sociology is not further reducible; on the contrary, it is the combination of its theoretical complexity, which views philosophy and social theory as dirempted halves of an integral freedom and reason, in tandem with a commitment to social justice that provides critical theory with its unique shape and trajectory.

At this juncture, one might complain against my proposal concerning what requirements a critical theory of society should satisfy that it illegitimately abstracts from the political and praxial demands that ushered critical theory into existence in the first instance and remain the pretheoretical touchstone for evaluating its adequacy. Lying behind this complaint is, I believe, a suspect assumption, namely, that a critical theory of society must not only provide the terms for a critique of modern societies, but that the satisfaction of those terms must yield knowledge which in principle could be action-guiding for the suppressed and dominated groups within those societies. One simple reason why one might believe this to be a formal requirement for a critical theory of society would be through consideration of its negation: would not a theory that lacked an immanently praxial dimension necessarily be 'traditional' in the condemned sense? And hence is not the praxial dimension, the connecting of theory and praxis, the primary requirement for a critical theory of society? And was it not this requirement that formed the ultimate motivation behind Horkheimer's contrast of traditional and critical theory?

One might even make this objection stronger. 'Does not your formal account of the requirements for a critical theory of society *accurately* demonstrate that the reiterated failure by Adorno, Marcuse and Habermas to provide it with a dynamic praxial dimension is not contingent but an inevitable and intrinsic feature of the programme? Insofar as the formal features and concerns of the project of critical theory are as you have outlined them, isn't it prohibited from attaining to the political significance it imagined for itself? Isn't the very fact that you could propose a formal account that lacked an unequivocal praxial dimension a tacit concession of defeat on this issue?' My formal outline, it is contended, gives point to and supports the most persistent and damaging objection to the programme.

Needless to say, I am unconvinced by this line of thought. My counter-thesis is that in locating a form of reasoning that is not instrumental, and which, remember, includes a cognition of ends, and a materialist conception of culture which is compatible with such a practical reason, we *exhaust* the demand that theory be practical, that there be a unity between theory and practice; and further, any more demanding and stronger requirement for a praxial dimension to theory will necessarily collapse the resultant back into traditional theory. In making this argument, I do not wish to claim that any particular critical theory is free from defects or that some of those defects pertain to the theory's relation to praxis.

Two objections are decisive against the requirement that a critical theory be immanently praxial in a manner stronger than the one outlined. First, whether or not, at any given time, the contradictions, suppressions and forms of domination in a society entail macro-potentialities for collective action is itself a historically contingent matter. To be sure, the logic and language of Marx's conception of burgeoning forces of production fettered by relations of production, when construed as a general historical logic, entail that at some moment in the history of every society, when the existing forces of production have been developed, such a moment for collective action will occur. Once this model of history is given up, as I have already suggested it should be since it implies both a reductionist conception of the unity of social formations and thereby of the social causes of human misery, and hence the implausible belief that there is a unique historical solution to the problem of human misery, then the grounds for thinking that there *must be* internal connections among structural contradictions in the society as a whole, crisis tendencies affecting its members' self-understanding as an expression of those structural contra-dictions, and macro-potentialities for collective action collapse as well. Further, once a simplified logic of history is surrendered, then the very idea of a 'macro-potentiality' for collective action must lapse as well. In classical Marxism the macro-potentiality related to growing forces of production subject to a reductive either/or: either privately owned and controlled or collectively owned or controlled, with the dysfunctionality of the former engendering the transition to the latter. Without the notion of class functioning as a kind of hermeneutical key to both the definitive structure of society and the practical collective identity of the groups within it, providing thereby the idea of a perfect mapping of economic structure onto social identity, then the idea of a praxial repetition of an unfolding historical logic disappears, and with it the logical linking of theory and practice.

Second, and more important given the familiar slant of the first line of objection, there is an equivocation in the very idea that theory must have a 'praxial dimension'. One way of taking that phrase is to read it as requiring that theoretical knowledge must be translatable, by means of a series of conceptually simple and necessary steps, into imperatives for action. What I have called the 'praxial repetition of an unfolding historical logic' conforms to such a pattern. The notion of 'repetition', however, eliminates rather than furthers praxis since within this outlook it is the philosophy of history at work and not action itself that is central. Action here appears to be relegated to the task of discovering sufficient means for bringing into being predetermined ends. This would make significant action and the form of reasoning appro-priate to it instrumental in the very sense fostered by traditional theory. Nor is this surprising since it is unclear why we should not conceive of a richly articu-lated philosophy of history as itself another version of traditional theory. In its original incarnation, critical theory and the empirical research projects of the Institute were in fact bound to an elaborated version of Marx's philosophy of history – witness Horkheimer's 'existential judgement' – with the question facing it of understanding the societal mechanisms then blocking the translation of social contradictions (the historical logic unfolding) into progressive political action (the praxial repetition of that logic).[14] Significantly, however, *any* attempt to forge internal connections between social structures and social identities that can secure macro-potentialities for action will possess the same logical form as the classical Marxist analysis. So the replacing of the proletariat by another dispossessed group will still involve reducing the possibilities for social meaning (as borne by social identities) to the projective demands of social structure. Insofar as the possibilities for social action are to be read off the possibilities projected from social structure, then the ends of action are bound by the combinatorial possibilities thrown up by structure. It is just this fact that reduces political action to instrumental action. Non-instrumental action must hence possess an irreducibly creative dimension. If this is correct, then the demand for a strong linkage between theory and practice necessarily undermines praxis and makes theory traditional, whatever its ends, rather than critical.

One could, and in the course of the 1930s research in the Institute did, question the empirical validity of Marx's essentially contemplative philosophy of history. In questioning the very idea of macro-potentialities for collective action and placing that philosophy of history on the side of traditional theory, my point has been to question whether the notion of a praxial dimension to theory, and hence whatever might be meant by the general desideratum of linking theory and practice, formally requires more than what is encapsulated in the three requirements for a critical theory already noted. That nothing more is required, as I have suggested, entails that at least one very common objection to the development of critical theory from the late 1930s on lapses, namely, that its pessimistic construction of the opportunities for significant social change drew it back into the arms of traditional theory. Adorno, Horkheimer and Marcuse may have been wrong in their diagnosis of postwar societies, and no one would deny that Adorno's sociological outlook in particular lacked nuance and a sense for the cultural complexities of liberal states, their cultural potentialities, but those faults in and of themselves are not sufficient to alter the status of their theories. On the contrary, it is more plausible to regard their theories as overburdened by a latent attachment to and nostalgia for the false Marxist notion of praxis *despite* the theoretical alterations which their differing conceptions of reason, each of which pursues the task of providing *micro-foundations* for radical social action, make to the paradigm of social labour and the philosophy of history it enjoins. This general thesis could be strengthened if one could discover a domain or problem of social meaning that could not be attached to social structure. In tracking the connection and difference between domination and nihilism we can uncover just such a domain.

20

DOMINATION AND NIHILISM

One way of capturing how the dual origin of critical theory in philosophy and sociology makes distinct but interrelated demands upon its theorizing is to examine how it relates to the substantive equivalents of those sources, namely, the problems of nihilism (hereafter: reason) and domination. Adorno's 1963 article 'Society' is revealing in this regard.

If any member of the Frankfurt School is routinely accused of surrendering its Marxist heritage for the sake of a philosophical engagement with modernity's suppression of a conception of reason other than the instrumental, it is Adorno. 'Society' belies this accusation. In its broad import, 'Society' contests what might be thought to be the neutral presupposition of social theory generally, namely, that it is the study of 'society'. According to Adorno, there is no such neutrally defineable object domain; rather, society needs to be understood in historical terms, terms which would contrast, for example, what it is to be a member of a society with what it might have meant to be a member of a clan, tribe, polis, or principality. For Adorno, the concept of society necessarily involves a certain 'inhumanity'; so, from the outset, he maintains that the 'specifically social' consists 'precisely in the imbalance of institutions over men, the latter coming little by little to be the incapacitated products of the former'.[15] Interestingly, this thought would bracket Honneth's contention that Horkheimer erroneously follows an institutional conceptualization of culture rather than an action-theoretic orientation through its tacit implication that those two orientations are not theoretical options but endpoints along a spectrum along which we are travelling from the latter to the former. Indeed, characterizing and underlining this movement is the leitmotif of Adorno's article.

In elaborating the cause of this continuous rationalization process, Adorno unequivocally points to the 'universal development of the exchange system', which, he contends, 'happens independently of the qualitative attitudes of producer and consumer, of the mode of production, even of need, which the social mechanism tends to satisfy as a kind of by-product'.[16] Adorno's theoretical gesture here is meant to begin the substantiation of two theses. Firstly, the expansion of exchange relations has a source in the dynamic structure of capital independently of the aims or intentions of those – which is everyone – who live and die in accordance with its machinations. Secondly, as a consequence, tendentially the notion of class domination, which presumed a mesh between the structural (economic) and cultural (sociological) senses of class, is being displaced into 'institutional' domination, hence making the idea of class position increasingly less sociologically significant as a marker for the potentiality for political change – at least within particular nation states. Class situation remains, only now 'transposed onto the relationship between nations, between the technically developed and underdeveloped countries'.[17]

Nothing in this brief sketch should lead us to think that Adorno is doing

21

anything other than providing a conception of society from a Marxist point of view. Nonetheless, the common notions of domination and exploitation are not the ones most applicable to the phenomena Adorno analyses. According to the standard argument, the transition from feudalism to capitalism involves the replacement of direct forms of domination by the indirect form of class as defined by ownership or non-ownership over the means of production. Questions of who has power over whom hence become fully answerable only when we turn away from the individual case as mediated through social role and analyse the logic of class relations and its consequences for class member-ship. While Adorno does not deny that domination and exploitation occur in this way, he believes that class domination itself is mediated through and dynamically sustained by the 'domination' of exchange value over use-value. But this is not domination in any direct morally or politically significant sense; rather it is a mechanism whereby any item's ultimate sense, meaning or value is gauged against a common standard which is qualitatively distinct from those of the item itself. With the expansion of the dominion of exchange value into all domains of society (the culture industry is Adorno's favourite example), not only do things become increasingly there for the sake of capital accumula-tion, and so increasingly fungible, but social practices themselves become increasingly subject to compliance with the demands of this process. By this route, the mechanism that sustained class domination, which, however mediated, was still the domination of some individuals by others, little by little becomes the domination of society over individuals.

This tendential alteration in the form of capital domination generates a bifurcation in the 'wrong' of capital. On the one hand, there remain straight-forward questions of social justice, questions of exploitation, of freedom and unfreedom, and of poverty and wealth. Yet as the patterns of ownership and power shift, ownership becoming more spread and the role of the state and bureaucracy more central to maintaining the market system, class structures become increasingly variegated and complex, and less directly a clue to power relations and life possibilities; further, with the connection between the struc-tural and cultural notions of class become increasingly irrelevant, class struggle becomes less and less plausible as the form in which contestation over power can take place, while power itself becomes more anonymous and pervasive as abstract, procedural demands come to be constitutive of the micro-practices of everyday life. So, on the other hand, a new set of deformations of individual and united life come on the scene: the dissolution of the living bonds of sense and meaning between the individual and his or her culture, the disappearance of the autonomous personality and so the possibility of freedom irrespective of the opportunity of exercising such freedom, the disintegration of notions of worth, value and meaning not sanctioned by the demands and needs of the market. Adorno ruefully comments that now although 'men must act in order to change the present petrified conditions of existence . . . the latter have left their mark so deeply on people, have deprived them of so much of their life

22

and individuation, that they scarcely seem capable of the spontaneity necessary to do so'.[18] Clearly, a range of Foucauldian emphases would have been congenial to Adorno. His conception of the rationalization of culture, as distinct from societal rationalization, tracks a tendential loss of meaning, a becoming meaningless of traditional ideals, norms and values. Adorno is not saying that as individuals we lack awareness of traditional values and ideals; rather, as the previous quote testifies, he considers meaninglessness to be announced in individuals' relation to norms and values: they lose their binding character and thereby, or equivalently, their power to motivate.

Yet Adorno recognizes, in a manner in which Foucault arguably did not, that the very nature of this changed state of affairs makes a non-ironic or non-hyperbolic statement of it impossible since insofar as the *experience* it refers to can be critically described, it is neither complete nor definitive. Acknowledging this point does not remove but rather intensifies the point of Adorno's rhetoric. First, and most obviously, because as human beings, and this side of despair, we naturally invest our lives and environment with sense and meaning, considering the 'situations' in which we act as constituted at least in part by our perspective on them; hence, we must consider our sayings and doings as our 'own', as things said and done by us because we believe what we say to be true and our actions a product of desire and belief. To think otherwise would involve collapsing the distinction between saying and repeating, speaking for oneself and being spoken for, acting freely and being coerced. To have a conception of oneself is to be able to distinguish oneself *from* society, to consider oneself a locus of speech and action rather than a mere conduit through which societal demands are channelled. As a consequence, we naturally perceive meaninglessness and constraint as 'out there', as external and at a distance. Hyperbole and irony permit us to see our lives 'from the outside', from the very distance subjective life necessarily refuses. Because the contestation of perspective between agent and spectator, inside and outside, is not further unifiable, one can only refer to the outside perspective ironically since the very *act* of announcing it suppresses the subjective conditions of announcement. Second, then, Adorno means to contrast the illusion of subjective freedom and meaning with objective unfreedom and meaninglessness just as Marx had contrasted the illusions of the sphere of circulation as the 'very Eden of the innate rights of man', the 'exclusive realm of Freedom, Equality, Property and Bentham' with the reality of class structures and domination. Ironic statement, then, rehearses a logic of illusion. Third, while not denying what freedom and meaning remain, Adorno wants to contend, as a component of a logic of illusion, that because these items are embedded in processes indifferent to them, then they must substantively partake of their opposite, making them real and illusory at the same time. Irony hence involves the holding together of these opposites. Finally, all this together is meant to disabuse us of the idea that historical change can intelligibly occur through the direct and political acquisition of centres of power, since while

23

there remain power and domination, power has no straightforwardly identifiable locus. Nor can there be a simple matching of collectivities to macro-
potentialities since, again, there are no *unequivocal* potentialites for either
justice or meaning stored-up but actual in our world. According to Adorno,
the very ideas of justice, of freedom and equality, only appear emphatically
through their absence. Ironic reflection seeks to attain to a perspective we
cannot have while refusing the seducements of a perspective we cannot avoid.
'The dialectical critic of culture', Adorno avers, 'must both participate in
culture and not participate. Only then does he do justice to his object and to
himself.'[19]

Cultural rationalization tokens a crisis of reason and meaning in that as
traditional norms and values lose their cultural place, they simultaneously lose
their critical force. From the agent's perspective, however, this process always
appears as something occurring elsewhere and to others; to conceive of it as
happening to oneself would be to devalue the worth of one's own life, the value
of one's own actions, the significance of one's own pursuits. This we cannot do
without losing a sense of ourselves as agents and as meaningful presences in
the world. Hence, again, short of despair, nothing could count for me as
evidence that my life has become meaningless. Adorno's intransigent
negativity, like that of other first-generation theorists, in the first instance
should be gauged against this resistance to their conception of the collapse of
an objective culture.

Horkheimer, Adorno and Marcuse all share a picture of the world having
negative shape. However, if I am right, we should not read them (the very late
writings of Horkheimer are, perhaps, an exception) as meaning to contrast a
fallen present with a utopian future forever beyond intelligible reach or
description, and as hence departing utterly from a materialist conception of
history. Rather, what their analyses all call into question is a unilinear,
developmental conception of history in which the future would emerge directly
out of a pregnant, conflicted actuality with people acting only as midwives in
the creation of their own future selves. Which is to say, the relentless
negativity of much critical theory is best conceived as opposed to the philosophy of history of classical Marxism, and thereby the conceptions of reason,
meaning, knowing and action which are presupposed by that philosophy of
history. These thinkers nonetheless remain materialists insofar as they view
history and historical practices as the sole locus for human meaning, and the
expansion of capitalism as the driving force of modern societies. It is sometimes claimed that what separates materialism from idealism is the former's
conviction that historical change results from the fulfilment of potentialities
latent in the present rather than from the pursuit of abstract ideals. This, I
have suggested, operates with a reductive conception of reason and action,
denying any role to human creativity, and thereby tacitly making all knowing
and reason instrumental. Horkheimer, Adorno and Marcuse never deny the
force of the ideals of the Enlightenment; what they deny is that we know now

what the fulfilment of those ideals would look like or mean. For them the *fulfilling* of the promises of modernity is possible only through their processual *transfiguration*; fulfilment and transfiguration operating as complementary features of human activity rather than belonging to opposing historical logics.[20]

Given what has preceded it, this last suggestion is bound to appear somewhat opaque. After all, it is not obvious that the impersonal and anonymous forms of domination that go under the heading of cultural rationalization, the 'domination' of institutions over people, bring in their train new logical and epistemological issues. On the contrary, when Lukács first introduced the problems of cultural rationalization under the heading of societal 'reification', he apparently believed that de-reifying activity would be at one with the collective capture of control over the forces of production, that the overcoming of societal domination (the problem of justice) and the overcoming of cultural domination (the problem of meaning) would occur through the same political gesture, a gesture fully bound to the conception of praxis that has been the focus of concern here.[21] While my description of the differentiated character of these two forms of domination makes Lucács's optimism suspect, it does not show it to be false.

It is precisely the questions of cultural rationalization, praxis and cognition that force critical theory away from social theory and into philosophy. In this respect, the famous opening sentence of Adorno's *Negative Dialectics* is misleading if read in isolation: 'Philosophy, which once seemed obsolete, lives on because the moment to realize it was missed' (*ND*, 3). If the last phrase of this sentence is understood as affirming a model of historical change through the fulfilling of macro-potentialities, then the sentence as a whole would entail that the 'living on' of philosophy involves only the search for a new philosophy of history that would, at the appropriate moment, become historically fulfillable in the same manner that Marxist theory had originally assumed. The Lukácsian formation of theory would remain, only now with a new content. In fact, the point of Adorno's text is to deny just this. Rather, philosophy's 'living on' is meant to invoke the necessity of a comprehensive reconsideration of the ontological and epistemological presuppositions determining Marxism and critical theory.

The premise underlying this necessity is that capital expansion can only be understood from the perspective of the expansion of the domination of exchange value over use-value, hence as a process of societal and cultural rationalization, and that the process of rationalization is not itself derivable from the dialectic between the forces and relations of production or the class theory of society that attends that dialectic. Lukács had perfectly understood that the development of capital depended upon cultural rationalization, and hence that a Weberian analysis of the disenchantment of society and culture was a necessary ingredient in an adequate social theory. However, for him rationalization was a mechanism through which class domination was secured, thus subtending rationalization processes under the aegis of the older dialectic.

That is why Lukács could remain loyal to the model of class praxis despite his significant alterations to the theory underlying it. Further, from this angle it now appears evident that both Horkheimer's and Marcuse's classic statements of the project for a critical theory of society are equivocal because they contain a systematic ambiguity between conceiving of rationalization as a function of class relations and conceiving of class domination as a component of societal rationalization. Without departing from a concern for class and the questions of social justice it entails, critical theory has developed fundamentally through its diagnosis of the meaning and consequences of rationalization.

From a philosophical rather than sociological perspective, rationalization processes possess three logically discriminable features that captured the attention of the critical theorists: proceduralism (formalism or methodologism as applied to social actions), substitutability, and end-indifference. A move from, say, judgment or decision to a (formal) procedure can be regarded as an advance in rationality because it works against arbitrariness, enjoining like results from like cases, and thereby unburdening social interactions from demands, subjective or social, extraneous to the endeavour in question. Successful procedures effectively 'liken' the objects and persons falling within their scope by taking into consideration only those features which permit such objects and persons to be candidates for their operation in the first instance. Proceduralism hence makes the rational principle of treating like cases alike causally efficacious by taking unlike cases *as* alike, thereby, over time, *making* the unlike alike. Insofar as anything is only an individual or qualitatively unique it is a mere contingency, and hence from the perspective of rationality arbitrary. Proceduralism is generative of substitutability, with non-substitutability appearing as recalcitrance to the demands of reason. Finally, a procedure bound to one unique end would fall below the level of procedural rationality itself by partaking in the contingency and arbitrariness of the end it served. Procedures proper are thus end-indifferent.

Collectively, proceduralism, substitutability and end-indifference form the logical infrastructure of the instrumental rationality constitutive of and for traditional theory. Yet, the actual opacity of instrumental reason is hidden by the presumptive 'ends' it secures, namely, the unholy trinity of profit, power and order, or, as the last is now denominated for liberal purposes, coopera-tion. Since power and order (or cooperation) are necessary ends for any social formation, and profit becomes a necessary end under market-dominated forms of production, then the end-indifference of instrumental rationality is refuted. The good of instrumental rationality is at one with the goodness of a social order organized on universalistic, non-hierarchical principles. This is the core of the ongoing appeal of traditional theory. It rests on a hermit-like modal conflation: to say an end is 'necessary' is to subsume it under a causal discourse which is itself indifferent to the language of ends. To claim an end is necessary is shorthand for 'necessary for such-and-such purposes', and hence not necessary as an end but only as a means. In the language of reason, rather than the understanding, an end is properly relative or intrinsic, either good as a means to some further end or good in itself. It is sometimes believed that intrinsic goods are necessary objects of volition, but this is mistaken. An end can be good in itself, say playing the violin well, without it being obligatory for any individual or group of individuals to pursue it. Hobbes and Kant have created massive confusion by conflating causal and moral discourse; for them, ends that are universally good as means – order or minimal cooperative arrangements – become thereby obligatory ends of action. But there are no obligatory ends, only actions are obligatory, and they are so or not only in context.[22]

Instrumental rationality is in fact cognitively and rationally opaque because it limits reasoning to items that are good only as means, including the 'universal' means of profit, power and order, thereby throwing into perpetual darkness the goodness or not of the actual ends of human action. Without a cognition of ends, judging the non-causal goodness of means is rendered impossible; since we cannot otherwise judge means except through their internally constituted terms of reference, then the order of means becomes cognitively unbounded. The reflective unbinding of instrumental rationality represents the destructive force of Enlightenment thought, while societal and cultural rationalization turns this same unbounded instrumentality into a historical actuality. Because instrumental reasoning is, at bottom, causal reasoning, with only causally bound criteria acceptable for determining what is rational, then any distinction between rational meaning and causal ordering collapses, with non-causal meaning sunk in the mire of preference and taste. This logical fate of meaning is materially realized in the 'domination' of society over people. It is this dual – logical and historical – fate that is diagnosed and challenged, however differently, in *Dialectic of Enlightenment*, *Critique of Instrumental Reason*, *Negative Dialectics*, *One-Dimensional Man*, *Eros and Civilization*, *Knowledge and Human Interests*, and *The Theory of Communicative Action*.

The logical and material advance of instrumental reason is nihilism, the path of the continuous devaluation of the highest values. Processual devaluation as analysed by the critical theorists is not austerely Nietzschean since for them it is not the highest values that devalue themselves; rather, they perceive a part of reason or meaning (instrumental rationality) as devaluing, by becoming logically and actually hegemonic, some other portion of reason or meaning. Adorno contrasts an identitarian logic with a logic of nonidentity; Marcuse seeks to recharge the utopian dimension of reason, re-fusing *eros* and *logos*, through the redemptive function of memory; while Habermas seeks to install the centrality of a communicative reason against the ravages of the subject-centred monologicality of instrumental rationality. Each of these proposals accurately targets an aspect of instrumentality, diagnoses its hegemony in terms of that aspect, and offers the obverse of the aspect in question as the key to its overcoming. Adorno targets the subsumptive character of instrumentality and its indifference to individuality (unlikeness) as the key; Marcuse focuses on the neutrality (end-indifference) of instrumentality, and thus its detachment from the order of desire; while Habermas perceives in the causal character of instrumental reasoning the reduction of cognition to a subject–object structure. Finally, then, each of these analyses entails a modified conception of the rationalization process: the impositional homogeneity of an administered society, the ahistorical continuum of a de-eroticized society, and the colonization of the lifeworld.

Without entering into the evaluation of these proposals, what nonetheless marks them out as belonging to a unified tradition is their perception of how nihilism and domination are entwined, and how the resolution of the problem of nihilism cannot be detached from the resolution of the problems of social justice. This, we might say, is the source of critical theory's philosophical bias, its apparent return to traditional theory. Yet, if my reconstruction to here is even only approximately correct, the move back into philosophy has its proximate cause in each case in a Weberian reinscription of the Marxist analysis of capitalism. That Weberian inscription, however, is precisely what provides critical theory with its dual perspective: from traditional Marxism critical theory inherits its concern for the problem of justice, while from Weber's appropriation of Nietzsche critical theory inherits its concern for the problem of nihilism and the question of meaning. Further, all the critical theorists explain the dual dilemmas of modernity, injustice and nihilism as having a common root, directly or indirectly, in the abstractive achievements of instrumental reason.

Traditional Marxism tends to focus on the question of injustice (with alienation, reification and fetishism as symptoms or consequences of capital's system of domination and exploitation), making its trajectory at one with the most advanced moments of liberal political theory. Conversely, the tradition of existentialism and phenomenology, with Nietzsche and Heidegger as flag-bearers, directs itself toward the problem of nihilism. Just as traditional Marxism and contemporary political liberalism remain insensitive to the problem of meaning, so the tradition of existentialism remains indifferent to the question of justice. Adorno's original insight, which I want to claim as fateful for the tradition of critical theory, was the identification of the common root of the dilemmas of modernity, and hence the demand for a theory that would address each dilemma without losing sight of the other. If we now reflect back on what I contended were the formal criteria for an adequate critical theory of society – a non-instrumentalist conception of reason and cognition, a non-functionalist conception of culture, and the harmonization of both of these – it becomes evident that the first criterion initially addresses the justice problem and the second the nihilism problem; but the harmonization requirement constrains the satisfaction of the first criterion such that it becomes answerable to the demands of the second. In this way, the substantive issues driving critical theory are at one with its formal ambitions.

Adorno's original insight, as I have called it, is what presses the project and tradition of critical theory to be multifaceted: critical theory is *necessarily* in debate with empirical sociology over the analysis of modern societies, with contemporary moral theory over the analysis of normative claims, and with contemporary continental philosophy over the issue of meaning. Yet if Marx and Weber are only approximately correct in their accounts of modernity, then modern social theory and contemporary philosophy cannot attempt less than what constitutes the basic outlines of the tradition and project of critical theory. The measure of Habermas's achievement is that he has fully taken on this complex and multifaceted project without losing sight of the demands it imposes.

From our present vantage point, it is not difficult to identify the nature of the debate between first- and second-generation critical theory. Fundamentally, they differ with the respect to the weight and focus they offer to the justice and meaning questions: Habermas believes that Adorno slights the question of justice in his engagement with the nihilism question, hence giving undue significance to the role of art in his theory and, by implication, espousing a position which could only be satisfied through a utopian re-enchantment of the social and natural worlds. From an Adornoesque perspective, Habermas's focus on the justice problem entails surrender over the question of nihilism, falsely assuming that total disenchantment would not be extentionally equivalent to total reification.

Habermas's complaint about his predecessors was their inability to provide adequate foundations for critique; implied in this criticism is a concern for rationality as defined by the problem of relativism. His theory of communicative reason hence emerges, primarily, as an answer to the problem of justice. Habermas, then, uses his normative theory of communicative reason to generate a *sociological* analysis and explanation of the problem of meaning in which functionally oriented subsystems of society invade and take over the heretofore communicatively governed interactions of the lifeworld:

Everyday consciousness sees itself thrown back on traditions whose claims to validity have already been suspended; where it does escape the spell of traditionalism, it is hopelessly splintered. In place of 'false consciousness' we today have 'fragmented consciousness' that blocks enlightenment by the mechanism of reification. It is only with this that the conditions for a *colonization of the lifeworld* are met. When stripped of their ideological veils, the imperative of autonomous subsystems [e.g. the economy and political administration as abstract systems dependent on monetary and power relations respectively] make their way into the lifeworld from the outside – like colonial masters coming into a tribal society – and force a process of assimilation upon it. The diffused perspectives of the local culture cannot be sufficiently coordinated to permit the play of the metropolis and the world market to be grasped from the periphery.

(*TCA*, II, 355)

Habermas images lifeworld practices, in very broad terms, along the same sort of lines that Wittgenstein offers to linguistic meaning in terms of public practices, language games and a shared form of life in his late writings, or as analogous to Heideggerian being-in-the-world as thrown projection, or, finally, as akin to what Hegel thought under the rubric of *Sittlichkeit*. The horizon of the lifeworld is 'formed from more or less diffuse, always unproblematic, background convictions. This lifeworld background serves as a source of situation definitions that are presupposed by participants as unproblematic' (*TCA*, I, 70). In ordinary actions, under conditions of modernity, Habermas thinks three formal dimensions or 'structural components' of the lifeworld are interwoven:

> Action . . . presents itself as a circular process in which the actor is at the same time both the *initiator* of his accountable actions [= the structure of personality] and the *product* of traditions in which he stands, of solidary groups to which he belongs [= the cultural level coextensive with tradition], of socialization and learning processes to which he is exposed [= the order of society].
>
> (*TCA*, II, 135)

In part, the rationalization of the lifeworld is equivalent to just this fracturing of the lifeworld into the three dimensions of personality (picking up modernity's conception of individuals as autonomous, accountable and self-determining beings), culture and society. Society is figured here in terms of the abstraction of social norms and the procedural institutionalization of what were the interpretive accomplishments of individuals, e.g. the developmental elaboration of legal systems and the juridification of ever more domains of experience, and the growth in the administrative handling of recurrent aspects of social reproduction (like welfare systems). Along with this process of differentiation there occurs a growing reflexivity about the contents of the cultural tradition – items losing their taken-for-granted character – and the consequent emergence of 'expert cultures' (science, law, technology, art criticism, etc.) cut off from everyday life. Growing reflexivity in its turn presupposes a systematic disentangling of the forms of social and cultural life from particular contents, for only under this presupposition can individual autonomy be respected on the one hand, and self-conscious innovation be given space within which to operate on the other.

In itself, Habermas conceives of the rationalization of the lifeworld as *progressive*: 'What is central to this notion is not, as for Weber, the expansion of formal or instrumental reason to more and more dimensions of social life, but an opening up of the processes of symbolic reproduction to consensual agreement among autonomous individuals in light of criticizable validity claims.'[23] Nihilistic disintegration of meaning for Habermas is a process that occurs on top of or as a deformation of the rationalization of the lifeworld. As the above quoted passage testifies, it is only when the communicative infrastructure of the lifeworld is invaded by particular subsystems of society that have themselves become rationalized in accordance with the generalized 'media' of exchange (money and power) that the loss of meaning and related pathologies (withdrawal of legitimation, anomie, alienation, demotivation, and so on) occur.[24]

Now it may appear perverse to claim that Habermas's diagnosis of nihilism is purely sociological rather than philosophical since his notion of communicative rationality is explicitly set against the claims of instrumental rationality and its invasion, colonization, of lifeworld practices heretofore constituted through communicative action and understanding. Hence, communicative action picks up the requirement for an alternative mode of reasoning and cognition, and its relation to lifeworld practices permits a non-functionalist account of the lifeworld and culture. Yet this simplifies what is at issue. Notice in the quoted passage that Habermas speaks of the 'spell of traditionalism', and of how traditional values' claim to validity has already been suspended. Tradition, for Habermas, is still the enchantment of societal practices; only norms vindicated through communicative interactions procedurally governed are not for him heteronomous. If we thus ask, 'Who (what) has suspended tradition's claims to validity?', at least part of the answer will have to be: communicative reason.

For Habermas, communicative reason is itself formal and procedural; for him only communicative reason itself, its procedural constraints on communicative interactions and argumentation, survive modernity's disenchantment of the social world. If understood aright, Habermas believes, cultural rationalization is progressive in revealing the rational core of Enlightenment progress: we are autonomous and self-legislating beings who are *dependent* on nothing else but the rationality constitutive of communicative interaction itself; as rational speakers engaged in communicative interactions we think for ourselves rather than permitting priests, monarchs and, where inappropriate, functional subsystems of society to do our thinking for us. The modern claim to the autonomy of reason is thus satisfied in the constraints governing communicative interaction. As a consequence, Habermas considers the decontextualization of beliefs and the demotivation that occurs when norms are no longer empirically derived, no longer traditionally enchanted, as part of the price to be paid for the undoubted cognitive achievements of modernity.

What makes Habermas's account compelling is that it both appears to be descriptively accurate and plausibly accounts for the new space given over to individual autonomy without relinquishing the fundamentally social constitution of rationality. Some version of the distinctions among personality, culture and society is necessary for us. Habermas appears to suppose that this decentring of society itself is logically incompatible with concepts of rationality that remain enmeshed 'with the substantive contents of a particular form of life, with a particular vision of the good life' (R, 219). So:

31

As a mechanism of socialization, the first act of reaching understanding itself set a dialectic of universalization, particularization and individualization into motion, a dialectic which leaves *only* the differentiated *particular* in the position of an individual totality [a closed form of life]. General structures of the lifeworld [society], collective forms of life [culture], and individual life histories [personality] arise within the structures of the diffracted intersubjectivity of possible understanding and are at the same time differentiated. The ego is formed equiprimoridally as a subject in general, as a typical member of a social collective, and as a unique individual. The universal, particular and individual constitute themselves radially, as it were – and no longer as moments bound within a totality.

(*R*, 219–20)

Let us ignore the metaphysical hyperbole invoked in the claim that the 'first act of reaching understanding' sets in motion the dialectic of differentiation and, by extension, communicative rationality, as if Adam agreeing to eat the apple already contained universal history within it. Is Habermas correct in his contention that decentration and ethical substantiality are logically incompatible, that once decentration is acknowledged then nothing like, say, a neo-Aristotelian conception of sociality is possible?

Even an apparently anti-modernist like Heidegger has space in his theory for the sorts of distinctions Habermas wants to draw: we are *products* as thrown from the past into a world of practices not of our own making and essentially shared with others (culture); insofar as we merely accommodate our performances to those around us, tradition becomes sedimented into a series of anonymous societal repetitions (the they-self as a prefiguring of society); while in acknowledging the groundless ground of existence in facing death as the horizon of our actions, we become authentic *initiators* of action. Or, somewhat differently, one could think of these three elements as equivalents of what Hegel analyses in terms of abstract right, the state (or ethical life generally), and the system of needs respectively. Both such accounts tell against Habermas. Consider Hegel's version; for him the overarching whole which would span the decentred and differentiated complex would not be communicative rationality as a moment standing apart from social life but regulative of it, but the modern democratic state as itself a form of ethical life, the most complete embodiment of the tradition of modernity, which was *presupposed* by our conception of individual autonomy (and the social spaces given over to it) and the market system as an abstract form of mutual interdependence. To be sure, Hegel also believes that our appreciation of the worth and rationality of the ethical life of modernity is not directly figured in participation in the state; modern reflexivity requires that such participation be reflectively comprehended. But the act of comprehension, the work of philosophy and the other forms of absolute spirit, cannot be conceptually detached from the life of objective spirit.

Uneasiness about Habermas's general schema need not translate into a denial of the phenomena he wishes rightly to support: reflexivity, autonomy and decentration. Rationalization of the lifeworld, of *Sittlichkeit*, might then be conceived of as indeed implying growing possibilities for communicative action; however, communicative rationality, as realized in processes of rational argumentation, need not be theorized as a newly discovered, if already implicitly present, *formal* property of communicative actions, but could equally well be analysed substantively as, for example, a value orientation tied to the development of particular institutional practices (science, education, democratic decision-making) which, as a consequence, would require *interpretive* study in order to be appreciated. For example, one way of reading Thomas Kuhn's critique of Karl Popper's methodology of conjecture and refutation, Popper's particular employment of the criterion of falsification, is to have Kuhn saying that being dogmatic, not accepting defeat because of experimental failures or logical inconsistencies in a theory, can be rationally necessary if theories are to be given the opportunity to develop.[25] What would count as a rational action would then have less to do with 'the force of better argument', which is what Habermas's constraint on communicative inter- action is meant to allow to emerge, and more to do with the very precise features of a practice itself. Dogmatism, the employment of rhetoric, tight strictures on the sorts of question that can legitimately be raised, refusal to move to higher levels of argumentation, and all the other phenomena that Habermas tends to lump together under 'strategic' uses of language, *may* in particular contexts be part of the *rationality* of a practice without which it could not successfully function.

With these acknowledgements and swerves around Habermas's theory, we can legitimately return to Weber's worries about cultural rationalization. After all, what Habermas ranges against the proceduralism of instrumental reason and the purposive-rational frameworks of the functional subsystems of society is another form of procedural rationality. Habermas's romantic critics, following Adorno, believe that formalism and proceduralism are themselves the primary *criteria* that make a form of reasoning instrumental, and hence believe communicative reason is a component of the very disintegrative process it means to remedy. Hence they take Habermas's acceptance of the demotivating consequences of cultural rationalization as a sign that his theory capitulates to the nihilistic, meaning-destroying processes of modernity.

This is a large and wholly philosophical claim incapable of being prosecuted directly. It can only be vindicated by a careful tracking of Habermas's thought through a range of topics. Two factors make this tracking difficult. Firstly, Habermas conceives the advance communicative rationality makes over Kantian moral reason as its salvaging of Hegel's intersubjective turn, entailing thereby that his proceduralism is already bound to social practice in a way that Kant's moral theory is not. What does or does not count as a fully intersubjective conception of self and reason thus becomes a recurrent question, with Habermas insisting that all that could be wanted from sociality without the enchanting dogmatism of tradition is provided by the linguistic turn into communicative interaction and rationality. Secondly, Habermas is forever awake to the type of Adornoesque and Hegelian criticisms that will be made in what follows; as a consequence, he has consistently attempted to accommodate his reconstruction (from the intuitive knowledge of speakers) of communicative reason to the demands that flow from his romantic critics without surrendering what he regards as the core of his theory. It can thus appear as if only a hair's breadth separates Habermas from his critics. Such appearances need to be undermined if the real differences are to become manifest.

No single argument, like the one just given concerning scientific rationality, can refute Habermas's theory of communicative reason; only the acceptability of his theory as it ramifies into particular topics and engages with particular challenges permits critical evaluation. Because with respect to each sub-topic (self-knowledge, ethical identity, judgment, etc.), Habermas is offering a communication's theoretic analysis, then inevitably in a purely philosophical reading of his theory the same *type* of counter-arguments are bound to recur. Nonetheless, what is at stake is not a flat yes or no to the idea of communicative reason, but Habermas's conceptual scheme as a whole in which communicative reason plays a controlling role versus the kind of conceptual framework implied by his critic. At the end of the day, sufficient reason to depart from Habermas's programme will not be provided until a worthy alternative to it becomes available. Adequately motivating the search for such an alternative and adumbrating its salient features thus become the first steps in the transfiguring of critical theory.

2

LIBERTY AND THE IDEAL SPEECH SITUATION

For Marxists the problem of liberty is centred upon those impersonal forms of coercion and constraint which restrict agents' opportunities to act upon given desires or choices among possible alternatives, as well as their capacity to conceive of and explore possibilities which, but for those impersonal forces, they could or would desire to pursue. Constraints may operate on either agents' given desires or actions or upon their understanding of what the available options truly are. The unhappy slave is prevented from pursuing particular goals, while the happy slave is prevented from even conceiving of pursuing what the unhappy slave overtly desires. In order to comprehend the unfreedom of the happy slave his position must be viewed counterfactually, that is, in terms of what he would (or, at least, could) desire were certain features of his situation different. What licenses the counterfactual construal of the happy slave's situation is its intuitive similarity with the situation of the unhappy slave. Since it is not at all obvious that the beliefs of all happy slaves are the result of deliberate manipulation, we must be prepared to accept the thesis that institutional structures via social roles can themselves induce illusory patterns of belief.

These considerations point to the two major respects in which Marxist accounts of liberty diverge from the traditional liberal understanding of liberty: firstly, not only actions but persons may be subject to coercion; and secondly, an agent's lack of freedom need not be the outcome of another agent's deliberate actions, but may equally be the outcome of the operation of impersonal social forces. In order to comprehend these two facets of the problem of freedom Marxists have fashioned a variety of theoretical concepts which attempt to capture the peculiarly social, but not necessarily intentional or deliberate, ways in which persons are deprived of their liberty: for example, alienation, reification, fetishism, ideology, and rationalization. Now each of these conceptions of the want of liberty has that characteristic which Berlin attributes to positive conceptions of liberty generally, namely, the employment of some distinction between a real, true, or autonomous self, and an empirical, heteronomous self, a self ruled by forces beyond its immediate control.[1] The defence of the Marxist conception of liberty must perforce

35

answer Berlin's charge that in such theories the autonomous self is often an 'occult' (counterfactual?) entity, whose non-empirical character permits those who claim to have knowledge of it to prescribe what is truly in the interest of the lowly, empirical self irrespective of its actual wishes and desires.[2]

Berlin correctly notes that the autonomy/heteronomy distinction tends to depend upon or reflect the rather more familiar distinction between what belongs to the world of human beings and history, where free actions are possible, and what belongs to the causally determined world of nature. Interestingly, in his critique of empirical political theory, as well as in his critique of the application of empirical, scientific models of explanation to history, Berlin himself employs a similar distinction when he argues, against the 'idea of a completely *wertfrei* (value free) theory (or model) of human action', that 'men's beliefs in the sphere of conduct are part of their conception of themselves and other human beings; and this conception in its turn, whether conscious or not, is intrinsic to their picture of the world'.[3] What Berlin is pointing to here is the idea that people's beliefs about themselves and what they are doing are more than subjective states of mind; they are, at least partially, constitutive of the actions, practices, and institutions that make up the social and political world. If this is so, however, it makes a difference not only to political theory but to political life as well, for if people conceive of political life as concerned with the regulation and control of the social world as if it were a natural process, then they will inevitably repress or deny distinctively human aspects of themselves.

Employing a critique of the positivist conception of social theory and the scientization of politics which is oddly congruent with Berlin's, Jürgen Habermas has attempted to construct a normative social theory which substantiates the Marxist refusal of the liberal theory of liberty, while avoiding the temptation to dogmatism inherent in positive conceptions of liberty.

THE PUBLIC SPHERE AND THE SCIENTIZATION OF POLITICS

Where ends are agreed, the only questions left are those of means, and these are not political but technical.

(I. Berlin)

Habermas's conception of the nature of political theory, and indeed, as we shall see, his conception of freedom as well, is largely derived from the classical tradition. According to Habermas the classical understanding of politics was normative; it was concerned with the constituents of the good and just life, and as such it was continuous with ethics. Politics referred to the sphere of praxis or actions done for their own sake, and was unconcerned with *techne*, the workmanlike skill needed to produce artefacts. Hence politics was thought to proceed not technically but pedagogically; it attempted to cultivate a virtuous character of praxis. Because of the changing and contingent conditions of social life, politics and practical philosophy were thought to require a different kind of knowledge and judgment from that attainable by the exact or rigorous sciences. A virtuous character was one which possessed *phronesis*, a prudent understanding of contingent conditions with a view to what was to be done (*TP*, 42). Hence the subject matter of politics was the changing conditions of social life, and its goal was the formation of citizens capable of virtuous action under such conditions. Questions of economy, personal welfare and contractual relations between persons for the sake of gain were not considered to be within the domain of politics, since in the case of economy and personal welfare success depends upon skilful means–ends calculations and not a virtuous character; while in the case of contractual relations, although public, legal regulations are required in order to ensure their orderly functioning, those who promote such arrangements do so as private individuals, 'as though they were separated: each of them regarding his own house as a city'. Thus, according to the classical doctrine of politics, not all public and legal arrangements make of a community a state: 'a community can only be called a state when it renders its citizens capable of virtuous actions and thereby a good life' (*TP*, 47).

The image of freedom conveyed by the classical doctrine is one of pure praxis, the political community representing an intersubjective realm of communicative action unconstrained by force or instrumental concerns. Habermas agrees with Hannah Arendt that the classical political conception of liberty is best understood as a structure of unimpaired intersubjectivity brought about through unconstrained communicative action, where the purpose of unconstrained communication is just the forming and maintaining of an intersubjective space where reciprocal speech is possible. This makes the praxis of speech the basic feature of cultural life, for it is only in the space of appearance engendered by reciprocal speech that human beings can reveal themselves as human beings, and as a consequence bind themselves together into a human community. Political community exists only through the intersubjectivity made possible through communicative action. On this accounting freedom is being imaged as pure politics.

Now the rigid separation of political and socio-economic issues which supports this conception of human freedom simply does not obtain in modern societies, nor, Habermas urges, is such a separation truly imaginable for us. Given the problems we face we would not desire 'a state which is relieved of the administrative processing of social problems', nor 'a radical democracy which inhibits its liberating efficacy just at the boundaries where political oppression ceases and social repression begins'.[4] To measure the modern state against the yardstick of the classical model would be to adopt an elitist, utopian stance towards the modern problems of politics and freedom – a stance more likely to produce frustration than critical illumination. This is not to deny that there is an aspect of the problem of liberty which would be lost if we ignored the model of freedom as pure politics; but it is urging that that conception of itself is inapplicable to our situation, that it must be reworked if it is to speak to our predicament. And in what he terms the 'bourgeois public sphere' Habermas believes he detects a modern analogue of the Greek polis, and hence a normative model of politics and liberty applicable to the modern situation.

By public sphere Habermas intends 'a realm of social life in which something approaching public opinion can be formed'.[5] What distinguishes a public sphere from other areas of social discussion is its goal of forming or bringing into being a public opinion (as opposed, say, to striking a bargain, or calculating an efficient means to some agreed-upon end). 'Citizens behave as a public body when they confer in an unrestricted fashion – that is, with the guarantee of freedom of assembly and the freedom to express and publish their opinions – about matters of general interest.'[6] What gives force to the opinions formed in the public sphere is that its debates are regulated solely by the criteria of rational argument and criticism, and hence without deference to existing forms of privilege, traditional customs, or collective prejudices. Finally, a public sphere is political when its discussions deal with concerns connected with the activity of the state: 'Although state authority is so to speak the executor of the political public sphere, it is not a part of it.'[7]

In modernity then, the state is displaced as the domicile of political action proper by the public sphere. Indeed, the bourgeois public sphere emerged in the eighteenth century in order to mediate the growing division between state and civil society. Its members were those large numbers of private individuals who were excluded from the then dominant institutions of government, but whose economic position gave them an interest in public arrangements. They sought, through newspapers and journals, to make government more open, accountable, and responsive to interests beyond those of the traditional elites.

Placing to one side his historical analysis of the rise and rapid decline of the bourgeois public sphere, what is distinctive here is Habermas's contention that it is the principle of the public sphere which articulates, gives meaning and point to the traditional liberal freedoms of speech, press, and assembly. Without something like a public sphere these freedoms become politically idle, for they are unable to serve the end of a discursive will formation in accordance with critical principles. The traditional liberal freedoms, when disconnected from the activities of the public sphere, deteriorate into vehicles for the promotion of private interests; 'public relations work', 'publicity', and media-controlled 'public opinion' are surrogates for the public sphere which allow plebiscitary support to be garnered for policies which may satisfy the wants of only a small sector of the population. What then gives value as such to the freedoms of speech, press, and assembly is their actual or potential connection with some public sphere; and what makes them political freedoms is their actual or potential connection with a political public sphere, their actual or

38

potential place in the formation of a public opinion capable of directing state action in a rational manner, and so rationalizing state power.

Considerations of this kind place Habermas's perception of traditional liberal ideals into a somewhat different perspective from that usually adopted by Marxists. As a first step in their ideological critique of liberal ideals Marxists argue that the criteria of generality and rational formality as norms of law derive from the market structure of liberal capitalism; and further, that it was the sphere of circulation, and the domain of private law necessary for the protection of contract relations, which generated the norms of personhood, reciprocity, justice, and equality. Because these ideals and norms have their true home, as it were, in the unequal and exploitive territory of capital market relations they are undeserving of rational assent: their ideological origin is indelible. In contrast, Habermas contends that the original force of these norms and ideals owes as much to the politically functioning public sphere in which public opinion was formed through unrestricted discussion as it does to the market economy. For this reason, if for no other, these ideals continue to contain an emancipatory core irrespective of the ideological ends to which they have been put. Since the democratic thrust of the universal principles of liberal theory depends upon a politically functioning public and a normative concept of public opinion, in the absence of a public sphere the application of these principles to public life means little or nothing; political and public freedom become, as Marxists maintain they always are under capitalism, merely formal and therefore empty.[8]

Political liberty exists truly only where there is a space free from domination where private persons can meet to form an enlightened critical public opinion concerning matters of general interest bearing on state activity. Without such a space individuals cannot transcend their role of 'private' persons. If the public sphere cannot make individuals virtuous in the Greek sense, it can enable them to act as citizens. Thus the normative public sphere takes up the function of political education, of social pedagogy which was so central to the classical doctrine of politics.

Initially, then, the surplus meaning required for legitimation of self-claimed democratic states was to be found in the catalogue of fundamental rights (freedoms) given in their constitutions. These rights were meant to underwrite and secure the normative presuppositions of the public realm. Going beyond the legal rights securing the autonomy of civil society, the freedoms of speech, opinion, assembly, and press gave point to the democratic claims of these states. While modern states are still required to protect these rights, in the absence of a politically functioning public sphere they no longer serve as the basis for the legitimation of state activity as such, that is, while the maintenance of the freedoms which formerly served to protect the public sphere is still required in order for modern states to claim democratic status, the evident lack of a public sphere makes these freedoms insufficient on their own to legitimate public policy proposals. Rather, Habermas argues, insofar as government action is directed toward the economic system's stability and growth, politics now takes on a peculiarly negative character. For it is oriented towards the elimination of dysfunctions and the avoidance of risks that threaten the system: not, in other words, toward the *realization of practical goals*, but toward the solution of technical problems.[9]

In his account of the classical doctrine of politics Habermas distinguished the practical (praxis) from the technical or instrumental (*techne*), associating the political domain with the former. Political questions concerned the nature of the good life, and therefore were essentially normative and ethical. In the bourgeois public sphere this concern with the good life was marginally maintained: government action was to implement the goals practically legitimated by the critical discourse of the public sphere. Insofar as the ideals of equality, reciprocity and justice were regarded as immanent constituents of that public discourse, that is, as what made that discourse truly public and democratic, the public opinion formed there was itself immanently normative. In contrast, the success of the current replacement programme depends on the suppression of practical, ethical questions as such, on the elimination of normative standards as appropriate to the evaluation of government policies. It is the disappearance of a domain of the practical, or rather, the elimination of the distinction between the practical and the instrumental which provides the justification for the government organization of social life without direct reference to normative assumptions or traditional values.

Extending the Enlightenment critique of religion and superstition from the world of nature to the world of social relations, the new ideology applies the value-free methodology of science and technology to the 'solution' of social problems, thereby reducing social problems to problems of technical control and manipulation. The inevitable result of this substitution of the practical by the technical is the 'depoliticization of the mass of the population and the decline of the political realm as a political institution'.[10]

Science and technology extend the reach of human freedom by extending human possibilities for coping with the environment when applied to nature or to those problems of social life which call for technological resolution; they come to occlude human freedom, however, when they are accepted as the only legitimate models for reflecting on 'practical' questions. The scientization of politics is precisely the repression of those modes of reflection and interaction which distinguish human social intercourse from our intercourse with the natural world: 'Technocratic consciousness reflects not the sundering of an ethical situation but the repression of "ethics" as such as a category of life.'[11]

For Habermas, then, the political public sphere, together with the normative conception of political life it supplies, represents the social instantiation of ethics as a category of life. For him man is a *zoon politikon*: politics is the social place where individuals realize their nature as rational beings. The universal application of technological rationality to social life drains the social world of its normative core. A fully depoliticized society would necessarily be a fully heteronomous society; in it no one would be truly free.

LABOUR AND INTERACTION

Liberation from hunger and misery does not necessarily converge with liberation from servitude and degradation, for there is no automatic developmental relation between labour and interaction.

(J. Habermas)

Habermas's account of social heteronomy in late capitalism, his image of social relations capable of being 'rationalized' to the point of stagnation through the application of enlightened instrumental rationality to social problems, echoes Marx's vision of alienation, together with Weber's theory of bureaucratic rationalization and, more directly, Lukács's and Adorno's rather different images of social 'reification'. From the young Marx Habermas has adopted the idea of social relations operating in such a way that the exercise of one fundamental human capacity comes systematically but subvertly (i.e. ideologically) to deny or repress some other fundamental human capacity. The account of science and technology as ideology makes sense only if it refers back to a normative image of human nature. Habermas's actual analysis, however, draws most fully upon the 'rationalization/reification' story as told by the three later writers. In each case there, it is suggested that the increment of freedom in one social domain issues in the restriction of human freedom elsewhere in the same social system. In Habermas's version this comes out as the claim that the very same technological forces and thinking which have provided for the growing human emancipation from external nature are now threatening a subjugation of human subjectivity. If this is so, then technological progress and political emancipation must be separate social processes tokening categorically distinct modes of social development. Such a separation is implicit in Marx's distinction between the technological forces of production and the social relations of production. In order, however, for this distinction to be developed in a consistent manner which avoids the temptation to assimilate the development of the social relations of production into the development of the forces of production – a temptation not always resisted by either Marx or later Marxists – Habermas argues that we must reformulate it on a higher level of abstraction, namely, as between 'instrumental' or 'purposive-rational' action on the one hand, and 'communicative' action on the other. These higher level abstractions are not, like the forces of production and the relations of production, components of social systems; rather they represent abiding features of human beings. Habermas apparently believes that part of the analytical and critical power of Marx's later writings stems from the fact that its organizing theoretical figure of a dialectical interaction between the forces and

41

relations of production assumes and depends upon what Habermas claims to be the more fundamental distinction between instrumental and communicative action.

According to Habermas, instrumental and communicative action designate two different, meta-empirical frames of reference in which reality is 'constituted' and knowledge accumulated; or, to state the same thesis more simply, they designate two fundamental, non-reducible ways in which we interact with our social and natural environment. Insofar as we remain human beings we must have an 'interest'[12] in (i) controlling and manipulating the natural world, and so in acquiring the kind of nomological knowledge appropriate to that activity; and (ii) understanding other social agents in order to facilitate the securing of our always fragile intersubjectivity. The former interest reflects the fact that as a species we reproduce ourselves through 'learning processes of socially organized labour'; while the latter interest reflects the fact that our species reproduces itself through 'processes of mutual understanding in interactions mediated in ordinary language' (*KHI*, 194).

As fundamental interests and meta-empirical frames of reference, instrumental and communicative action are always enmeshed in typical patterns of social experience. Instrumental action is inevitably situated in societal patterns of reproduction and adaption to the environment, which is to say, in societal structures of labour and work. Actions falling within this sphere are governed by technical rules based on empirical knowledge; hence the validity of the rules governing instrumental action depends upon the truth of the empirical propositions which support them. Failure to comply with technical rules or any lack of adequacy in the empirical theories supporting them leads to either incompetent behaviour or simple inefficacy. Communicative action is always enmeshed in patterns of socialization and social communication. It is governed by consensual norms which are objectified in ordinary language and are enforced through the application of conventional sanctions. Behaviour which deviates from agreed-upon norms is punished in some conventional manner. Whereas the validity of rules of instrumental action has an empirical backing, the validity of social norms 'is grounded in the intersubjectivity of the mutual understanding of intentions and secured by the general recognition of obligations'.[13] In the domain of instrumental action, then, the world is constituted in terms of a polarity of subject and object, where what makes something an 'object' is precisely the application of instrumental rules and reasoning to it; while in communicative actions there is always an assumption of reciprocity between self and other, ego and alter-ego. This last point is of central importance, for it grounds the anti-individualist train of thought that runs throughout Habermas's writing.

According to Habermas all human subjectivity, that is, all experiences by individuals of themselves as distinct persons, is grounded in intersubjectivity. Self-awareness does not arise through isolated, private acts of introspection or self-reflection. Rather, one begins to see onseself only through becoming

42

aware of how others see one. Self-consciousness, and hence subjectivity, is a social accomplishment wherein through acts of reciprocal acknowledgement individual subjects ('I') become aware of themselves as different from other subjects ('you'), all of whom are linked together through a recognition of their shared mutuality ('we'). Only where there are collectivities who can assert their individuality in relation to other groups can there be subjects who can assert their individuality in opposition to other individuals and against the demands of the collective. This complex accomplishment occurs above all through language. The framework of communicative action is that within which human beings are constituted as self-conscious subjects.

Because human beings are always and necessarily engaged in forms of activity fulfilling the requirements of the fundamental interests constituting instrumental and communicative action, human social life will always possess corresponding historically specific structures in which those interests can be realized: all societies must possess structures whereby they can reproduce themselves both materially and culturally. Each categorically distinct type of structure will naturally possess its own specific logic of repression and emancipation.

> While instrumental action corresponds to the constraint of external nature and the level of the forces of production determines the extent of technical control over natural forces, communicative action stands in correspondence to the suppression of man's own nature. The institutional framework determines the extent of repression by the unreflected, 'natural' force of social dependence and political power, which is rooted in prior history and tradition. A society owes emancipation from the external forces of nature to the labour processes, that is to the production of technically exploitable knowledge (including the 'transformation of the natural sciences into machinery'). Emancipation from the compulsion of internal nature succeeds to the degree that institutions based on force are replaced by an organization of social relations that is bound only to communication free from domination. This does not occur directly through productive activity, but rather through the revolutionary activity of struggling classes (including the critical activity of reflective sciences).
>
> (*KHI*, 53)

Emancipation from external nature derives from processes whose structure and logic are categorically distinct from the structures and logic governing the processes of emancipation from internal nature, from the institutional violence of social domination and repression. In concrete historical contexts there is, of course, an interaction between these two processes of emancipation; indeed, part of the work of social analysis involves deciphering the specificity of this interaction. At any particular time processes of political emancipation or repression will lead to concurrent processes of either growth or diminution in freedom from the constraints of external nature, and inversely in cases of pronounced expansion or contraction in our freedom from the constraints of external nature.

What the distinction between instrumental and communicative action allows, then, is a restoration of the classical separation of *techne* from praxis, as well as the congruent distinction between productive (instrumental) and reflective (practical) knowledge, for social analysis and political thought generally. With these categorical distinctions in hand it will follow that suppression of the essential spheres of communicative action in a society involves a massive restriction of human freedom; and further, that if that suppression is carried forward on the basis of a denial of the difference between instrumental and practical reason, then it is legitimate to claim that science and technology, the institutional bearers of instrumental reason, are operating as ideologies. Science and technology become ideologies when they encroach upon the domain proper to communicative action while denying the distinction between instrumental and practical reason. Clearly, however, not all political and social oppression is brought about through the ideological application of science and technology to the domains of social interaction; the scientization of politics represents but one of the ways in which freedom can be restricted. What is needed at this juncture is some general account of the logic of repression and emancipation in social interaction.

DISTORTED COMMUNICATION

> Paraphrasing Marx's dictum that all previous history has been the history of class struggle, we could say that all previous history has been a history of 'distorted' communication.
>
> (A. Wellmer)

The domain of communicative action, which involves non-verbal communication as well as speech, is governed by consensual norms objectified in ordinary language. Due to its linguistic constitution, the understanding of actions falling within this domain requires the employment of rather different methods of analysis from those used by the natural sciences. The argument for this claim goes roughly as follows. Social and historical reality is always a symbolically mediated reality; hence the data of social and historical analysis are themselves meaningful. Meaning, in this sense, is understood through contextualization, because meangingful relations are a species of internal relations. One understands the meaning of an event in a novel by locating it within the story being told; one understands a line of poetry or a poetic image through relating it to the poem as a whole; and one understands the meaning of a human action by knowing the reason it was done. But to understand any of these requires knowing the language and culture in which it has a place: childhood does not image innocence in every culture, and to recognize the nod of a head as a bid requires knowing the language game of auctions. The meaning, then, of any particular social or historical datum is determined by its place in the symbolic totality, the language game and form of life of which it is a part. Thus the comprehension of a meaningful element can require no more then relating it to the whole of which it is but a part; and the comprehension of meaningful totalities can require no more than seeing how their various parts unite to form a whole, or, again relating them to some larger social or historical totality. Now since we are always immersed in such meaning complexes, we can understand other meaningful realities only by relating them to our own. Thus the model of understanding here is not that of discovering a cause or making an inductive inference, but rather coming to understand another person, entering into a dialogue with another. All understanding of social reality, then, involves the understanding of social meanings; and the understanding of social meanings always commences from a given meaningful world and involves entering into a different and unfamiliar meaning complex by tracing its relations with one's own.[14] Let us call such an understanding 'hermeneutic understanding'.

If the claim for hermeneutic understanding is taken to be universal, that is, as representing the only adequate method for the understanding of social reality, then hermeneutics must be unacceptable to Marxism. Central to all versions of Marxist theory is the belief that history can and does work behind the backs of the individuals who make it. More precisely, Marxists claim that not only do social agents fail to grasp the interconnections between the various aspects of the meaning complexes they inhabit, that is, fail to realize the nature of the determinations operating on the different parts of their symbolic totalities (hence failing to see them as totalities), it is equally true that they are made blind by their understanding of given meaning complexes to the non-normative causes and conditions of those very same complexes. Habermas puts the point this way:

> It makes good sense to conceive of language as a kind of meta-institution on which all social institutions are dependent; for social action is constituted only in ordinary language communication. But this meta-institution of language as tradition is evidently dependent in turn on social processes that are not reducible to normative relationships. Language is also a medium of domination and social power; it serves to legitimate relations of organized force. Insofar as the legitimations do not articulate the power relations whose institutionalization they make possible, insofar as these relations merely manifest themselves in the legitimations, language is also ideological.[15]

On Habermas's reading, hermeneutics tends to idealize ordinary language communication firstly, by overestimating the degree of consistency and comprehensibility it possesses; secondly, by assuming there to be a greater potential for communication in a given context than is usually present; and thirdly, by presuming a degree of agreement (consensus) among speakers

45

which is almost never exemplified. These idealizations of ordinary language communication by hermeneutics has the undesirable effect of providing the existing self-interpretation of groups with a kind of normative inviolability, an ontological defence mechanism, against the interrogation of the truth of fundamental beliefs and the justice of operative social norms and values. In order to make more vivid what is at issue here it is helpful to imagine the way in which each of the three idealizations can be overturned. Habermas agrees with hermeneutics that normally there is a 'consistency' or mesh between verbal expressions, gestures, and actions. Each of these three aspects of communicative action interprets the others. What hermeneutic theory fails to note, however, is that inconsistencies here can themselves become habitual. When this occurs a part of the symbolic field becomes either incomprehensible to the speakers involved, or they give it a comprehensiblity it does not really possess (e.g. by 'rationalizing' the inconsistency in question). Secondly, as a result of the habitualized inconsistency communication becomes inhibited: non-verbal expressions, motives, desires, even doubts, uncertainties and 'felt' failures of understanding become incapable of being made verbal and thus communicated. As a result there are 'meanings' which are systematically excluded from public discourse. Finally, if communication is inhibited, then the consensus about beliefs and norms which is operative in public discourse must be deceptive or false. The difficulty for hermeneutics with a case like this is that the situation is as if there were a real consensus about beliefs and a free acknowledgement of norms as just; but a consent cannot be free if it is based on a systematic inhibition of communication. Because hermeneutics regards the given meaning complex as the point of departure for social analysis it cannot adequately distinguish between a real and a deceptive consensus, between true communication and pseudo-communication. If social analysis is restricted to the interpretation of meanings, if we always had to uphold the role of a reflective partner in a dialogue, then there would be no possibility of our detecting the false consensus underlying some given pseudo-communication: the self-interpretation of the happy slave and the satisfied master would be for ever inviolable.

In order to understand social reality we require something more than is provided by either the hermeneutical social sciences (symbolic interactionism, ethnomethodology, and the like), or the empirical, objectifying social sciences (functionalism, systems theory, and company) which repress the meaningful elements and hence normative dimensions of social interaction. We require what might be termed a 'depth hermeneutic', that is, a hermeneutic which connects agents' self-interpretation to the 'depth-grammar' of social relations which, operating like a natural force upon them (but behind their backs), distorts and mutilates their communicative actions. The Freudian account of the relations between the ego, id, and superego is one sort of depth-grammar; and Marx's analysis of the internal relations between capital and wage labour is also a depth-grammar; as is, of course, Habermas's own analysis of the operation of technological rationality in modern politics. What such depth-grammars reveal are the moments and causes of distorted communication in the life-processes of individuals and societies. By making causes of distorted communication visible, a depth hermeneutic places an individual or a collective in a position to remove the source of the distortion, and so to give voice to the inhibited meanings. The point of such analyses, then, is to allow for the abolition of the quasi-causal mechanisms they detect, to allow repressed meanings, interests, and desires to be formed and communicated. Habermas contends that the 'interest' guiding the depth-hermeneutical inter-rogation of social reality is an emancipatory interest; and a social theory guided by an interest in emancipation can properly be called a critical theory of society.

A critical theory of society is a normative social theory: it distinguishes real from false consensuses, true communication from pseudo-communication, and so the appearance of freedom from real liberty. But how can critical theory distinguish the appearance of human freedom from the reality? What does it mean to distinguish appearance from reality here?

THE IDEAL SPEECH SITUATION

The human interest in autonomy and responsibility is not mere fancy, for it can be apprehended a priori. What raises us out of nature is the only thing whose nature we can know: language. Through its structure autonomy and responsibility are posited for us. Our first sentence expresses unequivocally the intention of universal and unconstrained consensus.

(J. Habermas)

We have now truly returned to the world of happy slaves; the false consensus between master and slave unrelieved by critical interrogation; the liberal world where so long as none deliberately intervenes in the activities of others each is accounted as socially free; and the political liberty of each is assumed guaranteed so long as the apparatus of democratic participation is linked with the formal freedoms of speech, press, and assembly.

Habermas does not, of course, suppose that all want of political liberty is equivalent to a want of real communication and real consensus about social needs and values. What he does insist upon is that distorted communication is the inevitable concomitant of the ideological suppression of social needs and generalizable interests; and further, that without real consensus and true com-munication the appearance of freedom must be illusory. What his theory requires, then, is a theoretical wedge to insert between contexts of real and pseudo-communication; a counterfactual standpoint from which pseudo-communications can be discerned in order that critical reflection can begin. The theoretical difficulty Habermas faces is to justify a counterfactual

47

perspective which is immanently comprehensible to the agents to whom it is applied, while being sufficiently powerful to disturb the limiting pre-suppositions of the existing false consensus. If the counterfactual hypothesis lacks immanence, if it is merely ideal in the manner of classical utopian theories or theories of autonomy of the type Berlin castigates, then its compre-hensibility and acceptability to present agents must be in question. Alternatively, if the counterfactual hypothesis is too weak, in the manner of ethical theories which refuse a normative account of human autonomy, then it will end up legitimating the beliefs of some group of happy slaves.

If pseudo-communication is to be distinguished from real communication, then in the first instance what must be limned are the competences ordinary speakers of a language must possess if they are to engage in verbal com-munications with other speakers; that is, we must supply an account of what it is to communicate a meaning to another in general if we are to have a theory which can illuminate the various kinds of failure to which human communica-tion is subject. Habermas believes that the result of such an investigation will have point because communicative competence is not something we possess over and above our ability to speak a language; on the contrary, to understand language as such requires a theoretical comprehension of the kinds of under-standing available through language. While there are many forms of linguistic practice which are not oriented toward reaching an understanding (com-municating in the full sense of the term), Habermas regards these 'strategic' or manipulative uses of language as parasitic upon speech oriented toward achieving genuine understanding.

The normal case of human communication is precisely speech oriented toward understanding:

> Ordinary languages are incomplete and provide no guaranteee for the
> absence of ambiguity. Consequently, the intersubjectivity of ordinary
> language communication is always 'broken'. It exists because consensus
> is in principle possible; and it does not exist because it is in principle
> necessary to achieve effective communication.[16]

The limit case or realization of speech oriented toward understanding is, naturally, speech where there is understanding, what Habermas calls 'consensual speech actions'. Habermas employs the model of consensual speech actions, the model of smoothly functioning language games which rest on a background of consensus, in order to grasp what are the essential con-stituents of the more ordinary case of speech oriented toward understanding. He claims that consensual speech rests on a background consensus which is formed from the implicit mutual recognition of at least four types of validity claims. These four types of validity claims are: (i) that what is said be linguistically intelligible and comprehensible; (ii) that the propositional content or the existential presuppositions of what is said be true; (iii) that the speaker be truthful (honest or sincere) in what she says; and (iv) that what the speaker says (and hence does) is right or appropriate in the light of existing norms and values.

One can think of these four validity claims as conforming to the different dimensions of reality with respect to which all speech actions are related in virtue of being uttered; and as a consequence, as representing the different dimensions in which communicative interaction can break down. Intelligibility refers to immanent aspects of language itself: grammatical and semantic rules of language, consensus about the meaning of terms, and the like. Misunderstanding occurs at this level when we are unable to understand what is being said; the speaker's words do not make sense in some way, and so we ask, for example, for an explication, re-statement, paraphrase, or definition. Assuming we do understand one another at this level, consensus is threatened if we disagree about the truth of what is said, that is, if the relation between what is said and external reality does not appear to be the same for both of us. In order to vindicate a truth claim the speaker can try supplying some empirical evidence, or she can cite an authority, or merely provide more information. All speech actions are also related to the inner reality of the speaker. Signs of a breakdown in this dimension are evident when we doubt the sincerity or veracity of the speaker; we think the speaker is lying or trying to deceive us. Or maybe the speaker is self-deceived, and she is not telling us the truth of what she really believes because she cannot admit her belief to herself. Validation in this dimension is often fraught (doubt about another's honesty once implanted is difficult to remove) but normally it occurs by the speaker offering a variety of assurances: accepting demands, responsibilities, and obligations; or showing a willingness to undertake certain further (future) actions. Finally, all speech actions are placed into relation with a normative reality. Not everyone has the right, for example, to tell me what to do or not do, to arrest or punish me, to fail an essay, give a degree, or grant absolution. One can redeem a normative claim by citing a relevant precedent, or showing how the claim in question is connected with some other agreed norm, or through citing features of the situation which might have been overlooked (e.g. extenuating circumstances).

In consensual speech actions we recognize these validity claims, and therefore accept responsibility to attempt to redeem the validity of what we say if challenged in any of these dimensions. In the ordinary case of speech oriented toward understanding we cannot always reach an agreement; when this occurs a variety of possibilities are open to us: we can adopt a strategic or manipulative attitude towards the other, or break off communication altogether and resort to force. Both these possibilities represent a denial of the responsibilities to one another we have in entering into communication (the rules of communication are supplanted by the 'rules' of war). Alternatively, we can step outside the context of interaction and enter into a different type of communicative relation where problematic norms and contested truth claims are treated as hypotheses in need of thoroughgoing justification and defence. This new type of communicative relation Habermas terms 'discourse'. As opposed to ordinary communication ('interaction'), the goal of discourse is systematically to examine and test problematic truth and normative claims in their own right. And throughout history, in fact, a number of institutions have arisen which can best be understood as institutionalizing discourses of different kinds. For example, it is useful to think of the rise of philosophy in classical Athens as an attempt to institutionalize discourses which could systematically question the validity claims of mythical and religious worldviews; to consider the growth of modern science as the institutionalization of discourses in which validity claims concerning profane knowledge about the natural world could be systematically questioned and tested; and finally, to regard the growth of the bourgeois public sphere as the institutionalization of discourses in which validity claims connected with practical questions and political decisions could be (were supposed to be) continually questioned and tested.

Now in each case the shift from interaction to discourse by a communicative community tokened their commitment to the belief that a rational consensus could be formed concerning the validity claims at issue. Habermas contends that the grounds for this belief can be found in the nature of the argumentative rationality at work in discursive contexts. As members of a community of discourse, we presuppose that whatever consensus we do achieve be achieved solely through the force of better argument. And this can be a criterion for the rationality of our consensus only on the condition that our discourse is free from all forms of distorted communication, that all forms of force other than the force of better argument are put out of play. Needless to say, that condition is and has been only rarely realized; or to state the point more negatively, the belief that our discourse is free from all distorted communication is almost always contrafactual. Nonetheless, it is that belief which underwrites the rationality of discourse: 'on this unavoidable fiction rests the humanity of intercourse among men who are still men'.

In thinking of a discourse free from distorted communication we are imaging an ideal speech situation. In simplest terms, an ideal speech situation would be one in which all the participants had an effective equality of chances to take part in the dialogue. If this requirement is to be met then it is necessary to stipulate that all the participants in the dialogue have the right and the opportunity to initiate and perpetuate discourse on any issue; and this means they must have the right and the opportunity to question or defend any factual or normative claim. Further, if argument is not to be constrained by the existing assumptions of any particular linguistic framework, then each must have the freedom to radicalize the discourse by moving it to higher levels of abstraction and reflection, which in turn may require the modification of the originally accepted conceptual framework. Equally important is the proviso that the participants in an ideal speech situation be motivated solely by the desire to reach a consensus about the truth of statements and the validity of norms; and this requires that conscious or unconscious inhibitions to discourse (including strategic motivations) be overcome, and the norms of honesty and truthfulness be fulfilled. Finally, strategic motivations and inhibitions will not be overcome if the norms binding agents are not symmetrical, that is, participants to dialogue must neither possess role privileges, nor be subject to one-sidedly binding norms. The conditions for an ideal speech situation are not, then, linguistic in character; rather, they are social and material conditions.

DISCOURSE AND AUTONOMY

Only in an emancipated society, whose members' autonomy and responsibility have been realized, would communication have developed into the non-authoritarian and universally practised dialogue from which both our model of reciprocally constituted ego-identity and our idea of true consensus are always implicitly derived. To this extent the truth of statements is based on anticipating the realization of the good life.

(J. Habermas)

The ideal speech situation models an ideal form of life because ideal communication requires the realization of conditions which would underwrite the equality of effective chances for participants to enter into dialogue; which itself presupposes freedom from all forms of coercion and constraint which might in any way engender less than full discursive reciprocity. Truth, freedom, and justice cannot be thought apart from one another because the interpretation of each depends upon its connection with the others; each of these concepts is implicated materially and conceptually in the meaning of the others. A line of argument which illustrates this point runs as follows. One of the conditions necessary for the validity of a truth claim is the potential agreement of all others, since non-agreement entails that either the defender of a truth claim has provided less than dialogically satisfactory grounds for her claim, or an objector has put forward an objection which has failed to be satisfactorily answered. A statement may be true without our jointly being able to see that, and why, it is true. The dialogic process of objection and justification leading to a rational consensus is embedded in our *valuing* truth; truth without consensus would be, for us, empty (no better than brute authority or a claim of divine revelation). But the idea of a grounded consensus involves the idea of a speech situation free from coercion and constraint, where only the force of better argument is operative. And to image an ideal speech situation where this is possible requires conceptualizing a context of interaction where the forces which lead to lying, deceit, self-deception, indeed all forms of distorted communication (pseudo-communication and false consensus) are put firmly out of play: an ideal form of life.[17]

51

Unlike classical utopias, however, this ideal form of life is more than an end, a telos which we are a priori committed to bring about; it is equally presupposed in all actual discourses (and is effective or real in actual discourses to the degree to which the achievement of any given rational consensus must also be a partial realization of an ideal discourse). Dialogic partners are presupposed to be in a position either to accept or reject one another's claims on rational grounds. If we become aware that either there are, say, neurotic or ideological forces working on our partners, or they have ends other than rational agreement controlling their discourse, then we are entitled to, and can, change our attitude towards them. But our adoption of any kind of strategic attitude towards the other can only be regarded as a deficient or remedial mode of interaction, since even it could not be maintained except against a background consensus where the four types of validity claim were assumed (however tacit, implicit or buried that assumption was). The use of deceit presupposes the norm of truth-telling; and truth-telling makes sense only where we presuppose a distinction between what is true and what is false (one cannot rationally believe what one knows to be false); and finally, for truth-telling and truth to be able to have a place in our communications with others we must assume of them that they can and will respond to these norms, which is to say, we must assume that they are free to adhere to these norms, and that they are so motivated in their attitude to us that they will so respond. Again, it is important to admit that more often than not these assumptions are false; but we could not even begin a dialogue with others unless it were presupposed that these norms either were or could become effective. For Habermas the ideal speech situation can be posed as an end only because it is always already at work in actual ordinary language communications; and because it is a necessary end it can function in actual ordinary language communications as a reminder of just what we are committed to merely by virtue of entering into communication with others. The ideal speech situation is, then, at once ideal and real: as an ideal it is derived from the realities of human communication; and in its concrete manifestations it prefigures and alludes to its realization in an ideal form of life.

In part the significance Habermas attributes to the ideal speech situation draws upon his original imaging of the effects on individuals of distorted communications; above all on his conceptualization of the way in which a false consensus can involve a distortion of a person's relations with herself, how it can promote a disfigured self-understanding and self-interpretation. It is hence natural to suppose that the application of the ideal speech situation to the problems of practice would yield a model where conditions for valid self-interpretations were of central importance. And indeed, one of the most striking features of Habermas's thought is the way in which the problems of self-knowledge and self-understanding form the centre of his account of normative practical discourse. Not only does the ideal speech situation itself depend upon agents not being self-deceived, but positively, agents can attain a true understanding of themselves, of their needs, wants, and interests, only in the context of an ideal communication.

> The consensus-producing power of argument rests on the supposition that the language system in which the recommendations requiring justification, the norms, and the generally accepted needs cited for support are interpreted, is appropriate. . . . We call appropriate that language of morals which permits determinate persons and groups, in given circumstances, a truthful interpretation both of their own particular needs, and more importantly of their common needs capable of consensus. The chosen language system must permit those and only those interpretations of needs in which the participants in the discourse can make their inner natures transparent and know what they really want. . . . By virtue of its formal properties, practical discourse must guarantee that the participants can at any time alter the level of discourse and become aware of the inappropriateness of traditional need interpretations; they must be in a position to develop that language system which permits them to say what they want under given conditions with a view to the possibility of changing conditions, and to say – on the basis of a universal consensus – what they ought to want.[18]

What is wrong with the system of slavery, we might say, is not that the happy slaves have needs, desires, and interests which we can ascertain but they cannot; rather, it is that they are not in a position to discover, form, or know what it is they need and want. Only retrospectively can anyone know what the suppressed needs and interests of others are, and therefore what norms ought to have been binding in the original situation. This is because redeemable norms and generalizable interests are neither empirical entities waiting to be discovered by the vigilant investigator, nor are they simply and arbitrarily posited by individuals or collectives; rather, Habermas claims, 'they are, in a non-contingent way, both formed and discovered'.[19] The very idea of a rational will, here clearly imaged in a Rousseauian manner, involves making and finding. Without the emphasis on making and finding, Habermas's account of discursive will-formation would lose both its educative or pedagogical aspect, and its productive conception of historical change. What is discovered, on the other hand, is discovered only in virtue of, in the light of, the new interpretative language which replaces the language system of suppression (e.g. the 'language' of slavery, or the 'language' of science and technology). But it is because there are languages of suppression, language systems which promote pseudo-communication and false consensus, that we must be able to view concrete social configurations in counterfactual terms. With respect to any social system we must be able and prepared to ask how its members would 'have collectively and bindingly interpreted their needs (and which norms would they have accepted as justified) if they could and would have decided on the organization of social intercourse through discursive will-formation'.[20] No answer to such a question can be decisive, given what has been said about what such interpretations involve. Nonetheless, the mere granting of the legitimacy of the question, the demand that the question be asked, throws into relief the claim that our understanding of human autonomy and political liberty – complementing one another as the theoretical core of the ideal speech situation – forms an intrinsic part of what counts as understanding human social relations.

What distinguishes Habermas's vision of autonomy and liberty from those which Berlin criticizes is its assumption that the privilege of knowing what is truly in our interests and what norms ought to be binding for us cannot be had by anyone other than us. But not all situations are such as to allow those interests and norms to be formed in an autonomous fashion. Without the ideal form of life which would bring into being an ideal speech situation, our liberty and autonomy can only be partial.

A KINGDOM OF ENDS?

If we abstract from the person differences between rational beings, and also from all the content of their private ends – [we shall be able] to conceive of a whole of all ends in systematic conjunction.

(I. Kant)

It might be argued against Habermas that his ideal speech situation amounts to no more than a linguistic rewriting of Kant's Kingdom of Ends, that Ideal situation in which the dictates of the categorical imperative rule unchallenged.[21] Certainly, Habermas's search for the grounds of any possible rational consensus might be deemed to parallel Kant's search for the grounds of right action in general; and in sharing Kant's transcendental approach to normative questions Habermas ends up with the grounds for validity being both ever-present and projected into an indefinite future. However, before we press the issue of the ideality of the ideal speech situation, it is important to note two respects in which Habermas's theory diverges from Kant's. First, moral theory is 'monologic' in character, while Habermas's theory is consistently dialogic. Kant's moral law requires that valid maxims of action be capable of being universalized, that is, no intended action-type can be morally valid unless it can be consistently followed by all rational agents. Now this is monological (individualistic) in the naive sense that the procedure prescribed by the moral law for deciding whether a maxim is ethically valid is accomplished by a solitary subject who tests only whether other subjects could rationally will such an action. For Habermas the question of validity rests on actual dialogue – unconstrained communication – among agents, for the question of validity is whether other agents will accept a given maxim. And this points to a deeper sense in which Kant's theory is monologic.

By presupposing autonomy – and that means the will's property to being a law unto itself – in practical philosophy in the same way as he does the unassailable and simple identity of self-consciousness in theoretical philosophy, Kant expels moral action from the very domain of morality itself, Kant assumes the limiting case of a pre-established coordination of the acting subjects. The prior synchronization of those engaged in action within the framework of unbroken intersubjectivity banishes the problem of morality from the domain of moral doctrine – namely, the interplay of an intersubjectivity which has been mediated by overidentification and loss of communication.

(*TP*, 150)

For Habermas the problems of morality are always problems of intersubjectivity. Moral doctrine must concern itself with the forms of broken intersubjectivity and its reinstatement. Kant's ethics is an ethic of intention; according to it agents can be moral all alone.

This leads to the second point on which Habermas and Kant differ. Because right action for Kant is a solitary and private affair, the legal relations governing interaction between agents becomes a wholly outer or external issue. 'Right', Kant says, 'is the limitation of every man's freedom so that it harmonizes with the freedom of every other man in so far as harmonization is possible according to general law.'[22] Inner autonomy in the ethical domain must be complemented by maximum non-interference from others in the social domain. Hence the root problem governing Kant's conception of politics is that of securing negative freedom. That this should be the goal of a just state makes sense only if it is presupposed that the content (ends) of human desire is a private question without bearing on the public good; and conversely, that the structure of the public domain has no bearing on the content of human desires. But only a thoroughly individualistic theory can make such assumptions. As soon as one admits that human needs and desires are socially constructed and constrained, then the rigid distinction between morality and legality (politics) collapses. For Habermas, 'the validity of all norms is tied to discursive will-formation'. Autonomy concerns the conditions under which fundamental need interpretations and norms are formed. The ideal form of life required for an ideal speech situation provides an account of the meaning of freedom in general for beings who are social beings.[23]

Nonetheless, there is one respect in which Habermas's theory does appear subject to the same kind of criticism as that levelled against Kant's moral theory. While the model of the ideal speech situation may help theoretically to illuminate undetected areas of unfreedom in our present situation by focusing attention on those features of agents' conditions of thought and action which make it difficult for them to articulate their true interests and desires, it cannot guide those agents in making specific decisions since, in the last instance, rationality is defined by procedures operative only in the ideal speech situation itself. Marxists might put the objection this way: The universality of the model of the ideal speech situation depends upon its abstraction from concrete historical circumstances. In a world of class conflict it would be unreasonable to expect rationality to transcend class boundaries. Ends rational for the proletariat will appear irrational from the perspective of the bourgeoisie, even if both groups have generated their respective ends in a rationally discursive manner. And further, since the situation is not itself ideal, then the means for realizing those ends may be deemed less than ethically rational even from within a delimited class perspective. If the logical mesh between means and ends obtains only in the projected end state, then short of that ideal neither means nor ends can be expected to be fully rational. But to argue thus is still to view historical, class rationality as somehow deficient. Why not say that there is nothing but historical rationality, and Habermas's theory is a depoliticized abstraction from all that gives reason force and content?

Habermas's model of the ideal speech situation appears, then, to be a philosophical or theoretical model of human autonomy with no clear purchase on, or application to, existing social agents. In attempting to gain a vantage point transcending the historically defined circumstances of existing agents – a move, remember, which Habermas felt forced to make in order to distinguish false from true consensuses – he has equally gone beyond the conditions under which political ideas and ideals can have a rational appeal to social agents. 'The good for man is something that is encountered in human practice, and it cannot be specified in isolation from the concrete situation in which something is preferred to something else. . . . As a general idea, the idea of a just life is empty.'[24] While there is something to this criticism, to accept it at face value means relinquishing the critical perspective which the model of the ideal speech situation allows us to have. Would it not be sufficient to say here that the meaning of the model in relation to particular circumstances depends upon dialogue and discussion? That the theory injects an objective moment into the historical situation, but cannot itself provide agents with an absolute trans-cendent perspective? And given the nature of historical life, would we want a theory to do any more than this? Certainly after the time of *Knowledge and Human Interests* Habermas begins taking the hermeneutical objection to his theory on board, thus coming increasingly to conceive of the constraints of the ideal speech situation as negative and critical in function rather than projecting an ideal future. Whether this concession is enough, or whether the worries about formalism and abstraction that are first raised by Hans-Georg Gadamer in the above quote will form a continuous strand for the remainder of this study.

Habermas's conception of liberty is a complex conjoining of the liberal idea of free speech as modelled in the bourgeois public sphere, with the Greek idea of freedom as pure politics. What makes Habermas's theory more than a backward-looking utopia, and what allows him to link these two conceptions of liberty together, is a thoroughly modern understanding of human language and speech as a meta-institution of society which pervades all aspects of social life. Holding firm to the place of language in human life, Habermas is able to see the partiality of the classical Marxist emphasis on labour and technology, and the modern faith in objectivist scientific procedures. While this emphasis seems correct, the question arises as to whether the emphasis on communicative rationality can bear the critical weight Habermas places on it if it is considered in abstraction from the democratic practice?

3

SELF-KNOWLEDGE AS PRAXIS
Narrative and narration in psychoanalysis

Habermas's reading of Freud in *Knowledge and Human Interests* has often been criticized both in its role as a plausible model for a critical theory of society and as a reading of Freud.[1] In what follows I want to suggest that Habermas's reading of Freud exceeds the role assigned to it in his argument; and in so doing it provides a more powerful and radical model for critical theory than has been recognized.

Implicitly, and indeed in ways Habermas has tacitly come to recognize in his *rejection* of Freud and turn towards Piaget, Kohlberg, and evolutionary history, reconstructed Freudian theory delineates an emphatic sense of history and historical praxis incompatible with the universalistic and transcendental structures that are generally regarded as the Achilles' heel of the Habermasian programme.[2] To put the same point otherwise: Habermas interprets Freudian metapsychology in terms of a theory of depth hermeneutics; hence critical theory is to become a critical hermeneutics. Habermas believes that the 'critical' element of this project can be sustained only if a universalistic and transcendental moment is presupposed by depth-hermeneutical practice. This moment, the moment of the ideal speech situation, is not only required for a depth hermeneutic modelled on psychoanalytic theory, it is incompatible with it. This incompatibility is a consequence of the central and pivotal role of narrative in Habermas's account. Because of its narrative element depth hermeneutics remains hermeneutics – historical, contextual, productive.

DEPTH HERMENEUTICS:
REPRESENTATION OR INTERPRETATION?

As noted in the previous chapter (pp. 44–46), while Habermas accepts the core of the hermeneutical analysis of meaning and history, he rejects its claims to universality as forwarded by Gadamer (and Winch) on the grounds that its identification of social reality with the shared consciousness of its participants dissolves any critical appearance/reality distinction, and hence must be false at some level. How and under what conditions beliefs are formed, and subjects' relation to their beliefs, are components of their rationality. Even true beliefs if acquired through indoctrination or under conditions of censorship will bear the mark of their origin since if their holders cannot, in principle, provide an intelligible account of why those beliefs are held to be true then there is a sense in which they are not *their* beliefs at all. How can a belief be actually mine or yours if the mechanism through which it was acquired suppresses the conditions which permit true beliefs to be distinguished from false? Beliefs, even in cultures with very different justificatory grounds for evaluations from our own, carry with them normative implications referring to their ground and hence by extension their mode of legitimate acquisition. Beliefs, for us and within our culture, belong within the logical space of reasons. Habermas's notion of systematically distorted communication extends the idea that beliefs must be acquired through normatively legitimated mechanisms which agents implicitly or explicitly recognize as conditional for their goodness by providing a formal criterion of goodness (undistorted communicative relations in accordance with the norms of the ideal speech situation) which permits the identification of impersonal mechanisms that deform the rationality of beliefs. In the same way in which individuals can deform one another's beliefs through deception, coercion, withholding information, etc., so, Habermas avers, communicative relations among individuals can be analogously subject to forces that inhibit access to grounds, and hence to what could, in principle, reveal their collective beliefs to be justifiable. In cases of communicative relations distorted by impersonal mechanisms in societies like our own, because agents evince a sharing of values and traditions, with those values and traditions forming the horizon of their mutual understanding, then from a hermeneutical perspective the going consensus is indistinguishable from one formed where the appropriate mechanisms for belief formation are undisturbed.

If communicative relations can be systematically deformed or distorted – by social hierarchy, class domination, market demands, administrative structures of decision-making, etc. – then social theory requires a form of analysis connecting meaning complexes as evinced in agents' ordinary practices and self-interpretations with structural forms that deform those meaning complexes and thereby agents' self-understanding. A depth or deep hermeneutic is one geared to the elaboration of the connection between complexes of meaning and structural forms acting upon or mediating them. By eliciting the causes of deformed communicative relations, a depth hermeneutic permits the individuals or groups concerned to remove the source of the deformation, restore communicative relations, and so alter their self-interpretations, giving voice to suppressed claims (to rights, say) and need interpretations. By dissolving the quasi-causal mechanisms that distort intersubjective and so subjective life, agents can communicatively transfigure themselves and their relations with others. Since depth-hermeneutical theories allow quasi-causal mechanisms to be dissolved by being made visible, and since such theories hence operate in the name of emancipation, Habermas denotes them self-reflective sciences.

They combine hermeneutical theory's concern for meaning with objective theory's concern for detecting causal structures.

According to Habermas a depth hermeneutic is always a double hermeneutic: we come to understand the *meaning* of a deformed language game while and through the *explanation* provided of the origin of this deformation. Habermas's model of a depth hermeneutic adds to hermeneutic's interpretive procedure an explanatory dimension. The unique linking of interpretation with explanation in a depth hermeneutic is meant, again, to provide a conceptual schema for a science of self-reflection. In *Knowledge and Human Interests* Habermas offers an account of Freudian theory as an epistemological or methodical model for a science of self-reflection, and hence as a model which accurately delineates the respective contributions which explanation and understanding make to such a science.[3] In what follows I want to consider Habermas's analysis of Freud in precisely this light; that is, what is at issue in this reconstruction of Freud is not the truth or falsity of his theory (or theories) in general, nor will it concern itself with the question of whether there may be other kinds of therapy and other possible sources of mental disorder than those Freud proposes.

According to Habermas, Freud misunderstood his enterprise as forwarding an empirical, causal, theory of the psyche, and consequently he misunderstood analytic practice as an instrumental application of a natural scientific metapsychology. In so doing, Habermas argues, Freud was in danger of sacrificing the very points of the psychoanalytic enterprise: emancipation through self-reflection.

> Freud surely surmised that the consistent realization of the program in a 'natural-scientific' or even rigorously behavioristic psychology would have had to sacrifice the *one intention* to which psychoanalysis owes its existence: the intention of enlightenment, according to which ego should develop out of id. But he did not abandon this program, he did not comprehend metapsychology as the only thing it can be in the system of reference of self-reflection: a universal interpretation of a self-formative processes.
>
> (*KHI*, 254)

All the tensions in Habermas's account derive from the discordances among the three elements following the colon in the final sentence of this passage. What is at issue is an *interpretation*, but an interpretation which unlike interpretations generally, where context-dependence and limitedness are conditions of possibility, this interpretation is to attain to *universality*. Worse still, the interpretation is of self-formative processes, that is, processes of development for beings who possess the capacity for altering their agency through altering their comprehension of themselves.

Not only is Freudian metapsychology about a temporal sequence, and hence narrative in form; but it is derived from and refers back to the analytic situation of dialogue (pp. 237–45, 252–4), and hence is realized in a praxis of self-narration that is a self-transformation. Habermas acknowledges these aspects of Freudian theory as placing a constraint or restriction on the kinds of corroboration and falsification to which it is subject. These constraints, above all the fact that psychoanalytic inquiry cannot establish a 'methodologically clear separation of the object domain from the level of theoretical statements' (p. 262), are what distinguish it from the strict empirical sciences. Nonetheless, Habermas believes that in acknowledging these constraints and restrictions he is explicating the way in which general interpretations can attain to universality despite their specific differences from the strict empirical sciences. This acknowledgement is not sufficient. The gap between narrative form (the general interpretation) and narrative praxis is not the same as the gap between a universal and a particular it covers or can be predicated of; nor is it identical with a type and a token of that type (p. 264); nor is the situation here governed by a logic of exemplification. Rather, the realization of the Freudian narrative form in the narrative praxis of an analysand involves the queer idea of the narrative form *becoming true* because of the praxis it enjoins. Narrative praxis, it will be argued, is an excess beyond narrative form in virtue of which the latter gains its cognitive validity; the excess of narrative praxis beyond narrative form hence realizing at the cognitive level the excessive, self-transcending character human existence possesses in virtue of its temporal constitution.

So construed, one might object that narrative excess is nothing but the excess of human freedom itself; and hence that psychoanalytic narration is but another version of triumphal, self-mastering human subjectivity; the idea of becoming true a thinly disguised pragmatism and/or voluntarism. Such an objection would be true if psychoanalysis was nothing but an emancipatory project, another practice of self-liberation. It is not for two reasons: firstly, the constraints on what can be narrated, or to use a term from logic and mathematics, constructed, show that what is practically willed also has the character of and a claim to be a discovery. Secondly, according to Habermas, psychoanalytic self-transformations work through the operation of the Hegelian causality of fate. As we shall see this causality involves the acknowledgement (recognition) of an always already presupposed alterity which in its alterity conditions the self-possession of the subject. The narrative form that articulates or expresses the movement of the causality of fate is tragedy. Hence, there is a delimited and delimiting structure to such projects: emancipation is only possible as tragedy. Hence, human self-creating and self-transfiguring praxis is both cognitive and tragic in ways that, say, the Nietzschean version of the art of self-creation fails to grasp; but equally that Nietzschean emphasis on transfiguration is apt in ways that Habermas fails to fully appreciate. And, I want to suggest, the rudiments of that idea of a tragic syncopation of creation and discovery is just what Habermas offers in the idea of a science of self-reflection.

NARRATIVE REASON: THEORY AND THERAPY

One of the ways human beings assess and interpret the events of their lives is through the construction of plausible narratives. Narratives represent events not as instances of general laws but rather as elements of a history where a continuing individual or collective subject suffers or brings about dramatic, i.e. meaningful, changes. A change is meaningful in virtue of its relation to past and future events. Eating an apple is a pleasant but not generally meaningful act; Eve's eating of that apple, motivated by curiosity, is in that context an act of disobedience and defiance, which leads to banishment from the Garden, and the unending toil of men. Constructing narratives involves eliciting connections between events by describing them in one way rather than another. Sleeping with your wife is morally and legally acceptable, not to speak of desirable; but if your wife is your mother, tragedy is afoot. To describe an action correctly, then, means describing it under descriptions relevant to the story being told. Typically, we call the conceptual structure which binds the events of a story together a plot. Plots are not events, but structures of events. The meaningfulness of plot-structures is analogous to the meaning of human action in that they are governed by a teleological or purposive movement: 'A story's conclusion is the pole of attraction of the entire development. . . . [A] narrative conclusion can be neither deduced nor predicted (in the logical or scientific sense) . . . rather than being predictable, a conclusion must be acceptable.'[4]

Human self-reflection is dominantly, if not exclusively, either structural or narrative. In structural self-reflection we engage in self-evaluation, measuring character and personality traits against either accepted norms or their suitability for realizing desired ends. In narrative self-reflection we rehearse past events as turning points in a life-history. Only certain construals of past events cohere with present circumstances and self-understanding; but those construals, the descriptions narratively appropriate to them, can, and often do, fail to coincide with our original understanding of what had occurred. The understanding of past events, then, can require the searching out of new descriptions if our inarticulate sense of their meaningfulness is to be preserved. Sometimes this involves employing a language or vocabulary and concepts not available at the time the events in question took place. Psychoanalytic theory is such a language, and our childhood such a past.

The model of the three mental agencies, id, ego, and superego, permits a systematic presentation of the structure of language deformation and behavioural pathology. . . . They elucidate the methodological framework in which empirical substantive interpretations of [a] self-formative process can be developed. . . . They are interpretations of early childhood development (the origins of basic motivational patterns and the parallel formation of ego functions) *and serve as narrative forms that must be used in each case as an interpretive scheme for an individual's life history in order to find the original scene of his unmastered conflict.*

(*KHI*, 258; emphasis mine)

The model of the three mental agencies (derived from the experience of analytic dialogue), together with the roles, persons and patterns of interaction arising from the structure of the family, and the mechanisms of action and learning (object-choice, identification, internalization, and the like) are the materials which allow sufferers to form the narratives which would make their misery comprehensible in the first instance. Where pointless behaviour was, there narrative shall be. Therapy just is, in part, the constructing of a narrative, the making of a generalized biography into a specific autobiographical tale. The analyst

> makes interpretive suggestions for a story the patient cannot tell . . . they can be verified only if the patient adopts them and tells his story with their aid. The interpretation of the case is corroborated only by the successful continuation of an interrupted self-formative process.

(*KHI*, 260)

Around this feature of the analytic enterprise three essential philosophical problems of psychoanalysis crystallize: the validity of particular psychoanalytic interpretations; the validity of psychoanalytic theory generally; and the effectivity of therapy. Roughly, Habermas believes that the acceptability of particular analytic insights depends upon their acceptability to the analysand; and since analysis is the only place where the general theory meets reality, and the theory is a narrative schema, a generalized biography which becomes an *auto*biography through its acceptance by the analysand, then the empirical accuracy of the theory as a whole 'depends not on controlled observation and subsequent communication among investigators but rather on the accomplishment of self-reflection and subsequent communication between the investigator and his "object" ' (p. 261). Stated in this manner, Habermas appears to be merely specifying the kinds of evidential and corroborative constraints applicable to psychoanalytic theory in virtue of its narrative form and the significant place which an analysand's acceptance of interpretations has in the theory's projection onto the world. He does not appear to be arguing, for example, that psychoanalytic theory should be interpreted instrumentally. Rather, he is pointing toward the way in which the peculiar relation between universal and particular in psychoanalytic theory and practice distorts the standard picture of how theories are tested, corroborated or refuted. For all that, once we take account of these constraints on testing, psychoanalytic theory itself can still be interpreted 'realistically', not of course in accordance with the mechanistic, energy distribution model, but in accordance with the model of intentional structures pathologically deformed by the causality of split-off symbols and repressed motives. Now I want to argue that such an attempt to preserve a realistic core to our reading of psychoanalytic theory radically underestimates the significance of the materials which are used to demonstrate the necessity for there being alterations in our established procedures for theory evaluation.

In order to show what is at issue in this claim, let me instance a passage where Habermas is pressing beyond the bounds of his own interpretation.

> The process of inquiry can lead to valid information only via a transformation in the patient's own self-inquiry. *When valid, theories hold for all who can adopt the position of the inquiring subject. When valid,* general interpretations hold for the inquiring subject and all who can adopt its position only to the degree that *those who are made the object of individual interpretations know and recognize themselves in these interpretations.*
>
> (*KHI*, 261–2; emphasis mine)

As is all too obvious, the two 'when valids' of this paragraph are epistemically idle since they can refer to nothing beyond and nothing stronger than the *consequences* of the acceptance of the general interpretation for the analysand. And the reason for this is not simply that no firm methodological line can be drawn between theoretical statement and object domain, but rather that there is no firm distinction because the *existence* of the object domain is contingent upon the acceptance of the theory. The application of the general interpretation is, as Habermas insists, a translation (p. 264); further, 'the conditions of application define a *realization* of the interpretation, which was precluded on the level of general interpretation itself' (p. 266). The logic of 'realization' and what is 'precluded' on the level of the general interpretation reveals the non-representational core of the general interpretation. The relation between the patient's ordinary language and the language of the theory hence corresponds most closely to the Gadamerian notion of a fusion of horizons.[5]

What is properly, if obliquely, being stated by Habermas, despite himself, is that the schema of psychoanalysis can become true if agents can recognize themselves in it, and through that recognition continue their interrupted self-formative process and thereby gain emancipation. Nor is this claim surprising if human agents are the sorts of beings who can modify and alter their agency through altering their conception of themselves.

Nonetheless, the radically historical conception of truth implied by this, the thought that a theory may be neither true nor false in itself but become true through its employment, since it contradicts even our mildest representational (realist and/or naturalist) assumptions, is in need of backing, drawing on familiar materials. What we learn from a consideration of these materials turns out to be something already known to us from the history of narrative.

EMOTION, THOUGHT AND THERAPY

At the centre of Habermas's reconstruction of Freud is the thesis that the talking cure, the reversal of repression carried out through the analytic dialogue, would be incomprehensible unless the object of repression was itself linguistic. So, for example, he contends that instead of thinking of instinctual demands unable to find an acceptable outlet, we should 'conceive of the act of repression as a banishment of need interpretations themselves' (p. 241). On Habermas's reading, then, the id represents charged, split-off symbols charged because they have been split off and semantically privatized. The consequence of privatization, the binding of a symbol to a particular event or cluster of events in a life-history, is the formation of a symptom.

In urging these constructions Habermas is pointing to the familiar analytic thought that therapy would be impossible unless our emotional life had a large intentional component. Emotions which take objects logically require the having of some types of thoughts, and inversely, certain types of emotion are either appropriate or inappropriate to particular types of thought. To be angry, for example, one must have an object about, by or at which one is angry; therefore one must have certain true or false beliefs about this object; normally one will have appraised the object in question in unfavourable ways; and the content of those appraisals will be relevant to the justification of one's being angry if this is challenged as being in some manner inappropriate. The immediate object of an emotion must be an intentional object since only under an appropriate description can one have that emotion towards that object. This in itself generates two ways in which an emotion can be inappropriate: firstly, one's belief may be false ('You see, there is nothing to be afraid of'); or secondly, the appraisal may be inaccurate ('But the snake is harmless; it has no harmful – fear-provoking – properties'). Finally, objectless emotions are usually deemed to be caused, although we are willing to admit that conjectures, beliefs, doubts and related cognitive states may have a place in their genesis. Which is not to deny that joy, depression, free-floating anxiety, and the like, even if inaugurated by a belief, seem able to persist independently of that or any related belief, and hence without an object.

Even from this it is clear that a change in belief can under appropriate circumstances inaugurate a transformation in our emotional states; and finding the belief at the source of an objectless emotion *may* be the first step in dispelling that state. Now, as a first approximation, one might hazard that apparently pointless actions (or 'neurotic' feelings) are logically akin to objectless emotions, and hence what can yield relief from that latter may equally permit release from the former. Nonetheless, the analogy between neurotic feeling and activity, and objectless emotions is not altogether accurate, for in pathological cases the root cause of the emotional states and actions in question may be quite temporally remote from their occurrence. On further reflection, we shall also have to recognize that what makes neurotic activity or

feeling differ from their self-deceptive analogues is that the falsity or inappro-
priateness of the subject's beliefs about his state's object is often quite evident
to him. Phobics and obsessives are often quite aware of the irrationality of
their fears or the irrationality of their actions, and the same can often be said
for other forms of pathological behaviour. Hence, in order to account for such
behaviour we need to dig deeper.

In neurotic emotions, desires and beliefs, the object of the state in question
is not its true target. This simple form of displacement is familiar from everyday cases of, for example, venting the anger one feels against one's boss
against one's partner. Here it seems right to say that the cause and ultimate
target of your anger is what (you believe) your boss did, while your partner is
its object. In neurotic cases the causes are remote and the objects often super-
ficially heterogeneous: your anger at your boss is really an anger at all
authority figures which is really an anger at your father. When dealing, then,
with intractable emotions we, to use Amelie Rorty's lovely formulation, 'look
for the intentional component of the significant cause of the dispositional set
that forms the intentional component of the emotion'.[6] This procedure offers
us a generalized account of the method of 'scenic understanding' which
Habermas adopts from the work of Alfred Lorenzer.[7] Scenic understanding
seeks to establish equivalences between three locations: the everyday scene,
the transference scene, and the original scene. The establishing of these
equivalences *is* finding the intentional component of the significant cause (the
unmastered conflict of the original scene) of the dispositional set that forms the
intentional component of the emotion. The construction of the scenes and the
locating of equivalences is the means whereby symptoms are translated (or
retranslated) into symbols. Despite its reliance on intentional language, there
is nothing in this procedure itself, either in Rorty's generalized formula or in
the Habermas/Lorenzer account, which prevents us from regarding it as being
the case in a naturalistic and objectivist mode; objectively, this is being offered
as the correct, naturalistic analysis of intractable and anomalous emotions and
forms of behaviour. However, I want to argue, the intentional components of
this analysis do not really mesh with any form of naturalism, realism or
objectivism.

While there are a number of different aspects of the situation which might
be used to support this claim, I want to focus on what may be termed the
remoteness problem. Roughly, this refers to the fact that we tend to regard
intractable emotions as rooted 'elsewhere' than in a person's present, for if
merely present then it is difficult to see how anything other than conflicted
desires or beliefs could be at issue; and if this were so then a moral and/or
'existential' case would be the natural solution. And, indeed, this is precisely
our attitude to akratics and self-deceivers. But our sense that not all emotional
intractability is of this sort leads us to search elsewhere, for a remote cause of
the disorder. *Our* conception of childhood as formative for the 'character' of
our adult mental life, of personal identity as bound up with psycho-sexual

66

identity as rooted in early interactions with significant others (mothers and fathers), licenses and is congruent with the idea that present intractability represents a disturbed self-formative process, that past and present do not connect, that either we have a past removed from and unavailable to self-understanding, or a present that is lived in terms of an overshadowing, dominating past. As Habermas states, the entire analytic procedure was, from the outset, 'subject to the general anticipation of the schema of disturbed self-formative processes' (p. 259).

Now this feature of psychoanalytic theory, its regarding of intractable mental items as rooted in a disturbed self-formative process, takes on epistemological prominence when it is placed into proximity with the role of acceptable belief in psychotherapy. What I have in mind here is this: we may think that our pre-theoretical comprehension of childhood experience itself and its role in the formation of the adult is so unregimented, diverse, and alterable on the one hand, and our present access to it so necessarily oblique, on the other, that they consort ill with the quite richly theoretical constructions of childhood necessary for giving substance to the idea of a disturbed self-formative process. We might, that is, think that there are features of childhood experience which make for more-than-methodological difficulties, in providing evidence for a theory about it, and as a consequence there appears a more-than-ordinary gap between theory and practice. This gap will even appear larger once we begin assessing the degree of metaphoricity built into the conceptual schemes that elaborate infant experience. Compare, for example, Freud and Melanie Klein in this regard. Ironically, however, the interpretative character of theory and therapy inversely entails the utter inconsequentiality of that gap. Since in the last instance, if not the first, the acceptability of an interpretative suggestion guided by theory by fiat validates theory and interpretation together, assuming all other things are equal (by which I mean *all* available modes of theory confirmation, empirical and logical, having been satisfied), then the representational function of the theory disappears with or in its application: it *becomes* the analysand's self-understanding which inaugurates his cure.

Our pre-theoretical sense of what aspects of childhood experience are or could be formative for later mental life is so complex, diverse and indeterminate that any number of explicit theoretical narrative schemes might be shown to be internally consistent enough, empirically accurate enough (where this is subject to independent confirmation), and conceptually close enough to it to become acceptable to analysands on rational grounds. Oral and anal stages, the depressive position and the paranoid–schizoid position, the mirror stage and the Oedipus complex all could, logically, possess the kind of combined pre-theoretical reference and theoretical pedigree that would permit them to serve for the rediscription of childhood experience in an acceptable manner, so explaining the possibility of a type of disturbed self-formative process, and thus locating an acceptable significant cause of a disorder. So

Freudian, Kleinian, Lacanian, and akin theories all could be equally true. But this I want to say is unlike empirically equivalent but incompatible theories, *for what these reflective theories are about becomes different as the theories are accepted and so become true.* If there is some idea of being 'equally true' here, it is more like the way in which different forms of life may be equally true. The problem here is not the under-determination of theory by evidence, but almost the opposite: the evidence, the life-practice of the subject, appropriates the theory for itself, *giving it existential determinacy* of a kind unavailable to natural scientific theories.

'But surely,' an objector might argue here, 'if there *is* a significant cause for a disorder, then while given the under-determination of theory by evidence there may be a difficulty in saying which of two or more competing theories is true, only one of them can be true. And untrue theories will be therapeutically effective because they are approximately true. To drop these realist intuitions would be to jeopardize our primitive understanding of how theory and therapy connect. Worse, it would reduce therapy to pure instrumentality. Without the notion of approximate truth there can be no difference between self-knowledge and self-delusion. Hence, either you return to some form of realism or you accept some instrumentalist conception of psychoanalytic theory and therapy'. A purely epistemological answer to this might say that in the world of representation if two systems are empirically equivalent but incompatible, then they are both equally true; that it is only a picture of the relation between theory and world which leads us to think there can be but one true description of it.[8] If psychoanalysis were a descriptive theory, then this kind of reply to the metaphysical realist would be appropriate. Although what I want to argue is compatible with the neo-Kantian critique of realism, my fundamental suggestion has been that psychoanalytic theory is not properly a descriptive science at all; rather, I am tempted to say, it is a practical science in which normative and empirical elements are ultimately linked through practice itself. In order to see why this must be so, we must track down the connection between a significant cause and an acceptable belief. This will involve two steps: the first will show how the intentional component of a significant cause is necessarily unavailable for realist purposes; the second will show how the affective aspects of therapy are internal to its constitution as a self-reflective enterprise. Putting these two elements together in part explains in what sense we are self-interpreting beings, and how that connects with the ideas of a science of self-reflection.

When thinking about mental life it is important not to attribute to it more determinacy than it truly possesses; and this is more emphatically the case when dealing with 'unconscious' mental life. Consider the individual who has difficulties with authority figures. Note that it is only under some interpretation that we can collect the different persons with whom his disturbance manifests itself under the heading 'authority figures'. Different interpretive schemes might have suggested persons who are wilful or confident or aggressive or secure or masculine or domineering; and although there are manifest ways in which these concepts cluster, it is easy to conceive of regimentations of our ordinary usages which would produce different relations of inclusion and exclusion amongst these terms. Further, our individual's reaction might have been labelled as cowardly, angry, fearful, intimidated, passive, etc. In both cases the appropriate or correct description will be guided by the interpretive theory the therapist is employing. The point here is that implicit or unconscious beliefs, fears and desires *are* themselves vague, undisciplined, and semantically and grammatically indeterminate (on the assumption that they have a linguistic shape at all; if not then the effort of 'translation' is even more radical). In interpreting them in one way rather than another we are giving them a 'shape and accent previously absent; to convince [the analysand] to whom they are attributed to accept the new formulation is partly to draw out what is already there and partly to change it and its role in his life'.[9] The mistake which naturalistic interpretations of attribution make is to suppose that, on the one hand, the appropriate description of an implicit intentional component of a present dispositional state is a matter of straightforward empirical discovery; and that, on the other hand, the correct description of the intentional component of the remote cause of the dispositional state is equally a matter for empirical discovery. The movement from implicit to explicit is not an empirical matter because what is implicit is not identical with what is explicit but for the fact of its being unconscious. In the first place, locating the correct description of the intentional component of a present dispositional state is not detachable from locating the correct intentional description of its remote cause. But the latter, we have seen, requires the employment of some generalized and theoretical narrative system of development. Secondly, however, while there are axes of development which are or well might be straightforwardly empirical in character (e.g. developmental cognitive psychology), psycho-sexual and moral developmental schemes cannot be empirical in this way because they are determined by their terminus, their *picture* of maturity, autonomy, health, virtue or the good life for people which are not themselves subject to direct empirical questioning. Thirdly, then, accepting an interpretative suggestion, accepting, as in Habermas's account, a set of scenic equivalences, is an *act* of self-interpretation whereby one becomes, or attempts to become, the *kind* of person the theory normatively stipulates through acceding to its regimentation of our pre-understood self-understanding. So, finally, analytic suggestions unavoidably involve extending, refining, deforming and re-forming our given conceptual apparatus which simultaneously is a reforming, a transfiguring of the self.

To accept an analytic suggestion, then, is not like coming to believe, for good reasons, that one description of one's past is more accurate than another since what is to be described is constituted in part through analytic practice. Accepting an analytic suggestion, and so redescribing one's past, involves accepting a *regimented*, refined and explicit revision of our current conceptual scheme. But this involves more than agreeing to use a revised conceptual framework and apparatus (replacing one paradigm with another), for the framework in question is the one constitutive of our present self-under-standing and so present self-identity (broadly conceived). Thus, within the boundaries of a constructivist or ontological hermeneutic, that is, one in which who one *wants* to be has consequences for who one *is* (one cannot *be* a saint or a sinner in every conceptual framework, and hence what it is to *be* a man or a woman, a mother or father are not facts identifiable apart from conceptual schemes and the performances they elicit), acceptable belief in cases of analytic suggestions must be assimilated into the horizon of identity projection, where one is being asked, is asking oneself, to project one's identity, one's under-standing of who one is, along some new and different path. Hence the com-prehension of what is involved in accepting an analytic suggestion itself becomes assimilated into the comprehension of what is involved in acts of self-reflection which have an ineliminable projective or constructive aspect.

In purely epistemological terms, the deformed present is explained when the narrative of the present is placed within a larger narrative framework. This is the way in which one theory displaces another by being able to subsume the older theory – both its explanatory strengths and its anomalies and failures – in the new theory. Given this model, it is natural to suppose that Freud offers simply a new theory of the self. However, since theories about the self break the line dividing theory and object, there is only a new narrative of the self, general or particular, if the self can recognize itself in the narrative and so narrate itself. To narrate oneself is descriptive and performative at once since it requires, minimally, temporalizing oneself differently and so becoming qualitatively different thereby. The theory becomes true, if it does, as the self becomes a different self, if it does. Becoming a new or different kind of self is the discovery of the new conception of self promised by the theory. If the theory is true, it disappears as theory, becoming our taken-for-granted self-interpretation. Since hermeneutic understanding itself is always, properly speaking, an act of extending, altering, deforming and reforming one's own horizon of understanding, then theory-mediated self-reflection looks to be but a specific and explicit account of what is always at issue in acts of under-standing.

Now the necessity for this long detour might have been obviated if we had taken more seriously the thought that, at bottom, psychoanalytic self-transformation is a form of theory-mediated autobiography. It is a truism of our understanding of modern autobiography, a truism about autobiography since Rousseau, that in autobiography the self narrated is a construction, not a representation; and that in narrating a life the act of narration acts back upon the narrating self. Roughly, our intuition here is that the act of self-reflection which autobiography represents cannot be objective and representational not for lack of objectivity and honesty, nor because of humanly endemic self-deception; but because the *retrospective* construal of the significance of events, a construal constitutive of narrative sentences generally, entails a transcendence of the narrative emplotment of events beyond their original meaning. In a self-reflective narrative this transcendence folds back on the narrating self. The epistemological transcendence and productivity of narrative becomes onto-logical when the subject and object of the narrative are one and the same.

This feature of autobiographical discourse was unavailable prior to the development of secular autobiographies whose sole goal is the revelation – the producing and securing – of the identity of the narrated/narrating self. The common and consistent nervous reaction to this uncontrollable productivity has been to conclude that really autobiographies are not representations of a self in its travels through the world but art, creation, fiction. Psychoanalysis, theory-mediated autobiography, challenges this conclusion by revealing that the constitutively productive element of autobiography is but the consequence of the human temporal predicament when self-consciously realized in narrative praxis. Representational construals of narrative derive from regarding them as third person, observer constructs, as forms for epistemically appropriating external events. When narrative turns self-reflective, the tem-poral and practical predicament of all narrative irredeemably surfaces.[10] Habermas's attempts to neutralize narrative productivity fail because self-narration is the excessive truth of narrative form; autobiographical excess reveals the self as twisting free from form and universality even as it appro-priates it to itself.

What one might question in this schema is the fate of the 'other' narrated in autobiography. In autobiography the other is the id, the past, repressed need interpretations. Does this other suffer the same fate as the self appeared about to suffer from the scientistic self-misunderstanding of Freudian meta-psychology? Is narrative's capacity to render *unique and particular* events and life-histories in their uniqueness and particularity, which, after all, is supposed to define the epistemic specificity of narrative, but another fable of the domination of the object by the subject? An answer to this question will require two steps: first, a more precise reconnoitring of the practical, as opposed to contemplative, features of self-reflection and self-knowing; and then a probing of the materials governing Habermas's interpretation of psychoanalysis.

A PASSION FOR CRITIQUE

What is it to reflectively accept a radical interpretation of oneself and one's past? In order to answer this question we must necessarily ask: What might be involved in acts of self-reflection if not the mere discovery of some unnoticed mental item? On this question Freud himself supplies a valuable hint in a famous passage from his 'Observations on "wild" psychoanalysis':[11]

It is a long superseded idea, and one derived from superficial appear-ances, that the patient suffers from a sort of ignorance, and that if one removes the ignorance by giving him information (about the causal connection of his illness with his life, about his experiences in childhood, and so on) he is bound to recover. The pathological factor is not his ignorance in itself, but the root of this ignorance in his inner resistances; it was they that first called this ignorance into being, and they still maintain it now.

So long as we do not attempt to distinguish sharply what is repressed from the repression itself, thinking thereby of the repression and its object as two wholly different items, as Freud sometimes does, then this passage can guide us to an answer to the question posed above.

By construing the unconscious as a domain of ignorance a realist understanding of psychoanalysis naturally reads the therapeutic process in purely epistemological terms, as a movement from self-ignorance to self-knowledge. As a consequence, the realist reading of psychoanalysis is equally committed to a purely epistemic or contemplative account of self-knowledge: the activity of self-reflection just is the acquisition of significant items of information about oneself. With this conception of self-reflection go the beliefs that the effectivity of an unconscious item is a function of its exclusion from consciousness, and hence by bringing an item to consciousness its (dysfunctional) effectivity is eliminated. It is this automatic effectivity of knowledge which Freud is denying when he denies that the source of a disorder is located in simple self-ignorance.

What the contemplative reading of self-reflection obfuscates are the sources of resistance, and hence the sources of repression, which generate the particular kind of self-ignorance with which psychoanalysis deals. What is at issue in psychoanalytic self-reflection is not merely an unknown or unconsciousness item of mental life, but an item that has *become* unconscious, has been repressed, disavowed, disclaimed, and so excluded from consciousness. Conversely, then, for something to become conscious is for it to be avowed, recognized, assented to; its place in one's life must be thought through, its connections with other desires and emotions analysed and evaluated. The source, then, of self-ignorance is a certain set of attitudes toward oneself under the aegis of a particular evaluation and understanding of who one is. Correlatively, self-knowledge proceeds through the adoption of another framework of self-understanding which allows different attitudes towards oneself to be adopted.[12] In broad terms, then, it is a matter of coming up with an interpretation of a set of responses and coming to an acknowledgement of them. So my passivity may be rooted in a fear of aggression, which itself has its origin in an unwillingness to acknowledge a fear of and terrible anger at my father. The story is familiar. But the intensity of ambivalent emotions, love and anger, will not be resolved simply by coming to know that one has a suppressed emotion. To be able to avow one's anger is to be able to understand and accept it. Acceptance itself requiring an alteration in one's self-conception: I am indeed the kind of person who can have these death-dealing feelings which I previously denied even existed. The *kind* of person I am entwines normative and empirical beliefs that have immediate affective aspects since what 'normative' refers to here is what one values most. What one values most is what one invests in most, hence what one most desires. It is the reflective moment of this sort of conative state that self-reflective practices tap into: a state where our most intense striving reflects back on, and thereby reflects, who it is we *want* to be. Repressions and disavowals are the obverse side of the strivings which *are* our self-interpretation. If it is these powerful affects which are at issue, then the whole process of self-reflection will itself have to be constructed within an affective, value-oriented self-relation.

Analytic insights, to be effective, must have an affective basis; and the affective basis of a self-reflective therapy will be different from the affective bases of other therapeutic procedures. It is not sufficient in psychotherapy for the patient to desire relief from misery or to be returned to full functionality. Such desires may promote a cure, but not an analytic cure. 'Critique would not have the power to break up false consciousness if it were not impelled by a passion for critique . . . analytic knowledge is impelled onward against motivational resistances by the interest in self-knowledge' (pp. 234–5). The analysand's analytic insights are self-reflective not only because the understanding so happens to be an understanding of oneself, but also because the *need* for understanding arises in a context where some features of the patient's life are already inscribed as a practical issue: the significance for her life of 'these' feelings and acts are in question, they are yet to be resolved and require resolution. The self-questioning of self-reflection, then, is practical; to seek after 'the truth' about oneself and one's life is to seek after more than true beliefs about one's past, it is to grasp the significance of beliefs, desires, feelings and episodes as they determine one's relations to oneself and to others. The self-gathering of self-reflection is a praxis by means of which one might become who one (really) is; but who one really is is not something determinable external to the praxis of self-reflection.

The self-knowledge which analytic reflection brings is practical as well as epistemic. In analytic reflection it is the intelligibility and significance of the items composing one's mental life which are at issue; items must be scrutinized as to their connection and place within one's life as a whole, they must be evaluated and understood with respect to one's conception of oneself and one's fundamental aims and desires; and those fundamental aims and desires must be analysed as to their rightness with respect to one's fundamental norms and values, and so on. Analytic self-reflection, then, necessarily involves a willingness and a desire to make oneself different, to restructure and reconstruct one's life. And this, in turn, requires a different conception of self-relatedness than that offered by the contemplative model of self-reflection, the image of turning one's mental eye inward upon the landscape of the psyche, sanctioned by realism. Let me quote Habermas at length on this.

Because analysis expects the patient to undergo the experience of self-reflection, it demands 'moral responsibility for the content' of the illness. For the insight to which analysis is to lead is indeed only this: that the ego of the patient recognize itself in its other, represented by the illness, as its own alienated self and identity with it. As in Hegel's dialectic of moral life, the criminal recognizes in his victim his own annihilated essence; in this self-reflection the abstractedly divorced parties recognize the destroyed moral totality as their common basis and thereby return to it. Analytic knowledge is also moral insight, because in the movement of self-reflection the unity of theoretical and practical reason has not yet been undone.

(*KHI*, 235–6)

Emotions can be disavowed or avowed, acknowledged or not acknowledged. To disavow what is your own is more like denying responsibility than being ignorant, for ignorance is still absence and may be undone through the providing of more information. What is disavowed is actively denied, one removes oneself from where one ought to be or needs to be. Avowal involves finding a place in one's life for a desire or emotion, and this is more than discovering it is there, it is doing something with that thought. Hence the undertaking of re-narrating the events of one's life in accordance with the Freudian schema is a moral undertaking, and the insight it provides into one's character is inevitably and invariably a moral insight. In analysis one is being asked to take responsibility for one's feelings and actions; and the demonstration that responsibility has been taken is tokened by the progress of therapy, the capacity to write the narrative of one's life, and thereby to complete the disturbed self-formative process.

In all of this the self is conceived of as more than a body moving through space and time, or as a continuous series of overlapping mental events held together by habit and memory; the self here is a moral totality. As agents we can but conceive of ourselves in terms of those fundamental purposes, goals and values which orient the movements and directions of our life. As a consequence, the various parts of our life are not mere givens, but elements waiting assignment within the whole. That whole, however, is ineliminably normatively structured; the whole of a life always has the sense of a good or bad life, a life well spent or frittered away, a life worth living or valueless. So the narrative of a life is always a moral narrative, a narrative whose general meaning is provided by some narrative schema, some proto-narrative whose intelligibility involves a mesh between normative and temporal terms. Individual narratives employ the terms of the proto-narrative in order to interpret, and reinterpret, the events of a life. As is always the case with stories, the intelligibility of the events being recounted only comes fully into view at the end of the tale.

To enter into psychoanalysis is like undertaking to write a serious novel or to engage in radical political activity: activities in which the epistemic and the normative are staked in terms of a praxis without a predetermined end. In each case one begins with implicit, unconscious doubts, fears, desires, needs and thoughts; and in each case one presupposes that the source of the problem outruns available conceptual understanding: the narrative of the present is practically and cognitively inadequate. Self-knowledge requires preserving but going beyond present self-understanding, producing a narrative which has the narrative of the present, one's false or partial self-understanding, as one of its moments. New and different meanings have to be attributed to past events. But since these events are partially constitutive of the self, their redescription entails a reconstitution of the self. The reconstituted self, the end of the story, provides the vantage point from which the adequacy of the narrative, both general and particular, can be judged – although, of course, not the only or sole vantage point. Since the judgment of adequacy presupposes the validity of what is to be judged, then the judgment itself arrives too late. With self-knowledge at least, the owl of Minerva takes wing only at dusk. Because the vindication of a narrative scheme is dependent upon its practical realization, then practice itself must be conceived of as radically, theoretically and normatively under-determined. Conversely, how can we not say that at the end of this narrative process, as I acknowledge feelings and emotions through the acceptance of the particular scheme and alter my self-interpretation accordingly, that I have not learned and *discovered* new truths about myself and what it is to be a human being?

AN EPISTEMOLOGICAL INTERLUDE: CREATION AND DISCOVERY

At no point in the above analysis has the broad idea of a depth hermeneutic been questioned. Rather, the attempt has been to radicalize a central idea in Habermas's own approach, namely, to take the implicit disturbances in ordinary practice as the experiential basis for the reconstruction of those practices that can reveal a structural or systematic deformation of them that is not a conspicuous component of their explicitly understood intersubjective grammar. For example, political economy, on this analysis, would be an orderly reconstruction of concrete economic practices, hence a reflective articulation of the self-interpretation of economic agents, and *Capital* as a critique of political economy would be a critical reinterpretation of those practices. Because we have no determinate access to structures independently of interpretive understanding, no access to interpretive understanding except through agents' self-interpretations of their practices, and no access to agents' self-interpretations apart from their fundamental aims and values, then the 'test' of a theory is dependent upon individual or collective action on the basis of the insights it affords under the description stipulated by normative aims and values. In this respect, even a depth hermeneutic never leaves the perspective of participant understanding, and so of being a form of self-reflection; all that alters is the kind of item included in self-understanding. Therefore, it is inappropriate to say that reconstructive science or critical social science ever attain to *theoretical* knowledge; no naturalization of social knowledge is possible, no matter how 'naturalized' social relations become, because social theoretical knowledge must make essential reference to modes of human activity, modes of human activity are always bound to structures of self-interpretation, the identity of the agents, and the practical identity of social agents is always something found and created in equal measure, a praxis. To use the vocabulary that Habermas begins to deploy in *The Theory of Communicative Action*, knowledge of 'system', its invasion or colonization of the lifeworld, is simply highly mediated lifeworld self-understanding.

Yet the temptation to consider the detection of what Adorno calls forces of 'blind nature' in social processes as equivalent to the attaining of a third-person, observer perspective on ourselves cannot be easily shunted aside. Some reasons for this temptation are benign. So, for example, one might believe that since meaning, purpose and agency are internally bound together, then when the detection of structures or quasi-causal mechanisms that influence action are in question we must have departed from the perspective of agency. But being reflective about the conditions of actions does not entail leaving the perspective of agency; when I wonder whether my hangover is making me particularly irascible today, I am just being reasonably self-conscious about myself as agent. But if we are agents in the full sense only when capable of self-consciousness, and if self-consciousness is equivalent to having one's self-awareness mediated through other awareness, then for human agents first-person and third-person standpoints are not mutually exclusive. But this is only to say, to speak with the vulgar, that social scientists examining the social world are unlike natural scientists examining the physical world: the goal of the latter is to attain to a horizon of understanding that is not self-implicating, while even that goal would be a category mistake for the social scientist.[13]

Nonetheless, throughout this chapter deep realist and naturalist intuitions have constantly arisen and needed combatting; it is hence natural to suppose that the defence of a widened hermeneutical perspective entails an anti-realist commitment of some form. Yet, it has not been the standard epistemological vocabulary and issues of realism and idealism that have been the focus of concern. In placing the possibilities for self-reflection within a framework in which persons are conceived of as self-interpreting beings, 'perfectible' beings in Rousseau's sense of that word, the contention has been that acquiring knowledge of the self cannot be detached from acts in which the self is transformed or transfigured, become different, and hence that self-knowledge cannot be theorized within a categorically contemplative account of what knowing is. If a structural dualism has been the target of the analysis, it has been the dualism of discovery versus creation rather than the dualism between realism and idealism. If in this context we consider why experimentation is important in science, how the capacity of scientific research programmes to continue solving problems and make discoveries makes them progressive, why it is we think that certain patterns of explanations are merely ad hoc, then I suspect that our sense that science increases our knowledge of the world is tied to its capacity to make, and to continue to make, discoveries rather than any features of it that would bind it directly to standard epistemological positions (realism, idealism, empiricism). Hence there are reasons for thinking that the creation–discovery couple is more basic and more illuminating in considering questions of knowledge than textbook epistemological categories.

Arguably, the deep motive for thinking that there is a fundamental distinction between participant (subject) and observer (object) standpoints, is that we are wont to feel that there is a fundamental abyss separating the activities of creation (art) from the activities of discovery (science): phantasy imagines the world as it might be, inhabiting the domain of the possible, while science probes the world as it is, bound to actuality. It is equally plausible to believe that it is just that fundamental difference between creation and discovery that is the deep source of the debate between idealism and realism. There are other sources for that debate – say, all internal relations belong to the mental and are absent from physical nature (which here is being understood atomistically) or, in the philosophy of language, truth conditions versus warranted assertability conditions – but without the impetus provided from the distinction between what we can make in accordance with a plan of our own and what we find (with endeavour and probing), it is unlikely that the idealism–realism question would continue to intrigue.

Idealists are not concerned to claim that the world is somehow subject dependent; on the contrary, they want to explicate how the world is available to us, how something that is external to the mind can yet appear to it, touch it, and so be known. Their concern is to bridge the gap separating subject and object by coordinating the two: one is only a knowing subject in relation to an object domain conceived of as existing independently from one; to be self-aware as a knower is to be aware of what is known *as* independent. That is Kant's point in the Second Analogy in explicating the possibility of knowing an objective order in terms of the difference between objective and subjective succession, where objective succession is construed in terms of sequences of events whose temporal order is not reversible; non-reversibility designating what exceeds the power and freedom of the subject. Reversible sequences of events, say the order in which I view the façade of a mansion, are ones in which I create the order in which things are seen; in non-reversible sequences the order of my perceptions is not up to me, I discover what is happening or going to happen. If all sequences of events could be reversed in their order of appearance, then the very idea of a world existing independently of us would never arise; we would be world creators. Since we could not be self-aware without being able to distinguish what is subjective, belonging to the self, from what is objective, then the experience of self-awareness, of freedom (= reversibility) only arises against a background of what the self relates to but cannot control or manipulate (= non-reversibility). Our conception of ourselves as self-moving is internally connected to our conception of ourselves as originally passive and dependent; and that passivity is not brute, the fact of casual affection, but belongs to the order of cognition, the circle of reasons, as a pole of self-consciousness.

Realists are not concerned to deny that the objects of awareness belong to an intentional order; rather, they are concerned to assert that intentional constructions cannot constitute a world. If, in the Kantian idiom, even causality is a category *we* must presuppose in order to account for the possibility of self-consciousness, then even what belongs to the passive pole of self-consciousness is so only for us; thus that we must conceive of ourselves in relation to a world not of our own making is a way of constructing the world, of construing it from our perspective, thus cutting us off from the world as it is in itself. Realists hence want evidence that the order of reasons puts us in touch with *the* world rather than *our* world. If idealism appears paradoxical in claiming that the world is equivalent to what is transcendentally required if anything is going to count as a world for us, realism is no less so in demanding that the order of reasons be essentially truth related, where truth is defined in a wholly subject-independent way.

This has always looked like an irresolvable debate: in order for an item to matter, it must belong to the logical space of reasons; but the space of reasons is, definitionally, on the side of the subject. What belongs to the world is fact, there irrespective of any reasons we might claim for its being so or not; truth is reason transcendent. And, pictured in this way, this debate is irresolvable. But it becomes amenable to resolution when we shift paradigms; instead of worrying about reasons versus truth or warranted assertability versus truth conditions or what is subject dependent and what subject independent we should speak instead about creation and discovery.

The hypothesis underwriting the foregoing analysis has been that creation and discovery are not different intentional kinds (with created items and discovered items belonging to different ontological regions), but belong to a continuous spectrum or continuum with two impossible endpoints: pure creation or creation *ex nihilio* and pure discovery. To create out of nothing would be to create without materials and so without constraints of any kind. A pure creation would discover or reveal nothing because nothing would or could be at stake in the creation. Conversely, a pure discovery would be a revelation of how things are without mediation or perspective, hence without either temporal or spatial restrictions. Pure creation images a nominalist and existentialist God radically choosing to make a world; pure discovery evokes a Platonic God of perfect knowing.

Once the logical fiction of the endpoints are put out of play, then we cannot fail to note how creation and discovery are coordinated. Even the most creative endeavours are constrained by worldly materials not of our choosing

78

and thus in order to create one must respond to the possibilities and constraints that those materials and the history of their use dictate. Constraints
and responses are the conditions for discovery: for example, in modern
painting, the discovery of how what had been the fascination of landscape
continues and even intensifies as image is reduced to fields of colour (Richard
Diebenkorn); of how apparently impersonal expanses of colour in their brute
materiality evoke dimensions of our spiritual existence outside and apart from
explicit language, symbol or form (Mark Rothko); of how world without
human meaning eludes revelation as exemplified by the various projects that
sought to revoke human control, the imposition of meaning, by confining
themselves to the minimal conditions of painting, the placement of paint on
canvas, with their discovery of how unachievable the acknowledgement of the
flatness of the canvas is, how simply the placement of colour onto the canvas
yields depth and dimensionality, and so the suggestion of the possibility of
meaning (Barnett Newman). These discoveries – what else might we call
them? – are of a different order than the discovery of elementary particles or
the structure of DNA, but in both types of cases intensified practices of
creativity and inventiveness have their terminus in the disclosure of what
experientially or causally counts because it is only intelligible as transcending
want, desire, intention and will.

Constructive activities conclude in a finding: a new particle, a new
meaning, a new sense of colour, hidden desires or hidden sources of injury.
These discoveries *reveal* conditionedness and passivity, the world touching us,
the touch of the other. While the explicit *interest* of natural science may reside
in and be answerable to our capacity and need to control the physical world,
its *intrigue*, which is as palpable and persistent as that interest, resides in
discovery. Experimentation is more than theory confirmation, it reveals
entities and structures to consciousness as if we had suddenly touched, and
thereby been touched by, a hidden facet of reality. While the interest of art
may be identified with pleasure or expression, its intrigue is equally epistemic,
the *discovery* of meaning, as if until this moment we had never seen a flower or
tree before or known how, with the slightest fracture in a solid field of colour,
we could find ourselves spectating on the emergence of world and meaning.

As I shall discuss further in the final chapter when considering the relation
between communicative relations and language as disclosure, interest (communication) and intrigue (disclosure) can and do press in different directions.
In suggesting (no more is possible here) that we replace talk about what is
subject dependent or independent, the core of the idealism–realism debate,
with talk about creation and discovery, acknowledging that these are not
competing but rather mutually determining ideals, my express intent is to
defuse the anxiety that creation may be merely subjective and to deflate the
idea that the discovery of what is objective is incommensurable with the most
apparently object-independent forms of human activity. Metaphysically, the
reason why creation and discovery are necessarily entwined is that for humans,

79

unlike gods, possibilities are never pure but the possibilities latent in some materially and historically formed actuality, while actualities are always realizations or exemplifications of some field of possibility. Whatever Kant's confusions over formality, and hence over what belongs to the conceptual and what to intuition, the deep insight in his Copernican turn was his rejection of intellectual intuition, the activity of an intellect for which the possibility of an object (its concept) would entail its actuality. Human finitude, at the very least our spatio-temporal provinciality, entails that what is actual must be found through some activity on our part, that we must put ourselves into relation with the world. In *Justification and Application*, Habermas nicely states the matter:

> at one time, the passive moment of experience through which the world acts upon us predominates, and at another the active moment of an anticipation of possible effects upon us; but both moments, those of discovery and construction, intermesh, and the relative proportions vary already within the sphere of theoretical reason. From physics to morality, from mathematics to art criticism, our cognitive accomplishments form a continuum within the common, though shifting, terrain of argumentation in which validity claims are thematized.
>
> (*JA*, 30)

We could usefully consider these words as the outline of a research programme in comparative epistemology that would pick up the detailed and technical issues of the classical idealism–realism debate, pursuing them across different fields of cognition in the light of the dialectic of creation and discovery.

Within such a scenario, art and natural science look to be easier cases than social science since the former, unlike the latter, possess or can attain to a world-directedness capable of acknowledging and satisfying the intrigue which subtends explicit interests, the intrigue that comes to philosophical expression most radically in the voice of the sceptic. Social science, like psychoanalysis, begins, both historically and thematically, interestedly, with the experience of humans becoming unknown to themselves, finding what is most intimate to their lives, their place in a world with others, has become unrecognizable. The interest of social science is to illuminate for us our place in the social world, place our now atomized, highly individualized selves into relation with others, explain our lostness and thereby portend deliverance from socially induced misery. Analogously, psychoanalysis's interest is therapeutic and emancipatory, relief from psychological misery. The interest structures of both psychoanalysis and social theory can become detached from their intrigue, yielding bits of social engineering that address specific miseries with practical relief, as some modern therapeutic procedures promise to restore us to full functioning without the intermediary steps of self-reflection. Such instrumentalizations can be benign or threatening depending how we conceive of the misery and our role in the application of the instrument of relief.

If social science or psychoanalysis are more than interest driven, then they will possess a moment of intrigue: in order to find relief we must come to know ourselves, by knowing what it is to be a self, differently from before. Because human beings are self-interpreting, self-transforming and self-transfiguring beings, then in these cases what is discovered has a double accent: we can see ourselves differently only by interpreting ourselves differently, becoming different (kinds of) persons than we were before – which equally must be a condition for fundamental discoveries in science and art. In this light, social science and psychoanalysis will appear to be philosophical rather than empirical theories; the condition of social or psychological explanation involving the creation/discovery of a new sense of what being a person (socially or psychologically) is. Viewed in this way, notions like class, the unconscious, the Oedipus complex are neither straightforward theoretical entities (the realist hope) nor logical fictions useful for the sake of explaining recalcitrant phenomena (the instrumentalist despair), but possibilities for further articulating essentially indeterminate experiential fields. Articulating those fields in accordance with those possibilities, however, cannot be pure *theoretical* accomplishments, however subject they are to routine logical and empirical constraints, since those fields can have the shape designated by those creative interpretations only if agents can reinterpret their experiences in accordance with the stipulated designs and continue their narrative progress through the world. Hence the intrigue of social science and psychoanalysis is non-detachable from the discovery of a new sense of self, a new possibility for being a self; but new possibilities of self-understanding are themselves dependent on actual self-transfigurations.

Habermas broaches this fundamental dialectic only to suppress its trans-figuring intrigue within the confines of a fundamental interest. Still, its rude outlines are unmistakable in the following passage.

> The interest of self-preservation cannot aim at the reproduction of the life of the species automatically and without thought, because under the conditions of the existence of culture this species must first interpret what it counts as life. These interpretations, in turn, orient themselves according to ideas of the good life. The 'good' is neither a convention nor an essence, but rather the result of fantasy. But it must be fantasied so exactly that it corresponds to and articulates a fundamental interest: the interest in that measure of emancipation that historically is object-ively possible under given and manipulable conditions.
>
> (*KHI*, 288)

The lovely notion of an 'exact' phantasy and Habermas's construction of the meaning of 'good' are the Achilles' heel of this passage. Exact phantasy attempts to close the gap between possibility and actuality with the addition to the creative imagination of a calibrating power that obviates the difficult difference between a possibility, involving risk and transfiguration, and potentiality. Analogously, his construction of the 'good', rightly deemed neither an essence nor a convention, suppresses, as he knows full well, that each conception of a good life invokes a different conception of what and how a person is. By conceiving of the good as the object of an interest in emancipation, Habermas makes pursuing it more like the attempt to satisfy a desire than the discovering of new possibilities of selfhood. His interest structures hence read out of his account both the negativity of creation (the reduction of possibility to potentiality) and the intrigue of discovery (the element of finding that is a consequence of transfiguring action).

THE CAUSALITY OF FATE AND TRAGEDY

It is, or should be, evident that Habermas's reading of Freud is consistently governed by structures drawn from Hegel. He interprets repression and its overcoming in terms of the causality of fate and the dialectic of moral life. He concludes the 'when valid' passage discussed earlier by claiming: 'The subject cannot obtain knowledge of the object unless it becomes knowledge for the object – and unless the latter thereby emancipates itself by becoming a subject' (p. 262). In short, pathology is the becoming substance of subject, and cure the return in which all that is substance is understood as subject. This movement is doubly mediated: the analyst can only have knowledge of the object (the analysand) if the analysand transforms himself into a subject; and the analysand can only do this if he recognizes in the analyst his suppressed life. General interpretation is not realized within itself, it is precluded from so doing because analytic anamnesis is the theory-mediated performance of the dialectic moral life. Hence, transference becomes the scene of the speculative recognition of self in otherness.

> But the physician's constructions can be changed into actual recollection of the patient only to the degree that the latter, confronted with the results of his action in transference with its suspension of the pressure of life, sees himself through the eyes of another and learns to reflect on his symptoms as offshoots of his own actions.

(p. 232)

When Habermas first essayed the dialectic moral life in 'Labour and interaction' he did so as a refusal of Kantian moral theory where the antagonism between universal law and particular desire is resolved by subsuming the latter under the former. This, Habermas avers, 'expels moral action from the very domain of morality' (*TP*, 150), reducing moral action to strategic action: 'The positive relation of the will to the will of others is withdrawn from possible communication, and a transcendentally necessary correspondence of isolated goal-directed activities under abstract universal laws is substituted' (*TP*, 150).

Habermas turns to Hegel's model of communicative action as an alternative to the Kantian model. In Hegel love, fate and recognition represent alternatives to law. The 'form of law (and the law's content) is the direct opposite of life because it signalizes the destruction of life'.[14] Fate, on the contrary, is the complex movement of life itself.

> In the hostile power of fate, universal is not severed from particular in the way in which the law, as universal, is opposed to man or his inclination as the particular. Fate is just the enemy, and man stands over against it as a power fighting against it. . . . Only through a departure from that united life which is neither regulated by law nor at variance with law, only through the killing of life, is something alien produced. Destruction of life is not the nullification of life but its diremption, and the destruction consists in its transformation into an enemy.[15]

Habermas accurately presents the causality of fate in terms that should now strike us as familiar from his reading of Freud.

> In the causality of destiny the power of suppressed life is at work, which can only be reconciled when, out of the experience of the negativity of a sundered life, the longing for that which has been lost arises and necessitates identifying one's own denied identity in the alien existence one fights against. Then both parties recognize the hardened positions taken against each other to be the result of the separation, the abstraction from the common interconnection of their lives – and within this, in the dialogic relationship of recognizing oneself in the other, they experience the common basis of their existence.
>
> (*TP*, 148)

Love and recognition are, precisely, acknowledgements of separation and repression; such acknowledgements, however, are not dictated (by law), or logically required. They are acts of life, acceptances and acknowledgements. Recognition, acceptance, love and forgiveness (forgiveness as the act of love) are the opposite of autonomy and self-legislation; they are acts that cannot be commanded or demanded. On the contrary, they are excessive to what can be established by any subject independently of its others. What recognition recognizes is the heteronomous 'ground' of autonomy.

From 'The spirit of Christianity and its fate' and the 'Natural law' essay to the *Phenomenology*, Hegel associates the temporal movement of the causality of fate, and hence ethical life as opposed to morality, with tragedy. In tragedy, as opposed to comedy, the ethical order is composed not by abstract law, but through the structured recognitions implicit in communal practices, practices in which a group possesses a shared social and collective identity; and the individual accepts the moments of diremption, conflict and antagonism, including incommensurable social obligations, as the movement of the totality, not something visited upon it from without.

83

Tragedy consists in this, that ethical nature segregates its inorganic nature (in order not to become embroiled in it), as a fate, and places it outside itself; and by acknowledging this fate in the struggle against it, ethical nature is reconciled with the Divine being as the unity of both.[16]

The recognition of self in absolute otherness that is the goal of Hegelian dialectic (itself, surely, just the movement of the causality of fate) is not the sublation or dissolving of otherness, but its acceptance as ground. Life is aporia; dialectic is fate and tragedy.

Psychoanalytic narration cannot escape the dictates of the subsumptive model merely through contextualization (p. 273); rather the passion for critique, realized in and through transference, must equally involve the work of love; the acceptance of conflict – of loving and feeling murderous towards the other; of desiring what can never be possessed – and the acceptance of the otherness of the other as constitutive of the moral totality of the analysand's life.

Habermas's reading of Freud was intended as the working out, for a critical theory of society, of the logic of the causality of fate he spied in the early Hegel. Very quickly, and very approximately, Habermas argues that Hegel came to abjure the model of the causality of fate as he came to recognize its attachment to the idealized form of certain historical communities, on the one hand; and, on the other, came to recognize specific features of modernity – above all the logic of self-consciousness and the new model of civil society developed by the political economists – as different from and incommensurable with those idealized forms of past historical communities. Habermas's strategy has been to insert the presupposition of constraint-free communication at work in all speech acts into the place that the idealized forms of past historical communities had in the early Hegel.

This otiose move, otiose precisely because it attempts to replace historical reality by a transcendental or presuppositional structure, is unnecessary. What Habermas's reading of Freud shows is that our acceptance of the causality of fate and the writing of our tragic narrative must be theory mediated. As he himself states, 'Only the metapsychology that is presupposed allows the systematic generalization of what would otherwise remain pure history' (p. 259). Pure history is not our history because the moral and social totality which we are and of which we are part is empirically unknown to us. We can come to ourselves only through the mediations of theory. *Capital*, just as much as the writings of Freud, offers a general interpretation (of capital) and not a representation. As such, it is neither true nor false in itself. It can become true only if we can, through it, come to tell the story of who we are and so continue our disturbed self-formative process. That the process of self-formation is *disturbed* is the demonstration that the logic of the causality of fate is still operative. We have found new names for the transgressions of the moral totality – alienation, reification, rationalization, nihilism – but insofar as these new names refer us to a diremption of the moral totality of self and/or society, a totality only visible in its dirempted moments, then the ethical structure of the causality of fate remains. Because the structure of transgression and diremption becomes permanent when individuals accede to self-consciousness in an explicitly autonomous and historical form, when we take on the burden and responsibility for the meaning of history from within, then our narratives will remain tragic. Historicity and diremption are always equiprimordial; the negative self-relation implied by the modern conception of persons as self-conscious beings brings to light this structuration of experience.

To reiterate: what Habermas's deployment of the model of the causality of fate reveals is not the presupposition of communication free of constraints; but rather, that in our social practices an actual ethical totality is operative even in situations where the norms governing such practices and the structures reproducing them deny it. Habermas could avoid this point, and slip communication into its place, because at each moment where communication enters his argument another architectonic option is enunciated. Whenever communication is distorted, in Habermas's terms, the self, subject or ego necessarily 'deceives itself about its identity in the symbolic structures that it consciously produces' (p. 227). The force of unconstrained communication in Habermas is always parasitic on its being a transcendental marker for the 'we' which is the ground of each and any 'I'. In reality, however, this we, which is never just one, is constituted in and through practices which are 'neither regulated by law nor at variance with law'. (In later writings Habermas himself will acknowledge the existences of such practices under the title of the 'lifeworld', without, however, fully re-establishing the logic of the causality of fate in place of communicative rationality.) No theory or set of theoretical presuppositions grounds or founds 'united life'. On the contrary, only the act that denies life reveals it. Our tragedy is that this revelation is not an empirical accompaniment of our acts. Because our tragedy has become unknown to us, so has our life.

From this vantage point it is not difficult to see why Habermas's notions of undisturbed communication and the ideal speech situation run into difficulty: they are linguistic reformulations of transcendental intersubjectivity (which is for Hegel always at the same time fully empirical). Undistorted communication, however partial, however remote as presupposed and yet to be achieved, has *force* only if it is necessary for the possibility of maintaining oneself as a subject; thus it functions as the Habermasian transcendental marker for the 'we' which is the ground of each and any 'I'. Habermas's own quasi-transcendental form of argumentation, however, tends to elide what is central to transcendental argumentation, namely, self-consciousness. If Habermas's claims for undistorted communication are unpacked, then it becomes evident that its necessity is conditional: it provides a necessary condition for the possibility of self-conscious agency. If its force is weaker than this, then the general pattern of self-referentiality can no longer have a grounding function – an issue I deal with in my discussion of performative contradiction in Chapter 6 below. As in Kant's own transcendental presentations, what it is for anyone to be a self-conscious agent is left unspecified, or rather, in Habermas's theory, it is made a function of the categorical determinations of undistorted communication itself. Thus the conditions for subjectivity come to displace subjectivity itself, and, as Habermas's procedures elegantly demonstrate, subjectivity can be read out of the argument altogether. But this strategy begs the question at issue: What is it to be a self-conscious agent? And who is this agent? Like Kant's logical subject, Habermas's subject of an undistorted communication community is a logical fiction. Kant's argument wavers between according transcendental subjectivity its proper metaphysical status and leaving it an empty logical subject. Habermas attempts to rid himself of the problem of transcendental subjectivity altogether, but this he can manage only by an ellipsis in his argument which produces a rather evident *petitio*.

The direct result of making a science of self-reflection about the self is to displace emancipation from its position as being the sole object or goal of self-reflection. On the contrary, emancipation looks to be an effect or corollary of self-knowledge when it is comprehended as having an ineliminable practical dimension – no separate categorial 'interest' is thus required. In saying this I do not mean deny the operations of the causality of fate, individually or collectively, upon us; but I do wish to insist that any such curtailment of our freedom is a constraint upon the self (upon ourself – who we are). What we become emancipated from in the production of a self-reflective narrative are *false* views about ourselves, about our goals and desires, about who we, really, are. The emancipatory power of self-reflection is hence inseparable from its cognitive aspects; but the cognitive aspects of self-reflection are themselves inseparable from the practical activity of the reconstitution of self-identity which is the controlling end. By separating action from knowledge (true and false beliefs rather than the ersatz cognition of right and wrong), Enlightenment thought creates the illusion that who the self is and its (moral) freedom can somehow be analytically distinguished. But part of the force of the hermeneutic critique of Enlightenment ideology is to deny that questions of freedom and autonomy can be isolated from questions of self-knowledge and self-identity. In Kant this separation is pressed twice over: not only is the will separated from judgment (and so moral action from moral perception), but moral goods, which belong to the will alone, are firmly isolated from non-moral goods, which belong to the body. Since any identity we might have is an empirical matter, then as moral agents we lack a continuing identity. Like Kant, Habermas uses the ideal of autonomy, written now in terms of undistorted communication, as the *form* in which particular formations of self-identity may be inscribed; so, as in Kant, the distinction between autonomy and identity provides the leverage for a distinction between a priori (transcendental) form and empirical content. Hence communicative reason itself breaks the unity of theoretical and practical reason that Habermas applauds in the linking of analytic knowledge and moral insight (pp. 235–6). When the dualism between freedom and identity is overcome, then with it goes the kind of form/content distinction which legitimates Habermas's transcendental strategy. And with that gone, critical theory becomes all it ever can be: a critical hermeneutics.

If it is the case that the possibility of formally transcending our historical predicament is factitious, that the 'we' that conditions the possibility of self-consciousness and self-identity is always historically concrete through its immanence in social practices incapable of being wholly objectivized, then two important conclusions follow. First, individual acts of re-narration are never more than limit-cases of self-transformation. If individual subjectivity is but a weak precipitate of the 'we' that makes it possible, then substantial self-transformations require the re-formation of the practices conditioning individual subjectivity. And this may be another reason why apparently strong cases of re-narration, namely those found in modern autobiographies, not only appear as fictions but are fictions. No individual on their own can substantially remake him- or herself. Indeed, is this not the acknowledged pathos of Nietzsche's Zarathustra? Any transformation of the self would be a transformation of intersubjective practice; but this one cannot do alone.

Second, if the conditions for self-consciousness are, as sedimentations of past collective subjectivities, incapable of ever being fully objectivized, then while our narrative predicament is in important ways historically specific, it is not historically unique. A tragic dimension of all collective identities and their narrative representation is that the moment of self-recognition must always be wrested from a social substantiality that remains submerged in darkness. But this is just to say that the tragic pathos I have just attributed to Zarathustra must infect all narratives claiming insight into collective identity and collective fate. Absence of such tragic pathos is a sign of naivety, not of better insight.

Narrative is the form of intelligible discourse proper to human life. Disturbed self-formative processes are, in reality, disturbances of identity – individual or collective; but disturbances in identity are, for us, always disturbances of the temporal ordering of existence; disturbances that can only be re-formed through (re-)narration.

Modernity involves the occlusion of the ethical totality of which we are nonetheless a part. And this means: the tragic conditions of life have, tragically, been occluded from everyday practice. Who we are, tragic insight into our fate is now only possible via the mediations of theory. On this account, Freud and Marx are the tragedians of modernity; and the overcoming of modernity would be a kind of rebirth of tragedy.

4

MORAL NORMS AND ETHICAL IDENTITIES
On the linguistification of the sacred

CITIZENSHIP, DOUBLE MEN AND NIHILISM

In the opening pages of *Emile* Rousseau addresses the problem situation motivating his educational project, and thus by extension the existential aporia confronting his nascent everyman. We are born human beings and become persons. This becoming is the work of education, the cultivation of our natural aptitudes, capacities and propensities by forces internal and external. 'Everything we do not have at our birth and we need when we are grown is given us by education' (*E*, 38). This education, Rousseau continues, comes to us from nature, from men or from things. 'The internal development of our faculties and our organs is the education of nature. The use that we are taught to make of this development is the education of men. And what we acquire from our own experience about the objects that affect us is the education of things' (*E*, 38). According to Rousseau these three educations do not naturally syncopate. On the one hand, original consciousness disposes us to seek objects providing pleasure and to avoid those causing us pain. But, on the other hand, these original dispositions necessarily become refined such that we come to seek and avoid objects not upon this natural basis alone, but 'finally according to the judgments we make about them on the basis of the idea of happiness or of perfection given us by reason' (*E*, 39). The first teaching is that of things, the second that of men. The first teaching, were it autonomous, would relate the organism to the natural world only on the basis of what conduced to its solitary needs and wants, its survival in the broadest sense. This is an image of man as acting on 'preference' alone, and were those preferences to be rationally ordered, as preference maximizing. The second teaching relates those original wants and needs to their social coding in language and reason such that they fit the claims of the society of which the individual is a part. Given the intrinsic possibility of conflict between the two teachings, between the claims of self and those of society, we must ask what should be done when opposition occurs? 'When, instead of raising man for himself, one wants to raise him for others? Then their harmony is impossible.

Forced to combat nature or the social institutions, one must choose between making a man or a citizen, for one cannot make both at the same time' (*E*, 39).

Rousseau's account abruptly modulates from a consideration of a potential conflict between two sources of formation into a conflict between the self as preference maximizer and the self as citizen. And, indeed, it is impossible to disentangle within Rousseau's scheme his articulation of the relevant claims of the teaching of things and the teaching of society from his critical analysis of the duality between self and society, man and citizen. Within the context of his educational project, Rousseau will revert to the organizational schema given by the analysis of different forces of cultivation. But the education itself presupposes the corruptive and apparently intransigently disintegrating duality between man and citizen. So, at the commencement of *Emile*, Rousseau insistently places the latter before us:

> He who in the civil order wants to preserve the primacy of the senti-
> ments of nature does not know what he wants. Always in contradiction
> with himself, always floating between his inclinations and his duties, he
> will never be either man or citizen. He will be good neither for himself
> nor for others. He will be one of these men of our days: a Frenchman, an
> Englishman, a bourgeois. He will be nothing.
>
> (*E*, 40)

These beings, these nothings, Rousseau denominates 'double men': 'always appearing to relate everything to others, and never relating anything except to themselves' (*E*, 41). This is how society educates us now, an education into nihilism, into nothing.

This nihilism is a consequence of the mutual cancellation that the two sources of value, corresponding to the educative forces of things and society respectively, undergo when articulated by the dual structure of modern social formations: the duality of state and civil society. That it is this duality that is structuring the existential pathos of the disintegrated individual of modernity – a pathos we 'constantly experience within ourselves . . . during the whole course of our life', which ends without us having been 'good either for ourselves or for others' (*E*, 41) – is implied by Rousseau in his denial of the possibility now of public (political) instruction. Public instruction can no longer exist because 'where there is no fatherland, there can no longer be citizens. These two words, *fatherland* and *citizen*, should be effaced from modern languages' (*E*, 40). Against the background of this thesis, three questions arise for Rousseau's position. First, against the prevalent belief that one of the singular achievements of modernity is the creation of civic citizenship, where membership of the community is no longer tied to racial, ethnic, religious or even linguistic criteria, with what right or on what basis can Rousseau contend that there can no longer be citizens? Second, if an operative conception of citizenship is absent in modernity, is the analysis of that absence sufficient to explain nihilism in its strong Nietzschean sense?[1] Third, framing these two questions is the question as to why is it that Rousseau believes *being a citizen* is the appropriate opposite or counter-image to being a man, where the alternative of us choosing to be mere men is ruled out?

In making his claim that there can no longer be any citizens, Rousseau tacitly points back to the chapter on 'Civil religion' in *The Social Contract*. There he contends that in pagan times each state had its own cult and gods. As a consequence, each state made no distinction between its laws and gods: 'the provinces of the gods were, so to speak, fixed by the boundaries of nations' (*SC*, 129–30). This synthesizing of the political and the theological continued into the Roman era where, before taking a city, the Romans would summon its gods to quit it: 'They left the vanquished their gods as they left them their laws' (*SC*, 131). Citizenship, in Rousseau's sense, is possible only under these conditions: where (religious) belief and (political) loyalty are not differentiated. It is this state of non-differentiation that is disrupted by the appearance of Jesus, 'who came to set up on earth a spiritual kingdom, which by separating the theological from the political system, made the state no longer one, and brought about the internal divisions which have never ceased to trouble Christian peoples' (*E*, 131). Rousseau underlines this thesis a paragraph later: 'However, as there have always been a prince and civil laws, this double power and conflict of jurisdiction have made all good polity impossible in Christian states; and men have never succeeded in finding out whether they were bound to obey the master or the priest' (*E*, 132). With the dual jurisdiction of God and prince, citizenship, in the sense of one having primary and overriding allegiance to the state, collapses, and with it the binding force of laws. Now, one might consider the dual jurisdiction between God and prince to be properly interpretable in terms of the conflict between church and state. But this misidentifies the effect as the cause. The church's power to make claims on the individual is derivable from individuals having souls, where having a soul defines the overriding *interest* of the individual *qua* individual. Only with besouled individuals in the Christian sense does an individual or particular interest opposed to the interest of all come to be fixed: a Christian cannot but have an infinite interest in his or her own soul, in future salvation and everlasting happiness. Even the ethical drive of the Christian is reflexive, perfecting or ruining their soul, making it worthy or unworthy of salvation. The pathos of Machiavelli's declaration to his friend Vettori derives from the austere duality that the Christian soul doctrine introduces into the heart of the citizen: 'I love my native city more than my own soul.' If it is indeed his *soul* that Machiavelli is here referring to, then his love for his city is equivalent to the sacrifice of the infinite for the finite, and hence involves a tragic and infinite resignation.

Now it is precisely the fixed, or fixated, reflexive interest of the individual that gets transmitted into modernity to become the particular interest of the bourgeois, the interest pursued by the preference maximizer. Thus the dual jurisdiction between God and prince comes to be played out in the duality of civil society and state.[2] In both cases, an individual's primary allegiance is to herself (her soul or individual welfare and happiness), and relations to the state and so one's fellow citizens become conditional and instrumental.

Such constitutively divided loyalties would explain how the claims of law and social morality lost their binding character. But on such an analysis, it is far from clear why that loss has nihilistic implications, why the very idea of binding claims gets lost with the introduction of dual jurisdiction. To better focus the issue, we might ask the following question: Why do writers in the civic republican tradition, like Rousseau, consistently point toward the need for a civil religion as a necessary condition for republican virtue? A cynical answer would run: the common lot are so self-consumed that they will not put aside their self-interests for the sake of moral principles and laws unless they can perceive those principles and laws as deriving from a transcendent authority. Such an answer, even if true, would be question begging since it does not explain why having a transcendent source gives to principles and laws their authority. A better answer, one implied by Rousseau and the civic republican tradition, emerges if we retell this familiar story in more overtly Durkheimian terms. In this retelling, I intend my terminus to be the beginning of a vindication of Durkheim's difficult remark that 'morality would no longer be morality if it had no element of religion'.[3] The element of religion that must remain for morality to be possible is, I will contend, the element of belief – a cognitive relation to some conception of the good. In making this argument I will follow the path of Habermas's account of Durkheim, breaking off from it at just the juncture it most self-consciously departs from Durkheim. In breaking off at this point, my intention is to contest not just Habermas's construal of modernity, but equally his conceptualization of morality within communicative rationality. In the second half of this essay, I will consider the same set of issues from the angle of the questions of self-identity and practical self-consciousness, critically tracking Habermas's completion of his appropriation of Durkheim through a reconstructive analysis of Mead's social psychology of the self in terms of 'I' and 'me'.

What is less than obvious from this description of the trajectory of this chapter is its continuity with the discussion of Freud. My argument there was that the analysis of the therapeutic dialogue recapitulated the original dialectic of the causality of fate proposed by Hegel without the mediation of communicative rationality. It was able to do so because the logic of dependencies and independencies, recognitions and misrecognitions, desires and transference of desires of the analysand together with the therapeutic situation itself have all the closure and bindingness of primitive religious communities operative in the original model. The analytic dialogue is too much akin to the religious paradigm. In this respect, the turn to the analytic situation was unsuitable for Habermas's purposes because it remains continuous with the model of community from which self-conscious modernity departs.

In engaging with Durkheim's account of the religious foundations of morality Habermas is thus returning to the question of the causality of fate and its logical connection to primitive, religious social formations. The impression that *The Theory of Communicative Action* is the only one of Habermas's major works not oriented by the Hegelian paradigm is vitiated once we recognize that the opening of Volume II with the account of the 'linguistification of the sacred' is meant to demonstrate that the original dialectic of the causality of fate is itself bound to communicative interaction and its constraints rather than the forms of communal bindingness and the ethico-ontology of recognition and misrecognition implied by Hegel. If the construction of the analytic dialogue repeats the naive assumptions Hegel made about early religious communities that he attempted to rectify with his doctrine of, as Habermas sees it, trans-subjective Spirit, then it becomes impossible not to see *The Theory of Communicative Action* showing the communication theoretic 'road not taken' by Hegel in *The Phenomenology of Spirit*. Habermas's reconstruction of Durkheim, using Mead, is his reconstruction and rewriting of Hegel. Philosophically, then, the pivotal moment in *TCA* is neither the account of rationality in Chapter 1 nor the theory of communication in Chapter 3 since these analyses operate in a moral vacuum unless they can be attached to the dialectic of moral life itself; and Habermas cannot demonstrate that unless he can show that nothing of moral substance is lost with the passage into modernity – the very failed demonstration disrupting and ruining the Hegelian project.

In contesting Habermas's reading of Durkheim and Mead, in his and their own terms, my intention then is to begin contesting the linguistic turn as such and thereby begin the vindication of the model of self-reflective science drawn from the analysis of Freud. In order to achieve this end I must show the diremption involved in the separating of moral reason from ethical identity. This is attempted from both directions: revealing the role of social identity in Durkheimian morality, and revealing the moral reason invoked by each claim to ethical self-identity. The illusion of their separability is the history of nihilism: the shift from social integration as a cognitive achievement to the false belief in rational will-formation. This will leave dangling the question of whether or not the theory of communicative reason itself can intelligibly be thought to be a reconstruction of the causality of fate doctrine. I will argue for this claim in Chapter 6.

SOCIAL INTEGRATION AND OBLIGATION: FROM BELIEF TO WILL?

Durkheim's analysis focuses on pre-state norms in order to separate norms whose authority is parasitic on external sanctions and those whose (presumptive) validity grounds the punishment consequent on their violation. For the latter it can be said that we 'refrain from performing the acts they forbid simply because they are forbidden'.[4] It is this that typifies the obligatory character of moral rules, and it is this obligatory character that thus requires some form of explanation. In making that explanation Durkheim notes the impersonal nature of moral rules, the sense in which they make or can make demands upon the self that may run contrary to the self's immediate desires and perceived interests; and the dual nature of the feelings they trigger in the actor. The impersonal nature of moral rules refers us to their proto-universality, the sense in which they are directed at and hold for all members of the group of which the individual is a part. Durkheim's 'feelings' thesis points to the fact that, in order to be effective, moral rules must have the capacity to constrain individuals while *simultaneously* being of a kind that individuals are motivated to follow them. The *power* of obligation thus contains both logical and psychological elements. Their universality must be harnessed to their ability to constrain and motivate. By phenomenologically building into the obligatory force of moral norms their desirability, Durkheim constrains their theoretical reconstruction such that Kantian-style analyses that turn on the logical and rational vindication of universalistic claims are dropped from serious consideration. The justification for this move is just that any account that separates the logical from the psychological character of norms falsifies their role as action-guiding. For a norm or rule to be action-guiding it must have a role in an individual's motivational set. From this one wants to say: you cannot be obligated to do what you have no reason to do. Accounts that bypass the motivational requirement generate a curious two-step moral universe. In step one we demonstrate that certain rules are morally binding; in step two we take these free-floating moral rules and encourage or coerce others to adopt them. The strangeness of this is that in step one the rules are only logically binding. What is a rule that is, as yet, only logically binding? Perhaps this: one is logically bound to x means 'the binding rule x *ought* to be in your motivational set'. But we are then faced with the binding of this new 'ought'. And from here an infinite regress must ensue since rationally to vindicate the new 'ought' could only be to demonstrate that it was logically binding. Demonstrating the bindingness of moral rules, the entwinement of their logical and psychological features, thus becomes a requirement on moral theory – but one from which Habermas departs.

Durkheim's phenomenological analysis of moral obligation is explicitly directed at Kant, which is to say that it is part of a sociological critique of moral theory. Moral theory, Durkheim is implicitly contending, comes upon the problem of morality too late: it begins with individuals who already conceive of themselves as double men, who already believe themselves to have an infinite interest in their own persons as opposed to the good of the community. This oppositional relation is revealed in the discrepancy between the logical binding of a moral norm and its affective claim. That discrepancy in turn can be identified as the original difficulty that Kant's transcendental deduction of morality was intended but failed to resolve.

The structure of Kant's *Groundwork of the Metaphysics of Morals* provides evidence of this. The *Groundwork* begins by establishing the identity of a good will and a will that operates under the rules of the categorical imperative, and then proceeds, in Chapter 3, to attempt to demonstrate that the categorical imperative is necessarily binding for finite rational beings. Kant's deductive procedure thus intends transcendentally to close the gap between the meta-rule of morality and the volitions of concrete individuals, thereby circumvent-ing the interruptive variable and contingent judgments individuals are forced to employ in order to apply norms in standard cases. In the case of cognition, circumventing contingent judgment just means demonstrating that a rule, say the principle of causality, applies to a cognitive manifold as a necessary pre-supposition of the valid judgments individuals indisputably do make. But a demonstration of this sort cannot work in the case of morals since it would entail the bizarre claim that the willing under the moral law was presupposed as valid even in cases where agents happily and intentionally acted on unworthy maxims. Hence the goal of the deduction can only be the demonstration that the categorical imperative is the overriding law of the will, but since overridingness can never extend further than logical binding, then any such deduction must fail. The deficit left by the deductive procedure is the affective moment: that I experience the moral law as overriding for me. Because that experience and hence the reasons for my adopting the categorical imperative must depend upon the sorts of considerations to which it alone gives rise, then the deficit can never be made good by logical or conceptual means. This was Kant's own insight in giving up hope of a transcendental deduction of the moral law and adopting the idea of the 'fact of reason' in the second *Critique*.[5]

Durkheim's critique of Kant must be carefully weighed at this juncture since he cannot be claiming that he can empirically solve the problem of external reasons: if an individual can find no reason to be moral, then neither a philosophical demonstration that reveals that we are logically bound to morality nor a sociological demonstration that reveals morality to be isomorphic with socialization can bridge the gap. In conceding this point, however, we do not thereby accede to the idea that morality does have a logical element and an affective element, with the latter only playing the role of connecting the motivational constitution of the individual with the moral rule. This construal of the problem makes it look as if the complaint against abstract moral theory is that it fails to answer the existential question 'Why be moral?' Once this approach is taken, the anti-Durkheimian can take the position that there is no deduction problem and no charge to be answered: 'On the premises of post-metaphysical thought, there is no reason why theories should have the binding power to *motivate* people to act in accordance with their insights when what is morally required conflicts with their interests' (*JA*, 127–8; see also 75–6). But this simply bypasses Durkheim's fundamental claim which is about the *meaning* of moral norms and rules. What I have called the deduction problem is not a refutation in the sense of showing that the theory does not do what an adequate theory must do; rather, the deduction problem is symptomatic in that it reveals a misunderstanding of the constitutive sense of what it is for something to be a moral rule.

Durkheim's descriptive point about the affective dimension of the moral must be construed as demonstrating that the appearance of a gap or deficit is misleading because it has separated out the logical structure and normative *force* of morality into different domains, making the latter extrinsic to the very idea of morality. Insofar as this is the case, then the philosophical anthropology of moral theory becomes the anthropology of double men, as if we were truly beings whose possibility of being for ourselves could be firmly and logically disentangled from our being for others. Even in his departure from a deduction of the moral law, Kant conceptually installs the anthropology of double men as permanent. This is how a moment of brute arbitrariness and decisionism enters into even Kant's late moral philosophy.

> That the ultimate subjective ground of the adoption of moral maxims is inscrutable is indeed already evident from this, that since this adoption is free, its ground (why, for example, I have chosen an evil and not a good maxim) must not be sought in any natural impulse, but always again in a maxim. Now since this maxim also must have its ground, since apart from maxims no *determining ground* of free choice can or ought to be adduced, we are referred back endlessly in the series of subjective determining grounds, without ever being able to reach the ultimate ground.[6]

This is the same infinite regress from which this line of argumentation began.

The existence of this infinite regress, which is logically equivalent to the question 'Why be moral?', is for Durkheim the unequivocal sign that Kant has failed adequately to analyse what morality is. For the immoral person, morality will indeed appear as a set of abstract rules which he or she has no reason or motivation to adopt, and hence morality will appear as rules without force. But to accede to that appearance as correct is to understand the meaning of the moral from the perspective of the immoral: moral rules a priori are separable from what motivates an individual to adopt them. It is this thesis to which Durkheim objects, and which hence leads him to understand the binding validity of moral rules, what it means for moral rules to be binding, on analogy with the affective force of the aura of the sacred. Roughly, the separation of the sacred and the profane is taken as akin to the hierarchial relation between moral values and desires, with the aura that surrounds the sacred provoking *both* fear and love. Durkheim infers from the analogical overlap of the sacred and the moral that the latter has its foundations in the former. As Habermas succinctly puts it, Durkheim's thesis is that 'in the last analysis moral rules get their binding power from the sphere of the sacred; this explains the fact that moral commands are obeyed without being linked to external sanctions' (*TCA*, 49). This then transmits the question of the bindingness of obligations to the origins of the sacred, with the sacred being initially analysed by Durkheim in terms of society's transfigured and symbolically structured self-representation. The apparent leap in Durkheim's analysis from the sacred to society is navigated by means of the notion of absolute dependency: in the same way as the believer bows before God because she believes her very being depends upon God, so the moral individual can rationally accept the moral authority of society because it is the source and seat of the benefits that constitute civilization.

However unargued and ill-stated his account, it is through the fundamental experience of dependency, and hence through the experience of having the ground of our existence external to our individual consciousness, that Durkheim explicates the connection between the moral and the sacred on the one hand, and the sacred and the feelings of love and respect on the other. Initially, Habermas ignores this feature of Durkheim's account, focusing his attention on the avowedly peculiar relation between individual consciousness and society, where the former has the latter for its (intentional) object, which Durkheim assumes. Habermas finds this account's naive deployment of a philosophy of consciousness rectified in Durkheim's account of ritual practices where 'the sacred is the expression of a normative consensus regularly made actual' (*TCA*, II, 52). What Habermas emphasizes with respect to these practices is that their structural rituality dominates their content: the ritual expresses, repeats and renews normative consensus. There is an analogous shift in the concept of the *conscience collective*, stated by Habermas in these terms:

> Whereas Durkheim had first understood by this the totality of socially imposed representations shared by all members of the society, in the context of his analysis of rites the term refers less to the content than to the structure of a group idea established and renewed through identification in common with the sacred. Collective identity develops in the form of a normative consensus. . . .
>
> (*TCA*, II, 53)

Habermas's statement here rehearses a curious formalist twist. Durkheim does not believe that his account of ritual practices displaces his account of the sacred, rather he takes them to be complementary analyses of social identity, the first in terms of belief and object, the second in terms of expression. And this should be unsurprising: there is nothing untoward in the thought that there is no 'society which does not feel the need of upholding and reaffirming at regular intervals the collective sentiments and the collective ideas which make up its unity and its personality'.[7] What such rituals express, however, is a content, being Christian or Jewish or a member of the Labour Party, where for each of these conceptions of social identity there is associated a cluster of substantive beliefs, for example, there is only one God or all men are equal. Ritual reaffirmation establishes the group concerned as both a community of memory and a community of purpose. In memory the community is recalled to those events that have been formative for it; while those events themselves are ones in which a moral ideal is given to the community as a perpetual task. The double inflection of ritual acts thus invokes only those ideals which have a constitutive role for a community as being the community it is. Even if Durkheim is wrong to use a naively representational conception of consciousness and object in delineating the *conscience collective*, he is not wrong in insisting that such consciousness is reflective and cognitive as well as expressive. Habermas buries the difference or slips between the formal and the contentful conceptions of collective identity expressible in a 'normative consensus', since one can focus either on the consensus itself, *that* it is (together with the process involved in establishing *that*), or on *what* is being consented to by all. The slippage between *what* and *that* in Habermas's analysis in fact traces the slide from religion to morality wherein the experience of dependency and its acknowledgement is displaced into rules for cooperative behaviour. It is the suppression of substantive dependency (my being dependent on others for being a person *überhaupt*) in favour of acknowledging my need for the good will of others in order to pursue my ends (practical dependency) which enacts the slide into nihilism.

Habermas reconstructs Durkheim's account of the movement from religion to morality in *The Division of Labour* under his denomination for its progressive movement: 'the rational structure of the linguistification of the sacred'. He summarizes his account thus:

> I shall be guided by the hypothesis that the socially integrative and expressive functions that were at first fulfilled by ritual practice pass over to communicative action; the authority of the holy is gradually replaced by the authority of an achieved consensus. This means a freeing of communicative action from sacrally protected normative contexts. The disenchantment and disempowering of the domain of the sacred takes place by way of a linguistification of the ritually secured, basic normative agreement; going along with this is a release of the rationality potential in communicative action. The aura of rapture and terror that emanates from the sacred, the *spellbinding* power of the holy, is sublimated into the *binding/bonding* force of criticizable validity claims and at the same time turned into an everyday occurrence.
>
> (*TCA*, II, 77)

Habermas conceives of the rationalization process producing modernity not in terms of the 'unfettering' of the forces of production, but in terms of the 'unfettering' of the rationality potential of action oriented to reaching an understanding.

Durkheim's presentation of the transition to modernity is targeted toward the same problem as his earlier article, namely, how are we to account for the binding force of law once its sacred foundation is lost? Durkheim takes it for granted that short of the Leviathan, the binding force of contracts must have a non-contractual basis. Durkheim's answer to the question of obligation is as succinct as it is modern: 'It is not enough that the contract shall be by consent. It has to be just, and the way in which the consent is given is now no more than the outward criterion of the degree of equity in the contract.'[8] Consistent with his account of sacral authority, Durkheim sees the burden of representing justice, by which he understands Rousseau's general will, as providing justice with a basis in the social identity of those for whom it is to hold, as the task of the state. The state takes on this burden by producing out of the totality of representations evinced by its citizens a set expressing the general will. This is certainly problematic since the general will is still a will, an interest, and thus tied to the same logic of individuals' pre-social interests as motivating their recognition of the general interest as is the case in the Hobbesian account. Durkheim's account of organic solidarity achieved through the division of labour does nothing to mitigate or constrain the individual interest structures of modern societies. Nor would the morality of occupation groups do any better, for even granting such, they are still the product of a differentiation that effectively disintegrates social solidarity, and with it the binding force of general norms. In this respect Durkheim's account of the state simply replicates the logic of civil society from which it is drawn: the representations of the state are reflective arbitrations between competing wills to form a general will. It is this that reduces the claims of justice and equity to a matter of will rather than identity and belief.

On reflection, one is tempted to say that Durkheim's question and focus on the state is too close to Hobbes's vision of the state as the guarantor of contracts made by those who are functionally (i.e. defined in terms of their individual interests) strangers. Indeed, it is precisely his acceptance, despite himself one wants to say, of the modern self-portrayal as working a shift from a belief-based account of social integration to a will or consent-based account that bedevils his analysis. Putting the matter this way is contentious since one might believe that placing *rational* constraints on maxims or interests, like the moral law or Habermas's principle U (a norm is valid if 'all affected can accept the consequences and the side effects its general observance be anticipated to have for the satisfaction of everyone's interests'), is equivalent to making the moral cognitive. But this cannot be correct since all that is tested by the procedure is the acceptability of consequences and side effects for everyone by everyone; no beliefs about or insights into ethical or moral phenomena are thereby achieved. My will is brought into harmony with the will of others when I adopt such a procedure, but the procedure is morally blind: the *meaning* of the norm is wholly extrinsic to its rightness. But if the meaning of a norm is extrinsic to its rightness in this way, then in what sense is the procedure *cognitive*? Surely, the cognitive content of a moral norm, say contract keeping, would refer to what is involved in contracting, the value or goodness of having contracts as a social practice, and not simply noting that it can be universalized in the relevant sense.[9]

There is, then, a danger in identifying rational procedures with cognition, a danger suppressed by the very notion of a 'rational consensus'. While true, we must be able to evaluate what is at stake in the shift from a belief-based to a will-based account of social integration and so morality to the point of questioning the intelligibility of that shift. And it is the attempt to tease out those stakes toward which Durkheim's analysis of the moral is directed.

According to Habermas, the shift from mechanical to organic solidarity has three moments. Habermas conceives of these three moments as so many steps in the unfettering of the potential for communicative rationality. On the account being proposed here, these three moments rehearse societal rational-ization as a dialectic of nihilism. For present purposes, the third moment of the process is the most significant. Firstly, the rationalization of world-views that expresses itself 'in a process of abstraction that sublimates mythical powers into transcendent gods and finally into ideas and concepts and, at the cost of shrinking down the domain of the sacred, leaves behind a nature bereft of gods' (*TCA*, II, 83). This feature of rationalization, culminating in the dis-enchantment of nature, can be misunderstood and overgeneralized. I will argue in the next section that Habermas is guilty of both errors. Secondly, a generalization of values which disentangles laws and rules from the sacred, and gives to those newly emerging concepts an increasingly general applica-bility apart from local particularities. This same movement equally involves an increasing reflective relation to moral rules, and hence an increasing sub-jection of morality to rational vindication. As Durkheim states: 'One begins by putting articles of faith beyond discussion; then discussion extends to them. One wishes an explanation of them; one asks their reasons for existing, and as they submit to this search, they lose part of their force.'[10]

There is a fundamental disagreement between Habermas and Durkheim over this second thesis. Habermas construes this thesis as the unfettering of communicative reason; Durkheim's own statement is of Nietzschean origin: the highest values, ultimately here 'truth', devaluing themselves. For Durkheim rationalization is the mechanism through which moral experience, which is the experience of dependency, becomes subject to moral theory for its vindication. Because moral theory, in the philosopher's sense, presupposes the logical differentiation between logical structure and motive, then rationaliza-tion transforms morality into a configuration of rules that is necessarily logically independent of the motivational sets of empirical agents. In short, it is one thing to discover that representations of God are stand-ins for societal self-representations (Durkheim's thesis), and another to submit the social dependency of individuals as figured in moral norms to 'rational' procedures that are logically independent of concrete social practices.

Thirdly, and finally, there is modern individualism, which is both an idea, a belief in the individual person as autonomous and self-determining, on the one hand; and the processes of individuation that gives that idea social effectivity on the other. It is this third element, Habermas believes, that unites the other two and, I would add, gives to them their full nihilistic cast:

> According to Durkheim, this increasing individuation and growing autonomy of the individual are characteristic of a new form of solidarity that is no longer secured by prior value consensus but has to be achieved by virtue of individual efforts. In place of social disintegration through belief, we have a social integration through cooperation.
>
> (p. 240)

This new, general image of social solidarity models itself on the *presumptive* logic of civil society: autonomous, self-interested individuals cooperating (necessarily, since they in fact mutually depend on one another) through the formation of contracts. Two disintegrating forces re-enforce one another: as rules become more and more subject to reflection and rational vindication, the interests of the individual come more and more to form the criterion of legitimacy for those rules since there is no stopping-place prior to interest and need that can put a halt to the regress of justification. In this grimly Hobbesian picture, which Habermas will repeat and restructure in his account of the distinction between the moral and the ethical, moral rules and laws only bind to the degree to which self-interest, fear and enlightened insight adequately articulate with one another. But this binding is *not* moral binding, the experience of obligation, since, as the free-rider problem shows, moral rules and laws are accepted here as valid *only as instrumental goods*. It is this that the shift from belief to cooperation tokens and to which Habermas appears insensitive. In the pre-modern set-up belief in a moral ideal attaches to the identity of the self as a condition of will-formation; under conditions of modernity, the will deploys its interests and perspective as what regiments argumentation concerning general norms, while conversely rational argumentation is forced to demonstrate that, at some significant point, those interests are generalizable and shareable, making the acceptance of general rules worthwhile for the individual. Nonetheless, procedural generalizability only becomes applicable to claims that have already been de-socialized since they are being treated as if issuing from solitary and non-social selves. It is that presumption that makes the very idea of rational will-formation look necessary and reasonable.

As I have already hinted, this argumentation must fail since maximally it will be the case that for any particular will its interest will best be served if there are general rules that all follow except it. As Rousseau knew, the free-rider problem is the nihilistic nail in the coffin of all cooperation accounts of society.[11] Indeed, one can even say that insofar as an account of moral rules finds itself facing a free-rider problem, then *a fortiori* it is a will-based account that loses the link between the binding character of moral rules and social bonding. This is the point of Durkheim's critique of Kant. A maxim of action is shown by Kant to be morally illegitimate just in case it reveals itself to be non-generalizable. What a demonstration of this sort reveals is that acting on an unworthy maxim presupposes that others are not; if they were, then the conditions for employing the maxim would not exist, for example one can only usefully lie in a community of truth-tellers or usefully break promises in a community of promise-keepers or find coercion worthwhile in a community where coercion is not the rule. But to reveal this is to demonstrate that immoral maxims free-ride. This is, from a pre-modern perspective, true. Kant can demonstrate that free-riders are just that, but without an extra belief element that would give grounds for regarding others as deserving respect, as not deserving to be ridden upon, all Kant's account reveals is a liminal boundary where will requires a belief beyond itself if its perspective is to be transcended.[12] And, of course, Kant does flirt with transcendence in attempting to make the moral law sublime in its effectivity: an object of awe and respect. But this aesthetic moment begs the question at issue: there is nothing about willing, perceiving oneself as an autonomous willer, that can make sense of the idea of the goodness of the will being defined in terms of binding itself to a *possible* moral community. And again, the reason for this is that from the perspective of the will, and hence possible cooperative arrangements, its good really is not equivalent to strict universality.

These difficulties with the Kantian picture are simply replicated in Habermas's account of how norm-guided interaction shifts from the sacred to the everyday. At the centre of the collapse is the way in which 'social integration no longer takes place directly via institutional value but by way of intersubjective recognition of validity claims raised in speech acts' (*TCA*, II, 89). Even if we concede the logical necessity for the intersubjective recognition of validity claims, recognition of that necessity possesses nothing like the necessity of one's dependency on society. Indeed, Habermas seems to concede this point when he apparently replaces sacral authority with Hobbesian compulsion: 'the religious community that first made social cooperation possible is transformed into a communication community standing under the *pressure to cooperate*' (*TCA*, II, 91; emphasis mine). The presumption of an individualism that can legitimately conceive of itself as constituted externally to social praxis is what makes only the practical interest in cooperation a motivational force. Habermas is not of course that kind of individualist; however, by conceiving of the question of morality in terms of the generation of a consensus he perforce legitimates the position of the individual who reflectively places himself as external to all existing social bonds. It is because the Habermasian individual legitimately and necessarily possesses this degree of independence (through the idea of postconventional ethical self-identity) that cultural tradition cedes its role as providing the grounds for value-laden self-interpretations and becomes instead 'cultural knowledge' which takes on the function of coordinating action (*TCA*, II, 89).

In Durkheimian terms, whatever norms Habermasian selves come to accept as legitimate, and however fair those norms are in virtue of their mode of generation, they are not moral norms since the pressure to come to some cooperative arrangement is already non-moral in character. But this derives from the fact that Habermas begins with a non-moral perspective, namely, the problem of cooperation. If cooperation is a *constitutive* problem, then morality is no longer the issue, since by definition the question of cooperation only arises constitutively when morality has failed. The hypothesis driving this claim is that social order is an unintended consequence of effectively shared horizons of value, and disorder a consequence of the absence of such shared horizons. This is not to deny that moral communities can have cooperation problems nor that amongst strangers there can be rational cooperative arrangements; it is only to deny that the questions of social bonding and morality are fundamentally questions of cooperation.

If the pressure to cooperate is not itself moral, then a free-rider dilemma must ensue since the very reasons that lead to the search for some cooperative arrangement will always be available for free-riding on those arrangements. The reason why the free-rider problem is insoluble is because free-riders really are being rationally self-consistent. The fact that if everyone assumed the stance of the free-rider, free-riding itself would be impossible does not reveal the self-defeating irrationality of own-interested reason since it is necessarily hypothetical and conditional: self-interest has no reason to deny that it can be rational to come to cooperative arrangements. This is not to agree that the free-rider's beliefs are true. Their falsity, however, is deeper, concerning the character and extent of their dependency on others. Durkheim's way of making this point about free-riders looks decisive: the effective negative constraint of a moral norm is parasitic on the value beyond the self it enjoins. The price paid for transgressing a moral norm is shame, self-disgust, loss of self, not failure in achieiving desired ends. In conceiving of social bonds as bonds of cooperation, society as a whole is instrumentalized, which leaves the individual with only a practical but non-moral interest in it. As such, society is evacuated of morality, and morality loses its social meaning, which, if Durkheim is right, is equivalent to the disappearance of morality in real terms. Although Habermas intends his account to be only one of a shift from one form of consensus to another, since in the religious account consensus over cooperative arrangements is a by-product of value orientation and in the Habermasian account consensus becomes an intrinsic end, society is instrumentalized from the outset. While there are counteracting forces at work in Habermas's argument, above all in his account of the lifeworld, it nonetheless follows that in the linguistification of the sacred what actually transpires is the Rousseauian collapse from citizens to double men.

If this is correct, then the tendential nihilism of modernity is equivalent to the shift from social integration achieved through belief to social integration achieved through cooperative efforts. Since on the Durkheimian account the effectivity of pre-modern moral norms runs through the beliefs constitutive of social identity, and there can be no *moral* norms, no obligation, without such a passage, then it follows that *the force or binding effect of obligation is proportional to the degree of social bonding*; and nihilism stands in inverse proportionality to the degree of social bonding. This parody of Durkheim's suicide law is intentional since that account, for all its lapses, captures the same insight as his account of morality. Of course, *pace* Durkheim, social bonding cannot be cashed out in terms of social 'integration' or 'cohesiveness', for what social bonding refers to is the primacy of social identity, and the beliefs constituting it, in the construction of individual personalities within a community. What is denied by the argument to here is that moral obligation can be generated from the will alone, and hence from arrangements deriving from the will. Since the very idea of social cooperation and social consensus presupposes just such a form of binding, then neither pure contracts nor consensuses reached through valid argumentation bind in the moral sense.

As Rousseau – but also Hegel, Marx and Durkheim – knew well, we are double men since *we* citizens conceive of oursleves in terms of the contractual arrangements dictated by the cooperation-based structures of interaction in the market place; but this self-conception must be in some sense illusory, since there could be no market, no world of contract, unless, short of the Leviathan, conditions of need, trust and entitlement allowed us to contract. While interest and fear, the *forces* of cooperation, can form the outer limits of social integration, and the ordinary attachments and interpersonal relations acquired by children as a necessary component of development can provide a basis for trust, something more is needed if the aura of entitlement is to be present, say, in conceiving of ourselves and others as the bearers of irrevocable rights. For Rousseau – but also Hegel, Marx and Durkheim – these rights are ideologically misconstrued as natural rights; and insofar as they are so misconceived they are a negative force. In truth, natural rights are social rights, rights that *we* as *citizens* give to the solitary and self-interested *I's* composing civil society.[13] This is the asocial sociality of modern man, double men 'appearing to relate everything to others and never relating to anything except themselves'; or, as Marx states it: 'citizenship, the *political community*, is reduced by the political emancipators to a mere *means* for the conservation of these so-called rights of man and that the citizen is therefore proclaimed the servant of egoistic man. . . .'[14] Our degradation is our eschewal of the potentialities of citizenship. I shall pick up this thought in 'A community of citizens' (pp. 128–135).

DISENCHANTMENT AND THE UNLIMITED COMMUNICATION COMMUNITY

Habermas's linguistification thesis accepts the cooperation account of modernity, and therefore capitulates to the very nihilism it is attempting to combat. In saying this, there is no intention to deny the overarching point of validity both motivating and anchoring Habermas's thesis, namely, that language and linguistic communication play an essential *mediating* function. Difficulties arise because Habermas interprets that mediating function in terms of communicative actions oriented toward reaching an understanding, which, despite itself, both places the addressees of communicative action outside the normative consensus they are to achieve and reduces the relation between individual and norm to one of rational consent. This double jeopardy for Habermas's account is overt in his critique of Durkheim.

According to Habermas, Durkheim cannot adequately give a non-trivial meaning to the religious origins of institutions unless he takes account of religious world-interpretations as a connecting link between collective identity and institutions. This connecting link, however, cannot be established directly as Durkheim naively attempted. While Durkheim notes that we think everyday life through the conceptualities sedimented in the vocabulary of our mother tongues, he 'rashly subsumes both the communality of normative consensus accomplished through ritual and the intersubjectivity of knowledge established through speech acts under the same concept of collective consciousness' (*TCA*, II, 57). This rash subsumption consequently reads the mediated relation between world interpretations and cultural knowledge in modern societies as if they operated in the mechanical and 'subsumptive' way that produces social identity through collective consciousness in primitive societies. Thus the unsophisticated account of the meaning of ritual practices of religious cultures leads to Durkheim's undifferentiated account of modern societies.

For Habermas, the interpretation of concrete situations entering into everyday communications are indeed fed by religious world-views; but these world-views are themselves only reproduced by way of processes for reaching an understanding, thereby setting up a feedback mechanism between the demands of everyday practice and world-views: '. . . profane everyday practice proceeds by way of linguistically differentiated processes of reaching understanding and forces us to specify validity claims for actions appropriate to situations in the normative context of roles and institutions' (p. 57). What Durkheim failed adequately to note was that 'communicative action is a switching station for the energies of social solidarity' (p. 57).

Habermas provides communicative action with the role of a switching station for the energies of social solidarity not only for action coordination but equally for socialization where 'collective consciousness is communicated, via illocutionary forces, not to institutions but to individuals' (*TCA*, II, 60). For this analysis, Habermas replaces Durkheim by Mead. The advantage of turning to Mead is that while he shares Durkheim's view that personal identity results from taking over, internalizing, features of collective identity, a feat equivalent to building into the personality structure of the individual socially generalized expectations, Mead conceives of identity formation as taking place through linguistic communication. This occurs by the way in which an individual in learning a language is simultaneously learning the sets of expectations that go along with issuing speech acts in the first person; that is, to learn to make speech acts of certain sorts is to learn what the commitments of saying and responding are. Thus language learning proceeds through internalizing the match between speaker and hearer. This, crudely, is what Mead's conception of the 'me' is after. ' "Me" stands for the aspect that ego offers to alter in an interaction when the latter makes a speech-act offer to ego. Ego takes this view of himself by adopting alter's perspective when alter requests something of ego, that is, of *me*' (*TCA*, II, 58–9).

The tendential movement toward nihilism in Habermas's account arises at this juncture. The issue circulates around the idea of language as a 'switching station for the energies of social solidarity'. Where, in Habermas's account, are those energies? And how are those energies to be comprehended as oriented toward social solidarity? This question requires answering since, again, it is only the inner articulation of norms and social identity that is going to be able to explain the possibility of obligation.

However, even before we reach the question of social identity, there are grounds for questioning Habermas's initial theoretical gesture of identifying the binding effect of the sacred with the binding effect of the illocutionary component of linguistic utterances. Habermas feels justified in making this identification because he construes Durkheim's assertion that the association of the sacred with collective identity must be routed through an idealization of given society, forming an image of how that society ought to be, as itself a normative consensus: 'The normative consensus that is expounded in the semantics of the sacred is present to members in the form of an idealized agreement transcending spatiotemporal changes. This furnishes the model for all concepts of validity, especially for the idea of truth' (*TCA*, II, 71). Hence, the notion of society possesses a moment of ideality whose cash value, as it were, is that of an ideal consensus achieved in an ideal communication community. When this 'harmony of minds' is added to a 'harmony with the nature of things' then the notion of assertions as raising criticizable validity claims comes into being.

If I have understood Habermas aright, his claim seems to be that the notion of illocutionary force, which remember is meant to explicate the binding *force* of norms, is beholden to the idealized normative consensus. How does this answer the original question? *Does not this proposition rather raise the (further) question as to why we must affectively invest ourselves in an idealized conception of society in the first instance?* In answering this question, it is important to ignore the apparent impersonality or neutrality of the truth claims of modern science as a *model* for our investment in ideality, a model tacitly operating in Habermas's account. It was to this feature of Habermas's theory that I was pointing when I claimed in the previous section that he misunderstands and overgeneralizes the disenchantment of nature by natural science.

One good reason for placing this model to one side is that the institution of modern science has taught us that the truth or falsity of its empirical propositions relate to a world that exists independently of human experience. In saying this, I am neither affirming nor denying any epistemological theory, realist or idealist, about the world and our knowledge of it; I am only claiming that modern physics (followed by modern chemistry and biology) has constituted the meaning of the natural world as subject independent. Once the natural world is so constituted, it makes perfect sense to separate what we now believe to be the case from what is the case, so acknowledging the very idea of a natural world that exists independently of us. And from this it follows that the connection between a harmony of minds and a harmony with the nature of things must be routed through a double ideality: the subject independence of the world (the ideality of truth) is practically grounded in the idealization of the harmony of minds – the Peircean concept of a consensus achieved in an unlimited communication community. The Peircean removal of bounds from the communication community is simply the gesture through which a wholly human form of practice (the activity of science) acknowledges the meaning of nature as an object not subject to human determination with respect to its being or fundamental structures. But if that is the case, then the truth about the natural world, as figured by natural science, is necessarily a matter of indifference for our relations to one another. Indeed, this 'indifference' of the natural world as figured by modern science to our normative selfunderstanding is its disenchantment, its removal from 'mattering', except in the mode of indifference, with respect to our self-relations.

While in itself this indifference is a surprise to no one (however much it calls for another analysis about the natural and the human, one that can acknowledge the figure of a cold and indifferent natural universe and slip past it), in stating the point in the way I have, I do mean to make four suggestions. Firstly, and most evidently, I am attempting to tie Habermas's conception of the ideal communication community to the double ideality requisite for the acknowledgement of a universe capable of transcription in the language of mathematics. With respect to such a universe, it makes sense to inject a methodological moment transcending any substantive claims. While there may be reasons for injecting an analogous openness to revision with respect to other domains of experience, the ground of that openness will necessarily be of a different character from that of natural science since with equal necessity those domains lack the kind of subject independence essential to our construal of the physical universe. Hence, even if we grant the appropriateness of the double ideality which the Peircean unbound communication community provides, there is reason to doubt that it engenders a generalizable model.

Secondly, underlining the previous point, the indifference of nature to human meaning suggests an indifference, as it were, of this form of human endeavour to our understanding of ourselves as social beings. Its idealization of communicative relations necessarily tracks the meaninglessness of those relations, except as suitably neutralized, with respect to its object. What is thus projected by the image of the Peircean unlimited communication community is not an idealized version of ourselves, this society formally transfigured in its ideality, but the disappearance of the community as such before its forever subject-transcendent object. Peircean unlimitedness is, on the reading I am suggesting, a dynamic transcription of the removal of subjectivity from consideration in order that what is independent from communal mattering may appear. The unlimited communication community is thereby extensionally equivalent to the achieving of the 'view from nowhere',[15] that is the non-perspectival perspective of a science facing a wholly non-human world, and hence is equivalent to the absence of community. Or: the unbound communication community is community imaged as without bonds of solidarity; only as abstract, affectless exchangers of truth claims do we inhabit the ideal space of the unlimited communication community.

Thirdly, the idea of a subject-independent physical universe itself models a conception of truth as context independent, stretching out across space and time. This is not a point about truth as it is for either epistemology or philosophical logic; it is simply the thesis that if the physical universe is the way we have come to suppose it is, then true propositions about it cannot be thought of as indexed to any particular place or time. Hence, there is an idealization necessary in making truth claims about the natural world, but this idealization can be wholly accounted for in terms of how we have come to conceive of the natural world. Even an idealist who believed that our conception of the natural world was socially constituted would have to grant, given what that conception now is, that part of what we meant in issuing a claim about the natural world was that it should hold in a context-independent fashion. Other domains of discourse may also require idealizations with respect to validity claims, but there is no reason to think they are determined by the same considerations that underwrite context independence for propositions referring to the natural world.

Finally, from these points it follows that sphere differentiation, the separation of the practice of science from legal/moral and art practices, and so the separation of truth claims from moral/normative and aesthetic claims, does occur here, but arguably only here. And it does occur with respect to the truth claims of natural science not because of anything important about the nature of truth, and so about the nature of validity claims in general, but because of the subject transcendence of the (meaning of its) object.[16] In other words, the idea of truth-only cognition (which must be the Archimedean point which levers the account of independent spheres of validity), the sort of cognition which modern natural science provides, is such because its objects are *constituted* as without normative or aesthetic significance. However true that may be of the object of natural science, there is no reason to believe that such a separation of spheres of validity is applicable to other, socially constituted objects. By deploying the science of the disenchanted world as his model, Habermas furthers the disenchantment of human sociality, reading off substantive moral mutual recognition from the idealized case of the unbound communication community of natural science.

These are large claims that cannot be documented in full here, although it is worth noting that this account of the genealogy of the withdrawal of cognition proper from the social, the consequent generation of an a priori fact/value distinction and thus the logical trisection of reason that yields three autonomous types of validity claim is directly parallel to the same occurrence in Kant. In Kant the slippage occurs via the illegitimate inference from the thesis that the categories of the understanding, which are at bottom those of a wholly naturalized world, are necessary conditions for the possibility of self-consciousness to the thesis that those same categories are wholly constitutive of what it is for an object to be a part of an objective order. Even if the premise is true, the inference fails: there is no reason to infer that the minimal categorial set for an objective order is equivalent to the full range of categorial constraints on objectivity for all domains of experience.[17] Kant's difficulty with respect to teleological constructions in biology – both necessary and only as an 'as if' device – provides a good example of the aporetic consequences of that false inference.

While Habermas commits no analogous fallacious inference, it is plausible to perceive his trisecting of reason as driven by the disenchantment of nature by modern science with its demand for truth-only cognition, and hence to interpret the unlimited communication community as determined by the methodological necessities incumbent upon a community responsive to such a disenchanted natural world. But if disenchantment means objective nature becoming indifferent to our collective self-understanding, then scientific cognition becomes a marginal rather than paradigmatic instance. This hypothesis raises the conceptual question as to whether the rationalization of the lifeworld is intrinsically disenchanting, whether or not as a matter of sociological fact rationalization processes have produced a disenchanted *social* world? And to ask the question as to whether the rationalization of the lifeworld is intrinsically disenchanting is equivalent to posing Durkheim's thesis about the sacred origins of morality all over again.

What misleads Habermas into looking in the direction of illocutionary force as the linguistic core of social bonding is the correct insight that ordinary statements of all sorts about the world possess a normative dimension, albeit a normativity that is not explicitly 'moral' in character. What Habermas, following Mead and Durkheim, says about the meaning of moral norms provides the beginning of an account of this general, non-moral normativity.

> The authority of moral norms rests on the fact that they embody a general interest, and the unity of the collective is at stake in protecting this interest. 'It is this feel for the social structure which is implicit in what is present that haunts the generous nature and causes a sense of obligation which transcends any claim that his actual social order fastens upon him.' . . . The 'ought' quality of moral norms implicitly invokes the danger that any harm to the social bond means for all the members

of a collectivity – the danger of anomie, of group identity breaking down, of the members' common life-contexts disintegrating.

(*TCA*, II, 93)[18]

If we substitute the phrase 'the "ought" quality of social rules generally' for the opening words of the last sentence of this passage, then the general picture I want to propound begins to emerge.

While it is trivially true that the transgression of existing rules entails a failure of consensus, even on Habermas's account the dangers directly invoked are anomie, the breaking down of group identity and the disintegrating of common life-contexts. In pre-modern societies there seems no reason to restrict these threats to the transgression of explicitly moral norms: how one cooked one's food, addressed elders or persons of a different sex, dressed, greeted neighbours or strangers, viewed the relationship between the earth and the sun, etc., were all places where who we are and who I am in the life of the collective were at issue. Under such conditions, affective investment in social rules of all sorts, including those governing the issuing of assertions, derived from the absolute dependency of individuals on undifferentiated collective life, the particular order of the world that just was *the* world for those concerned, for the integrity of their individual identities.[19] And this plausibility would be the case generally if there were no deeper ground for the possibility of identity and society than the sharing and shared practices of social life itself. This is the fundamental thought underlying Durkheim's identification of the sacred with society. Hence what is important in Durkheim's identification is the connection between normativity as such and social bonding rather than that between *moral* normativity and social bonding.

This is not to deny that something goes terribly wrong in Durkheim's conception of the sacred as a domain of *sui generis* representations. What is required in order to overcome the idle claim that the sacred is *sui generis* is to insist, in a Habermasian manner, that the shareability of social rules entails their possessing an implicit moment of mutual recognition in virtue of which any infringement of a rule becomes an infringement upon the mutual dependencies constituting our united life – a picture of linguistic and social rules implicit in the writings of the later Wittgenstein. If we then image these mutual recognitions as forming the horizontal order of society, then the explicitly Durkheimian sacred arises as the vertical re-presentation of these horizontal structures of interaction. By this means the previously implicit horizontal order of dependency becomes explicit, thus giving back to the horizontal order its bonding function which, again, in fact issues from it.

According to the neo-Durkheimian account, we are explicitly and concretely dependent on the recognition of our peers as providing us with social recognition for the possibility of individual identity even though, necessarily, our conception of who we are possesses an ideality not reducible to existing social rules and states of affairs. The rationalization of the lifeworld puts intense pressure on this account since growing decentration and reflexivity at the very least open up both individual and collective identities to a continuous process of learning and innovation. Habermas believes that under these conditions individuals can no longer rely upon substantive social beliefs and rules as the source of the integrity of their personal identities; rather, they must come to *rely* on the idealized structures of communicative action oriented toward reaching an understanding as securing the social bond. It is precisely the difference between these two conceptions of the relation between individual identity, social identity and the social bond that is at stake in his reconstructive reading of Mead.

SEEKING SELF-REASSURANCE

In broad terms, Habermas defends the idea that our epistemic and practical self-relations occur through our relations to others:

> The self of an ethical self-understanding is dependent upon recognition by addressees because it generates itself as a response to the demands of another in the first place. Because others attribute accountability to me, I gradually make myself into the one who I have become in living together with others.
>
> (*PT*, 170)

An anticipation of Mead's distinction between the spontaneous 'I' and the self-relation that is intersubjectively constituted when I perceive the meaning of my acts as they are seen by others, the 'me', is to be found in Rousseau's contrast between *amour-de-soi* and *amour-propre*. *Amour-propre* is, like Mead's 'me', ego's self-conception as mediated through alter's perception of it. Similarly to Mead, Rousseau regards this entanglement of ego and alter as one in which ego strives to establish itself as having standing and worth in the world through alter's perception of it, that is, from the outset Rousseau conceives of the question of self-consciousness as indissolubly tied to the issue of self-reassurance.

In emphasizing this, Rousseau need not be considered as denying that our capacity to relate to the world generally occurs through (linguistic) socialization, and hence that even our epistemic self-relation involves, for example, the acquisition of the differentiated perspectival possibilities generated by the articulated syntax of identifications registered by the structured relations of pronouns – I, you, he/she/it, we, they – to one another. On the contrary, it is because we cannot stand in a self-conscious relationship to ourselves except through the possibilities these linguistic references dictate that our immediate and unreflective self-regard must take on a socially mediated form. This is the inference to be drawn from Rousseau's early introduction of language in his ideal histories. Socialization fractures immediate self-regard, requiring it to be established on a higher level. Once the ego can no longer act on the basis of its being the only individual of its kind in the world and so wholly indifferent to others, Rousseau's fictionalized transcription of pre-reflective self-regard, it must reconstitute its primitive desire for well-being in terms of others regarding it as being of worth. In the second *Discourse* Rousseau adopts the method of an ideal history with a fictional state of nature not in order to celebrate that state, but in order to underwrite the thesis that the fracturing of our immediate self-regard, *amour-de-soi*, is permanent, and hence that our most basic being for ourselves is always routed through our being for others. For this reason, it is a mistake to think that Rousseau's theory possesses two forms of self-relation; rather, we must regard either *amour-propre* as socially mediated *amour-de-soi*, or *amour-de-soi* as a fictionalized limit case of *amour-propre*. Either way, our minimal sense of ourselves as beings in the world who matter, even to ourselves, is always a mediated possibility; at best and at most we seek self-*re*assurance – our evaluative relation to ourselves always being in deficit to how we stand in the eyes of others.

Striving for self-reassurance, Rousseau's version of the desire for recognition is underwritten by two sources: sexual and those of *amour-de-soi*. The latter is 'a natural feeling that leads every animal to look to its own preservation' (*DOI*, 223n.); it corresponds to the teaching of things in *Emile*, and thus provides an anthropological source for identifying the 'interests' of any individual as opposed to that of any other. In Rousseau's fictional account of the emergence of sociality, the 'me' arose when 'men began to take the difference between objects into account to make comparisons; they acquired imperceptibly the ideas of beauty and merit, which soon gave rise to feelings of preference'. These preferences soon became competitive, a matter of 'public esteem' as comparison was harnessed to erotic competition and natural *amour-de-soi*: 'Whoever sang or danced best, whoever was the handsomest, the strongest, the most dextrous, or the most eloquent, came to be of most consideration' (*DOI*, 241). For Rousseau this is a liminal state, not unequivocally determined by the grammar of either *amour-de-soi* or *amour-propre*. It marks and images the idealized onset of individuation through socialization; only in the next moment of socialization does it become the case that self-regard becomes bound to others' views of me. Once this does occur, then for 'me' to survive in a plural world is to have a standing in it in the eyes of significant others; but for this to be the case they must accord 'me' a worth at least sufficient for minimal needs to be envisioned as social entitlements. A 'me' cannot demand less than this while procuring provision for itself in a social setting. Thus even under conditions of radical inequality, the 'standing' of a dominated 'me' must be sufficient for giving it worth both in being dominated (or impotent to overturn its domination) and in deserving what is received (socially and materially).

Now the point of Rousseau's story is to deny the Hobbesian belief in original egoism; *amour-de-soi* is a desire for well-being which knows no others, and thus it is not a preference for the self as opposed to others. In contrast to

111

this impossible state of affairs, often imaged as the immediate fusion of infant and mother, we in fact seek our well-being through gaining self-reassurance. Human beings can prefer themselves to others, but for Rousseau this enflamed or deformed *amour-propre*, which is the critical focus of the second *Discourse*, occurs only when the possibilities for acquiring self-reassurance are socially arranged in terms of fundamentally competitive structures, above all relations of production organized around private property and the market.[20]

My purpose in adumbrating Habermas's account of individuation through socialization with Rousseau's is to underline the affective stakes at issue in seeking self-reassurance, something that would have emerged in an analogous way if the story had been told in psychoanalytical terms. In seeking self-reassurance we are always seeking our well-being, which is equivalent to what we believe is our good, which in turn involves the satisfaction of even our most primitive desires. Our entire affective and conative being hence translates into and is staked on how we stand for others. Making this connection is necessary if what I referred to in the last section as the horizontal structures of recognition are to carry the affective charge that is vertically translated into the sacred. Our dependency on society for the integrity of our self-identities is more than practical: to have a conception of oneself is necessarily to have a conception of the worth of that self, its being regarded as of worth. Primitive self-concern hence must be inscribed in terms of some original self-evaluation, say, self-esteem or self-respect. These notions are not merely possible values the self can have for itself, but constitutive of what it is to have a self in the first instance.[21]

A self lacking some self-reflexive valuing of itself would lack reasons for believing that what it sought in life was good or reasons for believing that it deserved those goods or that it had the ability to achieve its ends if conditions permitted. But to lack any one or all of these is to lack a condition of selfhood. If the first condition were absent then an individual could make no sense of seeking after anything; he or she would lack reasons for giving priority to one good as opposed to another, and thus would lack the possibility of *actively* ordering his or her experience. One version of this inability would be to be or become a wanton in the sense Frankfurt has outlined. Seen in these terms, the first condition is simply a condition of human agency in general. If the second condition were absent then the goodness of objects of desire would be wholly dirempt from the self wanting or desiring them as good for it; or, to state the same thought from the opposite direction, our conception of fundamental goods is such that being deprived of them is being deprived of something integral to our being the selves we are. It is this idea that lies behind the otherwise mistaken doctrine that having 'rights' in the sense of having grounds for making legitimate claims on others is constitutive of being an individual self.[22] Finally, if the third condition is absent then the self lacks a sense of being connected to those goods and entitlements through the activities it performs.

It is considerations like these, I think, that led Rawls to list self-respect as

112

the most important primary good, and hence to believe that an adequate theory of justice must structurally secure the social bases for self-respect.[23] Supporting Rousseau's line of thought, Rawls thinks that normally the social bases for self-respect are satisfied if 'for each person there is some association (one or more) to which he belongs and within which the activities that are rational for him are publicly affirmed by others. In this we acquire a sense that what we do in everyday life is worthwhile.'

Now the hypothesis I want to forward from here is that Habermas's reconstruction of Mead's account of self-reassurance fails to sustain both the affective and self-valuing aspect of it, and that it does so in ways that parallel and explain his unintentional deracination of community in his critique of Durkheim. A certain awkwardness and complexity in making this argument is inevitable in virtue of the fact that Habermas believes that under conditions of modernity the original identity of morality with an individual's self-identity separates out into two, logically self-sufficient aspects of practical reason: moral discourse in which individuals seek consensus about the rightness of binding norms, and ethical discourse in which individuals and collectives probe their identity by reflecting upon who they are and who they want to be. Implicitly, my Rousseauian account has already presumed that this separation of the moral from the ethical cannot be sustained. And in retrospect, we can now see that the point of my defence of Durkheim was to make inroads against this same dualism. The present section, then, attempts an analogous line of argumentation, only now working from the perspective of ethical self-identity to the moral rather than from the moral to the individual. The awkwardness of the argument derives from the difficulty of knowing, at any particular instance, what is involved in seeking self-reassurance: are we engaging with just who we are and want to be or is something more always in question? To begin with, I shall let this indeterminacy remain, doing no harm to Habermas's theory thereby, since in it the logic of moral and ethical discourse parallel one another. Only toward the end of the section will I focus on the question of individuality and self-identity as such.

In pre-modern societies the social bases for self-reassurance and self-respect were secured directly through group membership, being one of us, and having one or more socially determined roles to perform. To be one of us and to have a socially legitimated role was to have a standing and a place in the world, with corresponding rights (to make claims) and duties. These descriptive conditions of self-reassurance come under pressure when being one of us stops being determinately secured through descriptive means (being born within a particular familial, religious or ethnic grouping) and the relation between roles and persons becomes contingent. Habermas correctly perceives this modern sense of self-reassurance emerging in Rousseau's autobiographical enterprises:

it is not a matter of *reports* and descriptions from the perspective of an observer, not even *self-observations*; rather, it is a matter of interested

113

presentations of self, with which a complex claim presented to second persons is justified – a claim to recognition of the irreplaceable identity of an ego manifesting itself in a conscious way of life.

(*PT*, 167)

Everything that is peculiar and deficient in Habermas's account is already available in these few words about Rousseau's performatively employed concept of individuality – the explicit focus of Habermas's theory. Habermas perceives the question of individuation through socialization as bound to the question of self-justification, that is, what underwrites or supports or would vindicate a claim to recognition. For Habermas, then, the question of self-reassurance becomes the question of how one can vindicate a claim to recognition once the descriptive conditions for self-reassurance have themselves become unavailable.

Now there is an evident overlap and distinction between what I have called self-reassurance and what Habermas calls self-reassurance. For both of us self-reassurance is connected to the question of how practical self-consciousness and thus individuality is constituted in relation to others. On my account, practical self-consciousness and hence individuality is grounded in the communal forms that provide agents with self-respect. For Habermas self-assurance refers not to the conditions for self-determined agency but to its achievement, the consummation of the movement toward individuality. So:

> self-consciousness is articulated not as the self-relation of a knowing subject but as the *ethical self-reassurance (Selbstvergewisserung)* of an accountable person. Standing within an intersubjectively shared lifeworld horizon, the individual projects himself as someone who *vouches* for the more or less clearly established continuity of a more or less consciously appropriated life history; in light of the individuality he has attained, he would like to be identified, even in the future, as the one into whom he has made himself. In short, the meaning of 'individuality' should be explicated in terms of the ethical self-understanding of a first person in relation to a second person. A concept of individuality that points beyond mere singularity can only be possessed by one who knows, before himself and others, who he is and who he wants to be.
>
> (*PT*, 168–9)

This conception of self-reassurance is connected to the previous discussion in the following way: for such a postconventional sense of practical self-consciousness the only valid horizon of address is to the ideal communication community; it secures for the postconventional self, which must continuously reconstruct itself and its self-understanding without the support of communally sanctioned identities, cut, as it were, from the fabric of tradition, the recognition which the now temporalized and hence continually superseded concrete community can no longer provide. In this respect, although practical self-consciousness emerges out of a concrete lifeworld, for Habermas that life-world is structurally displaced as securing ethical self-reassurance by the ideal communication community. Hence, structurally again, the *middle* of concrete, lifeworld reciprocal recognitions is eliminated in favour of the extremes of a highly individualized, postconventional self and the ideal communication community. Habermas thus takes seriously indeed the model of self-reassurance insinuated by Rousseau's confessional plea to God and eternity. In contrast, my consideration of self-reassurance in terms of the conditions for self-respect would locate the possibility for individuality in a concrete lifeworld whose *own* future self, and hence the future selves (or their progeny) of its existing inhabitants, would be the addressee of innovative social performances.

What we should find troubling in Habermas's account is the radicality of the shift from bound communities of recognition to the idea of communities so loosened from tradition and the reciprocal recognitions it allows that their denizens, namely ourselves, can be anchored in them only through recourse to the ideal communication community that includes everyone. Yet, this is cer-tainly the thought driving Habermas's analysis: 'Once a community of believers has been secularized into a community of cooperation, only a universalistic morality can retain its obligatory character' (*TCA*, II, 90); and what holds for moral claims, holds equally for claims to self-reassurance for Habermas. In Chapter 6, I shall note an apparent change of mind on Habermas's part on this matter. For the time being, let us treat the linguisti-fication of the sacred account of community as his standard doctrine.

It is important to remember at this juncture that Habermas is not proposing the ideal communication community as a stand-in for an absent set of com-munal solidarities; rather, in accordance with his 'unfettering' thesis, he regards the movement from bound communities to those that mediate them-selves through the ideal communication community as a releasing of the potential for communicative rationality. It is this idea which makes Habermas sympathetic to a passage from Mead like the following:

> The demand is freedom from conventions, from given laws. Of course, such a situation is only possible where the individual appeals, so to speak, from a narrow and restricted community to a larger one, that is, larger in the logical sense of having rights which are not so restricted. One appeals from fixed conventions which no longer have any meaning to a community in which the rights shall be publicly recognized, and one appeals to others . . . even if the appeal is made to posterity. In that case there is the attitude of the 'I' as over against the 'me'.[24]

Habermas notes that corresponding to this 'larger community' is a 'larger self', namely, an autonomous subject who can orient her action to universal principles.

What concerns Mead is the possibility of appeal and so of recognition once these can no longer be anchored in convention. Mead's way of stating the

115

issue, to which Habermas assents, should nonetheless cause some alarm since he treats the conventions established by tradition as *mere* conventions rather than perceiving in those conventions full, partial or inadequate forms of recognition, as if up to the moment of modernity the forms of recognition that traditional practices permitted were illusory through and through. Hence, Mead's strong claims: what is wanted is 'freedom from conventions', a move away from 'fixed conventions which *no longer have any meaning*'. Habermas's way of stating this thesis is equally frightening: 'No normative validity claim raised in the lifeworld is immune to challenge; *everything* counts as a hypothesis until it has regained its validity through the authority of good reasons' (*JA*, 120; emphasis Habermas's).

Let us ignore both the fallacious inference from nothing being immune to challenge to everything counting as a hypothesis, and, what is almost the same, the abrogation of the Peircean principle that nothing is to be doubted unless concrete grounds for doubt are provided. Habermas plainly takes modernity itself to invoke a universal scepticism or bracketing of the status of past claims (see *MCCA*, 126–7). On what grounds? Presupposed here are the first two moments of the process of rationalization, what I termed the dialectic of nihilism: the disenchantment of nature and the subjection of norms and values to the claims of disenchanted reason. The second thesis, which would involve the transmutation of the grounds of norms and values from God to society to social practices, is not sufficient on its own to generate the strong claim that fixed conventions no longer have any meaning for us. The mis-recognition of the locus of meaning, God instead of society, by itself might even entail us regarding values as more firmly grounded than before, or so Wittgenstein or Gadamer might argue. In order for conventions to be mean-ingless they must be construed originally as having the same naively subjective and projective character as did their attribution to physical nature. Which is to say, only for a natural world suddenly conceived of as subject indifferent would it be plausible to argue that previous predicate ascriptions were *merely* conventional, thus forcing us to regard all propositional claims about it as hypotheses. But the extension of this legitimate bracketing of claims about the natural world to the social world cannot go through without further argument since all social practices have an emphatically contingent and so conventional element.

But if this is correct, then the bracketing of conventions by treating them as hypotheses – my choice of the Husserlian locution here is intentional – is tantamount to *making* them meaningless. If previously norms and values were forms of recognition because acting on them was itself expressive of an acknowledgement of the manifold ways in which one's life was bound up with and dependent upon the lives of others, then the subjection of them to argu-mentative procedures must empty them of their cognitive content and trans-form them into mere generalizable conventions; will-formation thus coming to displace re-*cognition*. When I make a promise to you, for example, I am recognizing you as one to whom I can bind my future, how such binding is an act of loyalty or fidelity, and how going back on my promise would involve betraying you and so betraying a trust, and that trust, which implicitly makes reference to our mutual vulnerability to the will of one another, cannot ultimately be secured except by actions that continuously reveal us as trustworthy or failing to be so, etc. Promising is not simply a generalizable practice, but embeds a complex hermeneutic of will, respect, fidelity, trust; vulnerability, temporality, and so forth. In each of our most basic concepts a certain figure of the human is inscribed, a figure that reports and expresses a complexity of social practices with their history. In that sense, promising is a great deal more than a mere convention, and treating the maxim that promises ought to be kept as a hypothesis that could be dispensed with it if its consequences and side effects were found unacceptable threatens the revocation of that complexity of meaning before the pseudo-authority of consent – yea or nay.

My earlier suggestion, that the unlimited communication community as derived from the model of a scientific community facing an indifferent natural world imaged a community without solidarity, had this picture in mind. Habermas could reply that 'consequences and side effects' means to draw in the sort of hermeneutical considerations mentioned. But this cannot be correct since consequences and side effects relate to interests in a more familiar and direct way than can be elicited from an ethical or hermeneutical analysis. This must be so because maxims treat norms as isolable and discriminable items, while the hermeneutics of value concepts is holistic. While that holism entails a conservative moment, it is one which can be trumped; the thesis is not that if one concept is transformed or removed from the whole then the entire web will become unknit, it is only that if you treat *each* norm as if it were self-sufficient then you deny that there is a web there. But unless you treat each norm as isolable you cannot generate a maxim which can be reckoned as a hypothesis about just cooperative arrangements. This is why fallibilism, the thesis that no normative practice is immune from criticism, does not entail making each norm or value only a hypothesis. The price Habermas pays for securing a conception of justice is to give force to the dialectic of nihilism: each relegation of a norm to the needs of will-formation simultaneously cutting the bonds of intersubjectivity that unite individuals with one another. If 'bonds of intersubjectivity' is a plausible reinscription of what Nietzsche thought under the title of 'life', then it is indeed a nihilistic dialectic that is at work.

Perhaps part of what is at issue here is the difference between a logic of part and whole, and a logic of universal and particular, with the suggestion that the movement from the first to the second is what supplies illusory justice and universalism with their nihilistic thrust. That Habermas's route into universalism is through intersubjective communicative actions does not alter the fact that a fundamental shift from one kind of logical relation to another is what occurs when norms become conventions that are to be treated as

117

hypotheses for securing cooperative arrangements. Exactly the same type of disinterring is effected in separating the ethical from the moral, leaving ethical self-identity without a normative place within the fabric of the social. In order to see this, we need to put the above argument aside for the present, and return to Mead's original problem, namely, once social practices and conventions are subject to self-consciously explicit critical monitoring and innovation, what resources are available for vindicating those innovations? How can the community judge the validity of a claim that explicitly denies existing communal grounds of judgment? Mead's solution to the problem is the 'larger community' of past and future. This larger community is nonetheless more ambiguous than Habermas allows. In some instances, Mead's appeal to the larger community appears unequivocally as the larger community of rational beings; and this would match perfectly Habermas's conception of the ideal communication community. At other times, including in the above passage, the appeal is to *a future but not idealized continuation* of this community, to a transformed or transfigured extension of existing practices that would realize a potentiality in them denied by their existing configuration. In this case, my appeal would not be to everyone – how would they listen? on what basis could they hear or fail to hear me? how would or could I reflectively recognize that my performance met with normative constraints? – but to the members of my existing community (and to the members of any other communities sufficiently like mine for my claims to be relevant to their self-understanding) as they *both* are and could be, as they could be in response to how they are here and now. For these purposes my claims cannot be uniquely anchored in existing relations of reciprocal recognition; but that, as we shall see, raises no particular problems for a community which already takes itself to be postconventional in the sense of being subject to critical innovation.

The latter model has a variety of points in its favour. In it the appeal to 'you' remains concrete, acknowledging thereby more than the bare grammatic fact that innovative performances are logically bound to an addressee, but also my substantive dependency on my addressees as the final ground for the possibilities of my life and the claims I raise in the course of it having meaning even for me.[25] And this is because even a postconventional identity has for its *content* not simply experiences, events and their self-reflective sense, but a further (re)determination of existing practices of the self: being a man or woman, lover, friend, doctor, civil servant, builder, shirt manufacturer, cook, Christian, etc. While neither the content of these practices nor their placement within society is fixed, nor are the forms in which we combine them predetermined, nonetheless in all three registers indeterminate possibilities are being made determinate through autonomous agency. Hence, at least part of what is at issue in constructing a life is an ethical claim that my unique configuration of possibilities, if unique it is, reveals a potentiality for leading a good life, or at least the best life possible under adverse conditions, for *this society*. Thus my individual identity itself must be conceived as a further reconfiguring of what it means to live in this society *überhaupt*. My unique identity then comments on, judges and reinterprets what it is to be a self for us, which is to say that it is, or *should be*, even for me a critical construction responding to and answerable to the society I inhabit. That this society is far-flung or disaggregated does not typically lead me to refer myself to an abstract community of rational beings as my referential others, but typically leads me to look to a smaller group within the whole that for me stands for society as a whole with respect to its best possibilities: my family or church or friends or fellows in the workplace or fellow citizens. These, I assume, are the sorts of 'associations' Rawls has in mind.

In Chapter 1 I referred to this form of extending the indeterminately given in terms of a logic of fulfilment and transfiguration: the potentialities of the present are fulfilled through their innovative transfiguration. The orientation for such innovative practices is not derived from an ideal future, a measuring of the present against a perfectly hypothetical community, or, to be more precise about the unlimited communication community, critically measuring it against universalistic criteria conceived of as providing negative constraints, but, as Wellmer nicely states it, 'the present with all those pathologies, irrationalities, psychological blocks and inhumanities which may be empirically observed'.[26] In the absence of empirically observable inhumanity or transformable ideals, there is no orientation toward the future and the very idea of innovative transformation lapses from communal and individual life, however miserable. Anxiety over this possibility should not be overstated: such a drying up of resources for change is a human and terrible possibility, but we dislocate the achievements of modernity, which Habermas and Mead correctly read in the development of universalistic features of the civic state, if we disown responsibility for them by projecting them into a concept of rationality that is logically but not actually binding upon us.

One plausible way to consider the dialectic of fulfilment and transfiguration is as a temporalization of the logic of the sacred. On my reconstruction of Durkheim, the vertical axis of the sacred drew out the implicit but repressed recognitions embedded in the horizontal structures of everyday practice. This suppressed dimension of reciprocal recognition plays the same role in this account as communicative rationality does in Habermas's theory. The strength of the neo-Durkheimian account is precisely that it does not separate morality as a special sphere of norms, but sees the entwinement of recognition and misrecognition as a pervasive feature of all social interactions. Hence, for the neo-Durkheimian account not just moral norms and principles are significant for the possibilities of our having or failing to have a life, but each word and object can come to figure as a place or space in which our standing for ourselves and others may come into question.[27] Intuitively at least, this provides prima facie support for the amorphous belief that aesthetic or romantic or workplace experiences, for example, can appear to us as having all the weight of raising or failing to raise a moral claim, and that their possibilities, whether as realized or denied, can appear to be moral achievements or failures. This came through in the previous paragraph but one as my choice of identity being a comment on the life of the community as a whole.

If innovative claims exceed the grammatical possibilities of being vindicated in the present, calling thereby for its transfiguration, they do so in response to what cannot be suppressed here and now. The question raised by Mead's problem is: how can we recognize the meaning of that excessive claim except through the abstractions involved in the projection of the ideal communication community? But does such a projection make the innovative claim more recognizable? Arguably it is the converse that holds: we might come to see the meaning of the idea of reciprocal recognition, its weight and meaning for us, if we could see the failure of the present as revealed by the innovative claim. But if this is so, then only the perspective offered by the innovative claim itself, if recognizable as measuring the distance between ourselves now and our future selves, gives back to present interactions their ethical substantiality, only now in such a way as calling for change. Hence the horizontal and vertical axes of the sacred become the dynamic unfolding of a recurrently superseded present in the light of a transfigured figure. Durkheim's attempt at a syncopation of the negative or constraining features of morality with its presentation of an ideality is effectuated here in the thought that for us at least the negative force of moral (but not legal) norms resides in the judgment that an innovative claim makes on the present: change your life!

Morality becomes merely repressive, a making of wholly negative claims that lack force or meaning, and so appearing or coming to appear as only restrictive conditions that have purchase in virtue of rational self-interest, when it no longer appears as invoking a form of self-realization, when, we might say, superego and ego ideal come apart. The perception of morality as embodying an ideal consensus over rules for cooperative arrangements is a perception of it from the perspective of this collapse and separation; hence, the idea of morality as a system of rules of cooperation draws its image of morality from what is a defective case, and then idealizes that case as composing the whole. Because it begins from a defective state of the moral as such, it unsurprisingly devalues the ethical composition of the present, our misrecognitions, in favour of the abstract grammar of recognition as communicative rationality itself. Thus arises the philosophical problem of morality, Kant's deduction problem, namely, the gap between the logical binding of moral norms and their being norms for us. Even on my account, there is a gap to be closed between the fallen present and the transfigured future. An innovative claim acknowledges the gap as a call for a change, a transformation. That we can even begin to respond to such a call derives, again, from the concrete dependencies that already constitute our possibilities for self-reassurance. This concreteness can pull in both directions: my search for recognition trumping implicit ideals by leading me toward mere conformism – a life of all superego and no ego ideal. This possibility, I believe, is more than one way of responding to the desire for recognition for Habermas; *this mimetic desire is all the desire for recognition can be if it is not supplemented by the desire for recognition from the unlimited communication community*: 'The ego is also rendered vulnerable by the social interactions through which it is formed – by dependencies in which it becomes implicated and the contingencies to which it is exposed. Morality serves to counterbalance this susceptibility implicit in the very process of socialization' (*JA*, 131; see also 109). Hence what I claimed was the contingent separation between superego ('me') and ego ideal ('I') becomes on this analysis the permanent irreconcilability of the self with itself, a permanence that is revealed and affirmed in referring the authentic self to the unlimited communication community for moral relief from the demands of community and affirmation of its authenticity. To imagine that this is the case is to believe that we *are* Rousseauian double people: forever 'me' citizens and 'I' bourgeois. Like Rousseau in his most pessimistic moods, Habermas seeks a strategy for metaphysically comforting the necessary solitude of the 'I' with the only kind of community such an 'I' can have, one beyond space and time. This is a large claim requiring patient untangling.

In both of his accounts of Mead, Habermas tells two parallel stories: the first concerning postconventional morality and the second concerning individuation through socialization. They are parallel stories because both innovative or conscientious moral claims and autonomous life-histories raise the same Meadean problem of how what is fundamentally social can survive when what is claimed exceeds a given society's existing repertoire. They are distinct stories for Habermas because with the passing of social roles as constituting the parameters for personal identity, the possibility of building morality into the meaning of having a particular identity also lapses. Raising an innovative moral claim, which laterally raises a claim about one's autonomy as a moral being answerable only in terms of self-reassurance, and seeking self-reassurance about one's unique identity thus issue in analogous but distinct appeals to the ideal communication community. Because it binds morality and self-realization together, the neo-Durkheimian account has only one story to tell. Hence, if the neo-Durkheimian account is true, then we would expect Habermas's conception of individuality to fail in virtue of its separation from the moral.[28]

Habermas wants to argue that only on the basis of the idealizing supposition of a universalistic form of life in which all can mutually recognize one another are strongly individuated selves possible within a community; hence, strong individuation is 'the flipside of universalism'. To the idealization of a projected form of society, Habermas here adds a second idealizing consideration in order to underwrite a subject's claim to 'uniqueness and irreplaceability': to regard my own life-history '*as if it were* the product of decision for which I am responsible' (*PT*, 186). Habermas contends that my life could not be mine unless, counterfactually, it could be seen timelessly, as in the time of narrative retrospection, and thereby as performatively revealing me. But in order for this to be the case the notion of 'my life' must be equivalent to 'my existence as a whole – in the full concretion and breadth of the life contexts and formative processes that shape identity' (p. 186). Because then the issue is the whole of my life, no finite addressees could judge it. The wholeness requirement, which relates my life back to my choosing it, demands the forum of an unlimited communication community to make it binding. Only when so bound are my uniqueness and irreplaceability validated. These are distinctly odd and some-what opaque claims; that oddity, and the opacity which stems from it, derive from a reading of 'unique and irreplaceable' that is extensionally and inten-sionally equivalent to other, more familiar accounts of authenticity. But that concept of authenticity, I shall argue, fails because its notion of 'mineness' conflates the singularity of a life with its being autonomously chosen, where the good of autonomy is interpreted as a (unconditional) moral good. These matters are best approached obliquely.

As noted earlier, Habermas's conception of individuality is a secular and linguistic reformulation of the performative conception of individuality offered in Rousseau's *Confessions*. Despite the above argument, what remains mysterious in this analysis is in what sense my self-critical appropriation and continuation of my life-history would remain '*a nonbinding or even indeterminate idea as long as I could not encounter myself before the eyes of all*' (*PT*, 186; emphasis mine). It is difficult to understand what notions of binding and nonbinding are operative. There is some reason to believe that all Habermas intends to accomplish with these loaded notions is a *stabilization* (*PT*, 188) of the process of critical self-appropriation and continuance. Because there now exists no possible pre-existing objective end or goal to a life-history, then a life can at best be authentic; and it is authentic just in case it is indissolubly mine. Even that mineness, however, is subject to defeat since for us each present is charged with a consciousness of a future that eclipses rather than continuing it. Hence the totalizing gesture of critical self-appropriation, that is the narrative retelling of my life, transforms fact into act, and that act can then itself have the weight of finality, making the narrative binding, if its addressee is the unlimited communication community. But without some further thought, it is unclear as to why it *matters* that the future might eclipse my present narrative self-reconstruction, or how uniqueness and irreplaceability are somehow achieved through these idealizations. It is hard to see how Habermas's answer could be other than formal: without the closure provided by the double idealization of narrative totalization and recognition my individuation remains incomplete. So? And in what sense can two idealizations reflectively make an actually indeterminate process of individuation determinate?

Searching out the pre-history of Habermas's theory, while illuminating, will not directly support his case. The first substantive appropriation of the Rousseauian confessional model is to be found in Kant's idea of our empirical acts being expressions of our intelligible character. So regarding those acts makes them functions of choice irrespective of their actual origin. But the purport of Kant's thesis is futural: assuming the darkness of the human heart and thus the inaccessibility of real motives to self-scrutiny, I nonetheless must determine myself as if my acts were expressions of choice, otherwise they would not be mine. A contemporary version of Kant's notion of intelligible character that explicitly entwines futural and retrospective considerations is to be found in Rawls's conception of a rational life-plan: 'a rational individual is always to act so that he need never blame himself no matter how things finally transpire. Viewing himself as one continuing being over time, he can say that at each moment of his life he has done what the balance of reasons required, or at least permitted.'[29] Acting in this way entails that even if there occur untoward results, the agent has 'no cause for self-reproach'.

In order then to offer Habermas's theory a thicker notion of authenticity or integrity, we could consider its conception of a critical self-appropriation of one's life as a retrospective or narrativized version of Rawls's principle: typically our lives are not beyond reproach, but they can become so if our critical reappropriation involves a learning process such that the cash value for the claim that I take responsibility for my life, making facts into acts, is my placing past events into a history that makes where I am now and so where the narrative concludes a place of non-reproach. In this way the Rawlsian principle becomes both a regulative ideal and a schematism for the narration of my past. My life becomes beyond reproach to the extent that my telling of it makes compelling that I have indeed been blameworthy and failed in various ways, and these ways are now understood, so permitting me to acknowledge those failures, to take responsibility for them and so for myself, and thereby make my judgment of my life its sense and meaning. Whatever the strengths or weaknesses of this, and placing to one side Rawls's unpalatable desire to identify a stoically preserved sense of moral integrity with somehow being beyond reproach (as if I can only legitimately be reproached for what I intentionally do), both life-plan (prospectively) and narrative (retrospectively) pivot on the question of reproach; but the question of reproach is distinctly moral, relating to the goodness of our willings. What would thus issue from such a life-plan or narrative would be an account of my moral practical relation to myself, where that self-relation need not directly refer to any strong notions of uniqueness and irreplaceability beyond that implied by the principle itself. Better: the Rawlsian principle defines uniqueness and irreplaceability in terms of making myself unconditionally morally accountable for each and all of my actions. So I can offer myself to God with my conscience clear. But, of course, this was the original *moral* project of Rousseau's autobiography. In appropriating Rousseau's model of performative self-presentation for the purposes of ethical self-identity Habermas expunges the drive for moral purity that gives point to its excessive idealizing assumptions.

Although the explicit point of Habermas's reconstruction of Mead is to demonstrate how a linguistic and socialized reformulation of the idea of subjectivity and individuation is possible and indeed preferable to those

123

of the philosophical tradition, as my analysis so far amply shows, the theory itself is more speculatively loaded than its formulation suggests. As such, my fundamental objections to the theory are equally speculative – metaphysical, as it were – although I shall attempt to give them concreteness directly.

The metaphysical ideals embodied in Habermas's theory of individuality are traditional ones: activity is higher than passivity, being is higher than becoming, and necessity is higher than contingency. At least since Hegel and Nietzsche, these metaphysical ideals have become problematic for us, and hence to the degree to which they govern the overall orientation of Habermas's theory we must be at least worried as to whether the theory repudiates the very modernity it means to foster. If there is a pivotal moment in the account it is the hypothetical translation of fact into act: I am to regard my life-history '*as if it were* the product of decisions for which I am responsible'. Ethically, this seems to me unavoidable: unless I treat all that I have done as something decided by me to do, making failures, for example, to thoroughly reflect upon my motives at a given time equivalent to an act of omission, then I treat my actions as the consequences of brute nature and fail to distinguish myself from the world. Hypothetically translating past facts into deeds does not entail, as it may appear to, that I am responsible only for what I intentionally do. On the contrary, this principle asserts that I am responsible for whatever I do or have done, and I take responsibility for this by treating my actions and their consequences as if they had been intentionally done, chosen. As a moral principle, this does not emblemize the metaphysical ideals just noted since it presumes passivity and contingency as the recurrent conditions of action that are acknowledged by the necessity of having to treat past events counterfactually.

Habermas, however, does not treat his principle as moral in orientation; rather, it is a formal principle that permits the totalization of a life. As a consequence, its intention is to produce a closure that insulates that life in its meaning from further incursions from without. This is why the 'eyes of all' are its judge. But why should I do so much as wish to make my life not further answerable to those around me? If the answer to this is that its final terms of reference exceed those they subscribe to, then why is not my life a judgment *and* call on theirs? If it is not and cannot be thought to be somehow exemplary, making new sense of what a human life might be like, in what sense could the 'eyes of all' make it binding? What these questions challenge is the premise of Habermas's reflections here, namely, that postconventional selves have lives whose meaning is not given but self-determined. It is a sharply dualistic contrast between given and self-determined that drives Habermas toward a hyperbolical conception of individuality.

One reason why Habermas might have taken this view, as suggested earlier, is that he construes what I understand as only the contingent breakdown of the interconnection between superego ('me') and ego ideal ('I') as a permanent fate. The question then arose as to why anyone would believe that the relation between 'I' and 'me' was fundamentally antagonistic. My hypothesis at this juncture is that Habermas must believe that the empirical desire for recognition is only satisfiable mimetically, that is by offering to alter what it desires, and hence if my desire for recognition is directed toward my existing community it can only ever be satisfied by forgoing autonomy and authenticity. Conversely, autonomy requires removing myself from existing community, acting negatively with respect to its self-understanding. Therefore, if self-reassurance is social and recognitional in structure, then only an ideal community can provide my life-performance with an audience.

This should be a surprising place to find Habermas since the usual complaint is that his nostalgia for foundations leads him to give priority to the universal in the form of communicative rationality over the particular. Part of the slowness and convolutions of my account has been caused by my desire to show that it is precisely the opposite that drives his appropriation of Mead: the hypostatization of the unlimited communication community is a consequence of and driven by an extreme individualism, with the unlimited communication community entering only as a last gasp, anxious acknowledgement of sociality and the role of recognition in the constitution of self-consciousness. If, for the moment, we drop consideration of this final community and focus only on the logic of 'I' and 'me', then what we discover is the now familiar modern analysis of the irreconcilability of self and society. I hear in Habermas's distinction between 'I' and 'me' Heidegger's distinction between the authentic self and the they-self, or Mill's distinction between individuality and society (the 'eccentric' and the 'customary'), or Rorty's between private self-creation and public accommodation (irony and common sense, metaphorical and truth functional discourse).[30] Now the defiant note in these accounts that leads to the separation of the ethical from the moral, and thereby ego ideal from superego, is the thought that only an individuality, in Habermas's words a 'uniqueness and irreplaceability', that is demonstratively irreducible to the social can count as autonomous. Hence irreducible individuality becomes the *criterion* for autonomy, and autonomy realizes itself only as authenticity. Without this assumption it becomes opaque as to why individualism should be the flip side of universalism.

But this strong requirement for self-determination and autonomy is unnecessary. It is sufficient for my life to be mine that my reasons for adopting it are good reasons for me, where good reasons for me refer to existing values and ideals, their hermeneutical senses as it were, rather than the fact that others desire those ideals *simpliciter*. So what makes a choice autonomous is that it tracks a path of reasons and reason-giving rather than sheer givenness (by tradition or god or revelation or a sacred text). This path does not exclude tradition, for example, since I can autonomously choose a traditional way of life as a way of promoting solidarity. In that case, my choice of tradition would be conditioned by my valuing communal solidarity and in having reasons for valuing the good of solidarity in relation to other possible goods. And even if

125

my way of connecting 'this' traditional way of life with the value of solidarity were not presently part of the repertoire of our community, in virtue of how I reason it must be retrospectively confirmable as a possible way of continuing our life, first for me and then, in virtue of my characterization of it, for others.

What makes our society postconventional, to the degree it is, is that we take the requirement that life-choices be made autonomously in the way described as morally and ethically necessary. We do not regard any forms of givenness as providing good reasons for life-choices. But this is to claim that a post-conventional society is a social form of a particular type, with its own norms and rules for connecting its goals as a society with the particular lives of its inhabitants. Such a society would, if it were appropriately self-conscious about the kind of society it was, affirm the uniqueness and irreplaceability of each by generating conditions that conduced to autonomous lives in the sense speci-fied; this could be thought of, for example, as satisfied by its providing the social bases for self-respect in Rawls's sense.

None of this demands irreducible individuality or rules out repetition; I can autonomously come to see and affirm two plus two equals four as well as simply saying, because my community does, that two plus two equals four. To autonomously count does not entail my having to make those numbers add up differently. So it may be with being a train driver or lover or rabbi. That there are no first principles or Cartesian grounds for certainty does entail that there are limits on my reason-giving, and hence there are limits to my ability reasonably to claim that my reasoning is autonomous. But this only looks like a concession to dogmatism or tradition or conformism if we regard our place in society and history in wholly negative terms, as a forever unwanted constraint. Habermas cannot say that. Authenticity and individuation must be concrete social achievements.

Some view about universals (society) and particulars (individuals) must underlie accounts like those of Habermas and Heidegger and Rorty. But there must equally be some non-logical, human element in play that leads to the identification of authenticity with irreducible individuality. One plausible hypothesis would begin with the fact that because there are no first principles for ethics, first principles for a life being a good one, there are no definitive, objective criteria for autonomy and authenticity. Hence, we can never have Cartesian certainty for believing that our lives are autonomous; on the contrary, because all my reasoning is indebted to past lives, present social forms and the dark recesses of the unconscious, I can be led to wonder whether or not it is even possible for me to have good reasons for believing that my life is my own. And this can immediately generate the anxiety that in reality my life has been only a repetition, 'the horror' of finding myself 'to be only a copy or a replica'.[31] This is how Rorty, following Harold Bloom, conceives of the anxiety that leads to a strong, non-moral conception of individuality. Under the cold gaze of light shone by anxiety, sheer negativity and idiosyncrasy can appear to be attractive and even irresistible options. *Authenticity, now severed from moral claiming, is nothing but autonomy finding confirmation for itself in idiosyncrasy.*

Such idiosyncrasy, however, is subject to the reverse anxiety: being just idiosyncratic. This is the anxiety echoed in the concluding lines of the Philip Larkin poem from which Rorty takes his orientation on this question: 'But to confess, / On the green evening when our death begins, / Just what it was, is hardly satisfying, / Since it applied to one man once, / And that man dying.' On conceptual grounds, Larkin's anxiety is fully justified: if the sense of his life is reducible to what 'applied to one man once', containing nothing but his disappearing self, and thus exhibited nothing in the way of the possibility of what inhabiting the human is or could be, then no recognition, what Larkin calls 'satisfying', is possible. But if this is impossible, then in what sense might that life mean anything at all? Rorty, holding on to an exclusive either/or logic, wrongly distrusts Larkin:

> But in this poem Larkin is pretending that blind impresses, those par-
> ticular contingencies which make each of us 'I' rather than a copy or
> replica of somebody else, do not really matter. He is suggesting that
> unless one finds something common to all men at all times, not just one
> man once, one cannot be satisfied.[32]

Larkin does not appear to me to be suggesting anything so strong, nor need he. But equally, if Larkin had had the knowledge that those blind impresses did not contravene the negative constraints on communication, would this have been any different from sheer idiosyncrasy? Could this extra bit of Habermasian knowledge have proved those blind impresses satisfying in a way they were not before? I cannot see the difference between irreducible singularity and a singularity that conforms to merely negative universalistic constraints. If that is all that could be said of the blind impresses, if it is only the case that there is a logically possible world of rational, communicating agents that could recognize them, how could that bring satisfaction? To know that the shape of my life is not in principle unrecognizable does not entail, for mortal creatures like ourselves, that it is recognizable. The satisfaction of universal criteria does not of itself generate continuities (recognitions or satis-factions) where there were none before. If it is recognition that is sought, if in the green evening of my dying I bring my life before me, the blind impresses of experience like so many scars, joys and hopes marking it, then it is *your* recognition I desire, even if you would have to transfigure your life (and me, in those final moments, mine) for that to be possible. Real possibilities of going on, of inhabiting the world, are not a proper subset of communicatively rational possibilities; that is the logical or Platonic conceit animating abstract univeralism, however procedural.

A COMMUNITY OF CITIZENS

In essence, the defence of a neo-Durkheimian position and the critique of Habermas's reconstruction of Mead come down to the same concatenation of thoughts, namely, (i) that any diremption of norms and affects will generate Kant's deduction problem, which itself involves displacing ethical life with moral theory; (ii) that the most plausible way of connecting moral norms and beliefs with affects is through the connection between individual identity and social identity, a connection best conceived of, broadly, in terms of the desire for recognition, the seeking of self-reassurance; (iii) that in order for (i) and (ii) to go through we must reject Habermas's distinction between moral discourse, which concerns the rightness of binding norms, and ethical discourse, which concerns the identity of an individual as unique and irreplaceable; and (iv) that the consequence of separating the moral from the ethical is to hypostatize the distinction between self and society, and hence to legitimate the nihilistic dualism making us double people. The entire argument to here has thus been a defence of my Rousseauian opening.

In making this argument, no attempt has been made to challenge Habermas's theoretical proposal concerning communicative rationality, which will be addressed in the next chapter, or to demonstrate how and in what way Kant's deduction problem, which ultimately concerns the connection between the possession of norms or rules and the judgment required in order to apply them, infects Habermas's conception of binding norms; that is an issue of Chapter 7. Finally, no defence has been provided either for the claim that self-consciousness really is grounded in otherness or for a conception of the bindingness of norms; both these defences will have to await another occasion. Everything in this chapter has focused on the connections linking the authority of norms, society and identity.

One, somewhat quick way of throwing Habermas's account into question would be along the following route: if in the dialectic of the self the 'me' becomes equivalent to the superego and the 'I' becomes equivalent to the ego ideal, then were is the ego to be found? Within the parameters of Mead's analysis, we find either the 'me' mimetically adapting itself to the demands of alter or the 'I' projecting itself into a new intersubjective context, driven by either suppressed need interpretations or imaginative variations on existing norms, but there seems no place for a self which is neither submerged by existing norms nor dreaming and struggling itself free of them. Without wishing to dismiss the moments of domination and struggle, there nonetheless appears to be no place for the everyday self of social practice. Not every moment in the temporal unfolding of a self should be seen in terms of a repressive or ruined past and an ideal, better future. And even if we were to accede to that schematization of the temporality of the self, one would still want to know 'who' its agent was. Habermas fails to provide a self to mediate superego demands and ego ideals, hence stipulating their disconnection as constitutive of the self, while underwriting that constitution with a conception of the temporality of the self which leaves past and future unsynthesized. It is the absence of such synthetic mediation that leads to the hypostatizing of the moral and the ethical as discrete practical perspectives, the very same irreconcilable perspectives that Rousseau denominated as citizen and bourgeois. From a Rousseauian perspective, the idea that we should require a radical abstraction from the horizons of ethical self-realization in order to be able to count the value of norms as they affect others demonstrates only our failure to count their lives into our own in the first place. But in the absence of such a primary counting in of others to our ethical self-constitution, our reasons for taking up the moral point of view at some later stage must be abstract – the pressures of the need for cooperation and coordination. When the lives of others only come into accounting through a change of perspective, then our original stand with respect to them must have been one of dis-counting. For Habermas the question of who I am and who I want to be is structurally or grammatically self-sufficient without the voices of others (*JA*, 6–10). What then of the new perspective? In making ethical self-identity grammatically self-sufficient Habermas makes the voices of others ones I *have* to take into account, and perhaps, ideally, makes me want rationally to do so; I moderate or bracket my claims with respect to them. In making the moral a 'second' step we have already excluded others from what matters most. In this way the mode of recognition involved in the moral point of view is, in fact, a mode of non-recognition.

In the previous section, I contrasted two anxieties: that deriving from our lack of a positive criterion for autonomy, thus leading us to ground autonomy in a strong notion of individuality, generating thereby the idea of authenticity; and that deriving from hyper-individuality – Larkin's lament 'of only to one man once'. Logically and humanly, I contended, the first anxiety was, however real, ungrounded: nothing can demonstratively show our lives to be autonomous, but to want more than the indeterminate means available is to want self-reassurance to be conceptually equivalent to Cartesian certainty; and to want that for oneself is to want a self removed from the contingencies, both the continuities (recognitions and satisfactions) and discontinuities (mis-recognitions and injuries), that compose a life. I cannot see a logical space for Habermas's talk of the binding of a self-critical appropriation of a life or 'stabilizing' its temporal movement that does not come down to this wish to be free of the risks and contingencies of experience, and thus that is not a response to the indeterminacy of autonomy. Conversely, I argued that, *pace* Rorty, Larkin's anxiety, which we might reasonably construe as the logical consequence of the project of the modern poet, was impeccable, and further, that the late acquisition of an unlimited communication community would do nothing toward reconnecting such a singularity with the bonds of community.

Where one might wish to fault this account is over the motivational grounding of the desire for authenticity. After all, after the death of God and the pervasive acceptance of secularity, why should the desire for autonomy eventuate in a desire for authenticity? A sociological explanation here can add support to the original conceptual–psychological hypothesis. If life for a post-conventional self is good only if it is autonomously chosen, then at least part of what one wants for oneself is that one's life is self-determined, a life that flows from and is answerable to one's desires and choices. Autonomy is fundamentally a question about the sources of one's beliefs and desires, with the usual idea that only if beliefs and desires can be legitimated from within the circle of reasons can they be considered as 'belonging' to the self. Self-determination, in contrast, refers explicitly to actions rather than beliefs. Hence, for autonomous selves to lead autonomous lives they must lead self-determining lives, lives whose happenings 'flow' from their individual and collective choices. Conversely, autonomy without self-determination collapses into the stoical freedom of the existentialist: I can freely 'decide' when to confess to my torturer. In what sense are we free and autonomous selves if our actions and hence our lives are determined from without? If we now add the thought that the fulfilment of the relation between autonomy and significant self-determination is a condition for self-respect or self-worth, itself a condition of selfhood, then the opening of the modern anxiety over autonomy comes clearly into view.

Despite the substantial opportunities for autonomy in modern societies, those opportunities have not translated into substantive possibilities for individual or collective self-determination, or at least so it would appear from the perspective of the classical sociological thought of Marx, Weber and Durkheim. It is equally implied by either Adorno's conception of the domination of society over persons or Habermas's analysis of the uncoupling of life-world and system. Now if autonomy is a condition for self-respect, then there is bound to be a substantial and persistent doubt over whether one's actions are really autonomous when the world seems to be determined by forces having nothing to do with autonomous lives. Under these conditions, only lives and actions that can stand apart from the structures determining society, that do not fit because irreducibly singular, can *appear* as one's own. According to Adorno, it is just this logic that lies behind modernism's recurrent longing for the new.[33] The conception of authenticity which perceives it as involving strong 'uniqueness and irreplaceability' conforms to this very same logic of modernism. Authenticity and modernism are symptoms of the same dilemma and pathology of modern life: the diremption of autonomy as a reflexive capacity of the individual from its fulfilment in the practices of everyday life. However much we are autonomous selves, our lives are far from being self-determined.

Even if this is accepted, this argument might still be thought to suffer from a formal inability to square the possibility of autonomous existences with the neo-Durkheimian commitment to a solidaristic conception (vertical structures of recognition) of sociality that does not collapse into Habermasian abstract universalism. Rather than Habermas's slogan of perceiving individuality as the flip side of universalism, I suggest we opt for autonomous lives as the flip side of democratic citizenship. While backing for such a Rousseauian idea would be an elaborate affair, its rude outlines are perceptible.

Contrary to appearances, modern democratic societies cannot support or affirm value pluralism. Value pluralism – of traditions, lifestyles, fundamental beliefs, and so on – is accepted by Habermas as a given of our situation, and hence as a given for philosophical reflection. Its factual presence together with the lack of the prospect of any change is what first leads him, as well as philosophers like Rawls, to consider that rules of justice can only be rules for fair cooperative arrangements between individuals and groups whose ethical orientations onto the world, which is just their possibility of having a world, are incommensurable with one another. In this scenario, value pluralism replaces the disaggregating role that metaphysical individualism and natural egoism had for the early defenders of social contract liberalism. Once such a disaggregating premise is accepted, then the diremption of moral values and ethical life is preordained. Value pluralism, however, is not a fact of modern life but an interpretation susceptible to reconstruction and reflection.

What is required for reconstruction is not the denial of the phenomena pointed to, but a reconsideration of its grammatical and logical features. In the Rousseauian account, all the values, identities and practices in a modern democratic society are properly conceived of as *modes or ways of inhabiting it*. Hence, Habermasian ethical self-descriptions, ones in which persons affirm who they are and who they want to be, are syntactically incomplete: the phrases, for example, of wanting to be a good teacher, bagel maker, poet, friend, sister, and the like, in each case require the further substantive 'in a democratic society'. Individual ethical self-descriptions are best construed as predicates or qualifications of the essential ethical self-description of being a citizen of a democratic polity. For this to be the case, the idea of democratic citizenship must not be taken as an external constraint on the permissible modes of life for modern individuals, as a boundary or limiting condition – the perception that leads to the idea of a distinct moral point of view through which I come to fair cooperative arrangements with others. On the contrary, being a citizen of a democratic polity is itself an ethical form of life through which we realize the value of leading an autonomous life. And we can realize that value only through autonomously adopting more specific identities and values that are the concretizations and expressions of the perfectionist ideal limned in the more general ethical self-description.

Value pluralism is the illusory appearance form of the range of options necessarily available to a citizen if she is going to lead an autonomous life. If there were not this range of options, and if they did not form incommensurable and non-compossible sets with respect to the lives of particular individuals, and if the possibilities of synthesizing commensurable and compossible sets of goods and values was not radically underdetermined, then autonomy would become a liminal ideal.[34] As Joseph Raz states, 'appropriate mental capacities, an adequate range of options, and independence' are conditions of the good of autonomy.[35] Such conditions are intrinsic and hence necessary features of a form of life where autonomy is a fundamental good. If a life cannot be good unless self-chosen, then the conditions and possibilities of choice must be available. Hence, a diversity of goods and values which are comfortable to the good of democratic citizenship are intrinsic to it in a way directly analogous to the plurality of roles in pre-modern societies.

The evident premise of this view is that unless we regarded autonomy as a fundamental good we would have no grounds, other than pragmatic self-interest, for respecting others' choices. That we can and do value lives which we would not choose is recognition that those lives in part realize and exemplify the ideal of democratic citizenship which we share, and further, that because our own life is only a mode of exemplifying the general good of democratic citizenship, other good lives complement and affirm the value we attach to our own.[36] In this respect, the logical form of the relations between autonomous lives is equivalent to the logical form of the role-bound structures of life of pre-modern societies: complementary distribution bound together by an overall ethical conception. The transition to modernity transfigures how the neo-Durkheimian analysis is realized, but does not alter the basic structure.

In the absence of an argumentative defence for this conception, evidence for it can be found in our attitude toward educational practices within our own societies that deprive its recipients of autonomy.[37] If mere value pluralism was the premise of the democratic state, then systematic refusal to provide children with the capacities for and appreciation of choice would not be an issue: unchosen, fundamentalist religious lives, for example, would just be one more value and life. We would naturally require that exit from such lives be possible eventually, but we would have no grounds for complaining about such an education *ab initio*. But we are inclined to complain here, and rightly so. Exit without voice provides only a negative liberty. Yet in these circumstances it is parental voice that is being given the power to trump since only parents can be proper members of the community of argumentation. And if we ask the Habermasian question of them and ourselves, namely, could control of a child's education by its parents be a principle the consequences and side effects of which could be freely accepted by all affected?, the answer appears equivocal. Certainly an affirmative answer would not be obviously impossible or in any way untoward. Yet fundamentalist religious education does contravene the good of autonomy which in religious matters regards only *free* religious belief as worthy of respect. Education for us involves education for autonomy, thus education for a certain form of life and participation in a specific form of community.

Unfree beliefs, except in the case of still closed because remote societies, must appear to us as cases of coercive socialization, brainwashing or the like. We cannot separate the goodness of a belief from the way it is held; unless an agent *can* take a reflective and critical relation to her own beliefs we shall not count it as hers at all. This entails that the fundamental meaning of values and traditions alters once they are submitted to the melting pot of autonomy and democratic citizenship. In saying that only free religious belief can have a role in a democratic society of autonomous persons, we are not merely placing on its believers the constraint of voice and exit. For religious beliefs to continue to have a role is for them to have the status of being choice-worthy, or potentially so, for persons inhabiting a society that itself remains secular. To accede to this demand, religious beliefs must pose themselves not as absolute, exclusive truths but as ethical orientations deserving of being chosen and affirmed. Precisely this is what distinguishes the writings of, for example, modern Catholic novelists (say, Flannery O'Connor) and poets as opposed to pre-modern religious writers. Because divergent values and traditions now become potential ethical identities, then they must reveal themselves as furthering the good of an autonomous self, which might, for example, involve demonstrating the good of surrendering choice over certain ranges of activity by locating oneself in a tradition by accepting some 'arbitrary' rules for the practice of everyday life (e.g. keeping a kosher kitchen). In each case, however, such traditions must reveal themselves to be compatible with the assumption that they are just one possible way of inhabiting the world; they are values and traditions *for* citizens. The ethical horizon from which we cannot abstract without simultaneously abrogating the force of the multiple values and traditions available is that of ethical citizenship: it configures the hyper-good which gives meaning to the plural good lives composing it. Whatever is incompatible with the hyper-good of modern citizenship, a further *articulation* of it, cannot be accorded the status of a 'good' at all.

Issues like religious education bring into focus the question of whether our universalist beliefs are either intensionally or extensionally equivalent with 'impartiality of judgment' (*JA*, 48), with neutrality in whatever form. In raising this question, we need not deny that the Habermasian principle can have a role in our ethical projects; it is to deny that there is some coherent concept of the moral point of view, and further that Habermasian principles (U and D) capture the specific contours of our valuing the lives of others. In the present context, it is through the possibilities of ethical self-identity that we are posing this question. The belief that there is a separation between ethical and moral points of view comes down to the intelligibility of Larkin's 'only to one man once' formula since it expresses the conception of an ethical self-identity that is restricted to the horizon of the question 'What is good for me?' Habermas believes that however far such ethical questions extend, they are not yet moral since they do not touch upon 'the regulation of interpersonal conflicts of action resulting from opposed interests' (*JA*, 6). That Habermas should begin from the assumption of conflict as raising the question of the

133

moral point of view is decisive. If the interests of others do not satisfy the condition of complementarity, how can I acknowledge their significance? Coming to *see* that other life-choices are complementary, add to and elaborate our form of life, may indeed require discursive elaboration, but that is quite different from being generally acceptable. Conversely, if the interests of others are potentially complementary in the specified sense, then we are not beginning from conflicting interests, but from *different epistemic sightings* of our ethical life. The idea of different epistemic sightings of our ethical life makes questions of conflict hermeneutical in the precise sense that we are not asking about a proposal whether it is valid but whether or not it successfully elaborates the good of the life of democratic citizenship. And this hermeneutical question is clearly continuous with the narrow conception of the ethical question of self-identity.

Real conflicts of interest, on the other hand, call for compromise and negotiation; interests that lack complementarity because those pursuing them lack ethical insight or sensitivity, and thus are still immersed in the egocentric perspective, require strategic handling, not ethical consideration. That we are willing to compromise and negotiate, when we are, derives from two sources: either considerations of power give us no choice or we wish to engage with self-interested others in an ethical manner despite their egocentric perspective. In this latter case, we are not moved by others' interests deserving consideration, but from belief that others themselves are best treated as if unconditional members of the community because that is the most promising route through which they might become so. In acknowledging real conflicts of interest in this way, I am not acknowledging real value pluralism, but the less sanguine contention that political life must persistently engage with persons and perspectives that remain outside the ambit of the ethical life of modern citizenship;[38] the ethical life of modern citizenship is, following Hegel, the rose in the cross of the present. Because the cross of the present is itself permanent, then political questions will remain, in part, determined by questions of power and strategy. (Once he came to perceive this unfortunate fact, Rousseau was led to complement his account of citizenship with a series of experimental analyses of solitary ethical self-realization. This is the hidden despair that drives Rousseau's confessional self to seek self-reassurance in God, nature and eternity.) It is the conflation of the fact that some or even all persons (in part) refuse or suppress the ethical claim of citizenship, thus opening up the terrain of non-moral conflict, with value pluralism that leads to a simultaneous rejection of the inseparability of the ethical and the moral on the one hand, and the idealizing and moralizing of political discourse on the other.

When Rousseau demanded that the word 'citizen' be effaced from the language he was voicing an ideal of ethical life he believed expressed in that concept, namely, that only in our most basic ethical self-understanding and self-identity as citizens can we uphold the universalistic goods of liberty and equality since only that identity first expresses and articulates those goods.

Once they are abstracted from their place in the life of citizens communally bound, they become free-standing moral ideals compatible with the ethically indifferent stance of the bourgeois. Only from the outside, which is to say by making them correspond to restrictions on our willings, do universalistic ideals appear as constraints. Within the life of the ethical democratic polity, what can appear now as universalistic negative constraints operate as positive goods through which we recognize and attempt to foster the lives of our fellow citizens. One, blunt way of expressing this thought is to say that there are no negative rights; all rights are positive since rights are for the sake of furthering the self-realization of autonomous individuals *as* members of a democratic polity. Rights conduce to the end and good of democratic citizenship.[39] If we concretely believe that only in others realizing the ideal of democratic citizenship can we realize ourselves, then there can be no logical space for a duality of perspective.

If we begin from the perception of conflict, that is because we have forgotten our place in society. The modern idea of citizenship, which arises only when we *must* Hobbesianly take the perspective of others into account, discounts them from belonging to our ethical self-understanding. Hence we become citizens not for ourselves but for our being with others; as bourgeois we relate everything to ourselves. That we have these dual perspectives is the disintegrative dynamic of modernity: abstractive individualism being the flip side of abstractive universalism. Although guided by the idea of legitimating the intersubjective perspective, in following Mead's bifurcation of the self into 'I' and 'me', and providing the distinction between the ethical and the moral with the dignity of grammatical and rational self-sufficiency as perspectives, Habermas ends up sanctioning the lives of modern double men – nothings.

5

THE GENERALIZED OTHER, CONCRETE OTHERS

Seyla Benhabib's *Critique, Norm, and Utopia*[1] is the most philosophically acute and learned history of the critical theory of society yet to be written. Because the intentions of Benhabib's work are systematic rather than historical, her history is equally a major contribution to critical theory which will prove to be a powerful focus and catalyst for future research.

Benhabib subtitles her work *A Study in the Foundations of Critical Theory*. Her point of departure is the now familiar aporia of Adorno and Horkheimer's totalizing critique:

> If the plight of the Enlightenment and of cultural rationalization only reveals the culmination of the identity logic, constitutive of reason, then the theory of the dialectic of Enlightenment, which is carried out with the tools of this very same reason, perpetuates the very structure of domination it condemns.
>
> (p. 169)

For Adorno and Horkheimer this aporia belongs not to their theory but to modernity. For Habermas, however, it marks the place where the question of foundations must be resurrected and answered anew in terms of language and communication. Benhabib's study concedes the question, and at least the form of Habermas's response. What distinguishes her study is its subjection of Habermas's Kantian-inspired communication theory to Hegelian critique.

As she admits, her conclusion amounts to something of a 'belated vindication' (p. 336) of one of the central insights of early critical theory. My contention will be that Benhabib's final vision requires more than her admittedly large concessionary nod to early critical theory; in order to sustain her remarkably bold and compelling vision she will have to take on board the core of Adorno's philosophy of nonidentity. Indeed, precisely through her desire to avoid the impasses of Adorno's philosophy, her austere presentation of the shortcomings of Habermas's theory amounts to the fullest vindication of Adorno yet to appear.

136

THE PHILOSOPHY OF THE SUBJECT

Throughout *Critique, Norm, and Utopia* Benhabib deploys and develops a subtle and elaborate theoretical apparatus with which she interrogates her chosen authors. Central to this theoretical scheme is what Benhabib calls 'the philosophy of the subject'. Benhabib isolates four presuppositions as being constitutive of this philosophy: (i) a unitary model of activity based upon Hegel's phenomenological conceptualization of labour; (ii) the model of a trans-subjective or unified collective subject; (iii) a conception of history as the story of trans-subjectivity; and (iv) the ultimate or inner identity of constituted and constituting subjectivity (p. 54). Each of the components of this model possesses a comprehensible and often sound theoretical motive. The rationale behind the development of (i), the dialectical model of transformative activity, which is world- and self-spiritualizing/humanizing, depends on a generalization of Kant's conception of the constituting powers of self-consciousness that acknowledges the material and social conditions of constituting activity. Once Kant's categories can no longer be assumed to be given a priori, then they and the world they project must be historical products. If so, then reason must be both historical and fundamentally practical even in its epistemic striving. Behind (ii) lie two thoughts: on the one hand, it was obvious to Hegel that natural right theories tended to project into the state of nature images of reason derived from their understanding of their own concrete historical experience. It hence became necessary to recognize that reason was not an ultimate term of analysis or a raw given, but a historically conditioned product. On the other hand, however, it was equally obvious that reason tended to forget or repress its historical and social situatedness, and to regard itself as naturally or metaphysically transcendent to the work of history. Since reason was not, at bottom, 'in the head' anyway, but rather was manifest in complex social practices, and could only be perceived from the perspective of an outside observer–thinker, it looked plausible to regard the 'object' observed as 'the', trans-subjective, subject. Once this thought is harnessed together with (i), (iii) and (iv) follow quite unproblematically.

In hardly any of the writings Benhabib considers does the model of a collective, singular subject that exteriorizes itself and subsequently reappropriates what it has exteriorized operate in isolation from a contrasting model. We get an idea of what is involved in this contrasting model if we examine Benhabib's suggestion that throughout *Capital* two strands of analysis, corresponding to two distinct social epistemologies, are followed. The first perspective is inter-personal, considering individuals as always enmeshed in complex social relations with other individuals; corresponding to this participant perspective is a crisis theory which presents crises as '*lived* phenomena of alienation, exploitation, and injustice' (p. 123). The second perspective, implying the philosophy of the subject, views the movement of capital from the perspective of a third, of a thinker–observer; and corresponding to this perspective there is a crisis theory which regards crises as the failure of the functional logic of the system. Benhabib theorizes these two perspectives in terms of Lockwood's familiar distinction between social integration and system integration. System integration takes place through 'the functional interconnection between the consequences of social actions' (p. 127). Adam Smith's concept of the 'invisible hand' and Hegel's account of the 'system of needs' can serve as adequate models for what is at issue here. Social integration requires the co-ordination of social actions, and this occurs through the harmonizing of action orientations. Individuals can orient their actions to one another because, Benhabib says, 'they understand the meanings, social rules, and values in question' (p. 127).

These perspectives are the social equivalents of the traditional philosophical distinctions between first and third person, agent and spectator, inside and outside perspectives, and are as irremovable, discordant and recalcitrant to easy reconciliation as they are. Benhabib never suggests that this duality can be dissolved; on the contrary, her critique of the philosophy of the subject is precisely that it brackets and then, forgetfully, dissolves interpersonal experience in the objectifying gaze of the thinker–observer. What is required here is not an act of dissolution, but rather a workable account of how these perspectives can be mediated.

Nonetheless, it is no accident that the system perspective has come to dominate since, in the first instance, it was not the theorist who objectified, reified interpersonal activity but capital itself. The logic of capital works behind the backs of the agents of capital, and its comprehension therefore necessarily invokes the perspective of the thinker–observer. Since the perspectives with which the critical theorist operates are theoretically and socially pertinent, then unsurprisingly these perspectives coordinate in complex ways with both the forms of critique and the accounts of overcoming (capital) employed by critical theory from Hegel to Habermas. And this, directly, implicates the dual perspectives of social theory in the question of the normative foundations of critique.

Benhabib distinguishes between immanent and defetishizing critique, and between categorial and normative critique. Immanent critique has its origin in Hegel's critique of natural right theories; Hegel proceeds by demonstrating how each apparently a priori criterion of right is in fact a posteriori. However, according to Benhabib, Hegel can only sustain this critique by illicitly contrasting the ideal of the ancients with the fact of the moderns. Marx, taking up Hegel's thesis concerning the illicit substitution of a priori norms for a posteriori facts, sophisticates Hegel's procedure by operating an immanent critique which is both categorial and normative. Categorial immanent critique involves demonstrating how the accepted definitions and significations of the categories of political economy turn into their opposites without the intervention of a separate categorial framework. For example, if capital is defined as self-expanding value, and if the reason for the increase in the value of capital is sought in the sphere of the exchange of commodities, then either the exchange of commodities violates the principle of equivalence or the self-expansion of the value of capital becomes unintelligible.

(p. 106)

Immanent critique can also be normative when the categories of the political economist are normative. In this case critique involves comparing the norms of bourgeois society – e.g. 'Freedom, Equality, Property, and Bentham' – with 'the actuality of the social relations in which they are embodied' (p. 107). Normative immanent critique thus reveals the apparently a priori norms of experience to be distorting, albeit factual, appearance forms of the social relations they help to articulate.

Defetishizing critique has its origin in Hegel's reinterpretation of self-reflection as involving the recuperation of the historical and social conditions which have produced the self. Once this position is articulated with the labour model of activity, defetishizing critique can be read as the critical motive for and consequence of the philosophy of the subject. According to Benhabib, Marx's critique of Hegel in the *1844 Manuscripts* is not a rejection of this model, but a 'materialistic' continuation of Hegel's discovery (p. 21), wherein Marx 'simply replaced "Spirit" with "mankind" or "humanity" ' (p. 54). Again, the deployment of defetishizing critique in *Capital* is more nuanced; it presupposes only that the categories of political economy are theoretically refined versions of the social discourse it is theorizing. Political economy handles these socially given categories as if they were natural, and as a consequence 'fails to uncover the social constitution of its own object domain' (p. 108).

Now if, on the one hand, we consider the occluded value-producing agents of capital to be 'the proletariat'; and, on the other hand, consider defetishizing critique as analysing theoretical versions of everyday forms of social consciousness with reference to a future actuality, where that actuality is cashed out in terms of systematic crisis (the falling rate of profit, unemployment, and so on), then it again becomes quite natural to put into operation the discourse of the philosophy of the subject. Only here the language of class, class interest, and the like replaces 'humanity' and 'mankind', and the interests of one particular class, the proletariat, are regarded as being universal precisely through their occluded but constitutive place within the capitalist system of production.

While Benhabib does not wish to deny the appropriateness of the thinker–observer perspective, she regards its articulation in terms of the philosophy of the subject as amounting to the virtual dissolution of the interpersonal perspective. Briefly, she argues that, firstly, the category of 'objectification', as employed within the labour model of activity, is inadequate to characterize communicative activities; secondly, that this model of activity is fundamentally monological, moving from ideas in the head to actions in the world, and hence abstracts from the linguistic mediation of desires, intentions and purposes; thirdly, in so doing it illegitimately suppresses the interpretive indeterminacy of human action; fourthly, it is only as a consequence of the suppression of the interpretive indeterminacy of human action that the model of a trans-subjective subject comes into being, but such a subject involves a denial of the inescapable fact of human *plurality*; finally, the model of self-actualization operative in the philosophy of the subject assumes 'an epistemologically transparent self, who seems to possess unequivocal knowledge for determining what would "actualize" him/her' (p. 137); as such, it suppresses the very situatedness that characterizes interpersonal existence.

As mentioned above, throughout her account of the domination of the illicit model of the philosophy of the subject in Hegel and Marx, Benhabib etches a counter-story of the interpersonal perspective. She sees this counter-story at work in the dialogic dimensions of Hegel's *Phenomenology*; in Marx's analysis of sensuous finitude in the *1844 Manuscripts*, and in the historical chapters of *Capital*. What is important here is not simply the existence of another perspective, but the fact that it entails a different account of human emancipation. Roughly, in accordance with the model of the philosophy of the subject, emancipation amounts to the *fulfilment* of the possibilities and potentialities of the present. However, in accordance with the model of interpersonal, communicative relations, emancipation involves the qualitative transformation of our needs, pleasures, and self-understanding; in short, it conceives of emancipation as *transfiguration*.

With these elements before us we can now, quickly, anticipate the predicament of contemporary critical theory. Given its historical situation, early critical theory was led to deny that there were any potentials in the bourgeois world worth fulfilling; on the contrary, it looked to Horkheimer and Adorno as if enlightened reason and the philosophy of the subject had already and disastrously been fulfilled in Nazi Germany. However, since they accepted the Hegelian critique of the a priori, then there were no norms, immanent or transcendent, on which they could base their critique. Hence their project of interrogating the very reason which had undermined the ideals it had previously generated and espoused with its own tools. Their presumption was that this reason, identity thinking, *itself* harboured an alternative which immanent critique could unlock. For Habermas, Adorno and Horkheimer's self-consciously aporetic and speculative practice is to be rejected precisely because it is aporetic and speculative. Worse, it fails to actually break with the philosophy of the subject. Hence, he attempts to reground critique by displacing the philosophy of the subject with a theory of communicative action, which will simultaneously salvage the emancipatory potential of the Enlightenment conception of bourgeois rights and self-reflection. This programme, however, can only be carried out through a surreptitious continuation otherwise of the discourse of the philosophy of the subject, and through the restriction of emancipation to fulfilment.

HEGEL v. HABERMAS

Almost from the beginning of his career Habermas has been anxious to argue that the growth of western rationality does not entail a loss of freedom. On the contrary, if we can categorially distinguish technical from communicative rationality, then we can demonstrate that there is an emancipatory potential in communicative rationality which the technization of society, brought about through capital expansion and the altered role of the state in the postwar period, has suppressed. For Habermas 'the constituents of cultural modernity – decentration, reflexivity, and the differentiation of value spheres – are binding criteria of rationality' (p. 254); the emancipation of society would involve the fulfilment of these criteria.

Benhabib considers Habermas's claim for the bindingness of communicative rationality as resting on three assertions, each of which she rejects. Firstly, Habermas claims for communicative rationality a quasi-transcendental status based on a rational reconstruction of the anonymous rule systems or deep structures underlying cognition and action. More precisely, he claims that the criteria of communicative rationality are the results of a non-reversible or developmental process of social learning or evolution whose compelling logic is underwritten by the quasi-empirical reconstructive sciences of cognitive psychology, genetic epistemology and generative linguistics. Against Habermas's claim for the quasi-transcendental status of communicative rationality it has been argued that he presupposes that there is just one correct explication of linguistic competence etc., ignoring the fact that for each of the phenomena he considers there are competing explanatory frameworks. This entails dropping the uniqueness claim associated with transcendental arguments generally; and from this it follows that the line separating reconstructive narrative from hermeneutical narrative may not exist.

Secondly, communicative rationality, with its insistence on the validation of claims through argumentative procedures, correctly captures the growing 'reflexivity' characteristic of the cultural tradition of modernity. How could such reflexivity not be binding for us? Notoriously, however, as the whole of Habermas's evolutionary schema suggests, this claim simply begs the question when faced with the claims of other cultures, cultures which do share our penchant for reflexivity and argumentation. Habermas, in fact, is not averse to offering to the critical theorist a privileged epistemic situation from which he can judge the comparative 'health' or 'sickness' of different societies. 'If we do not wish to renounce altogether standards of judging a form of life to be more or less misguided, distorted, unfortunate, or alienated, if it is really necessary the model of sickness and health presents itself.'[2]

Finally, Habermas claims for communicative reason an existential irrevocability; for him the developments of scientism, universalistic morality and post-auratic art represent ' "irreversible developments, which have followed an internal logic", and which could be reversed only at the cost of regressions'

(p. 276). This contention is deeply reminiscent of speculative philosophies of history, where the 'normal' or 'true' future is already latent in the present. Not only does such a thesis provide history with a closed logic, but it regards the fulfilment of the legacy of modernity in theoretical rather than practical terms. As Benhabib states: 'The question here is: does such a demand for fulfilment of modern reason project the image of a future we would like to make our own?' (p. 277). And here one wants to say: Habermas has denied that we can have such a question (without being irrational or mad).

This is not to deny that the standpoint of modernity and the norms of communicative rationality are in some sense binding for us; Benhabib's contention is only that this binding is cultural and contingent, not trans-historical and logical, and hence the binding itself can always be brought into question. In this sense she is conceiving of modernity as a self-conscious tradition, a tradition in which the question of tradition is always reflectively posed. She hence perceives modernity as a form of life, a tradition, that always stands in a reflective and critical relation to itself. Because for her modernity is just tradition become reflective and reflexive, then she must think that the crisis of modernity is in part constitutive of it since it is always in a critical self-relation, and hence always divided from itself. In this respect its reflectiveness is both irreversible and always in question. Although she does not say so, this would make modernity constitutively aporetic. Habermas certainly refuses this aporetic stance; Benhabib's relation to it will be canvassed below.

Benhabib's account of Habermas's programme for a communicative ethics, which draws from the idea of communicative rationality the presupposition of an ideal speech situation embedded in all discursive argumentation, is, disconcertingly, compulsively sympathetic and austerely critical. Habermas's thesis is now familiar: discourses are forms of speech which rationally examine controversial claims concerning truth and normative rightness that have arisen in the course of ordinary communication. The 'ideal speech situation' specifies the 'formal properties that discursive argumentations would have to possess if the consensus thus attained were to be distinguished from a mere compromise or an agreement of convenience' (p. 284). These divide into a two-part symmetry condition and a two-part reciprocity condition. The symmetry condition states that each participant must have an equal chance to initiate and continue dialogue; and an equal chance to make assertions, recommendations, etc. The reciprocity condition states that each participant must have an equal chance to express their wishes, feelings, etc.; and they must act as if, in action contexts, systematic domination was not a feature of their relations with others. It must be noted here how strong the reciprocity condition is; it not only requires honesty and sincerity (a dubious *social* virtue),[3] and I think by implication the non-existence of self-deception, but further makes essential reference to action contexts where inequality and subordination of a systematic kind can play no part. Habermas believes this to be a necessary idealization, a counterfactual belief, necessary to communicative relations as a norm governing them.

Initially Benhabib considers the now standard objections to Habermas's programme. As we have already seen, the attempt to provide a strong justification, which would ground a communicative ethic on the fundamental norms of rational speech through the establishment of a quasi-transcendental connection between the structures of rational speech and a communicative ethic, must fail: it illegitimately discounts at the very least other competing explanations; at worst narrative praxis. Other arguments against Habermas suggest that:

(i) his theory is circular:

> universal pragmatics cannot justify the step of abstraction which defines the transition to a universalist ethics, because it presupposes it methodologically . . . already [assuming] a moral attitude corresponding to a *universalist ethical* standpoint that disregards all existing natural and social differences as irrelevant in defining the moral core of one's humanity.
>
> (p. 291)

> In this his theory becomes extensionally equivalent to Kant's notion of reason, sustaining the difference between the rational will (*Wille*) and the actual will (*Willkür*);

(ii) his theory presupposes a richer semantic content than the symmetry and reciprocity conditions in general entail; and

(iii) once we reach the stage of universalist moral orientation, the formal criteria demarcating that orientation (impartiality, universalizability, etc.) are no longer sufficient to arbitrate between competing moral theories.

Habermas now contends, following Karl-Otto Apel, that the relation between argumentative speech and communicative ethics is neither deductive nor inductive, but rather invokes the idea of a performative contradiction. That is, the sceptic who doubts that validity claims can be settled through rational argumentation immediately gets involved in a performative contradiction. This shows that the ideal is 'unavoidable' and 'uncircumventable' without, however, claiming that it can be non-trivially justified. I will deal with the status of performative contradiction at length on pp. 180–90 of the next chapter.

It is at this juncture that Benhabib reformulates the Hegelian objections to Kantian moral theory to make them applicable to Habermas's revised communicative ethic. Hegel raised three essential objections: (i) the objection to Kantian formalism; (ii) the institutional objection that Kantian theory illicitly abstracts from the functional interdependency of practices; and (iii) the objection to Kantian moral psychology that it falsely contrasts reason and emotion, disallowing the formative capacities of reason. Benhabib's reformulation of these objections follows Hegel's pattern of argumentation.

(i) Habermas's discursive, procedural reinterpretation of Kant's categorical imperative, called principle U, states that every valid norm must fulfil the following condition:

> *All* affected can accept the consequences and the side effects its *general* observance can be anticipated to have for the satisfaction of *everyone's* interests (and these consequences are preferred to those of known alternatives).
>
> (*MCCA*, 65)

This thesis is, in fact, weaker than Kant's since, minimally, the rules of argumentation do not entail it as uniquely satisfying their requirements, and hence other universalist principles seem compatible with the general requirements of argumentation; and maximally, it does not seem to be able to prohibit a group from consenting to a principle which entails the violation of that principle. In contrast, Kant's conception of the categorical imperative asks if others *could* act on the maxim of the agent if universalized. Habermas attempts to circumvent this objection by claiming that the principle of universalizability belongs among the pragmatic presuppositions of argumentation, and thus cannot be materially violated without (a pragmatic) contradiction. However, as Benhabib demonstrates in a careful analysis, this reveals the principle of universalizability to be, as Hegel would have it, still either redundant or inconsistent. Benhabib states:

> Either this principle explicates the meaning of rational consent in such a way that nothing new is added to the available explication of the argumentation procedure in practical discourse; or this principle defines the meaning of rational consent in some additional way, but this definition is neither the only one compatible with accepted rules of argumentation, nor can it be said to follow from the rules of argumentation without the introduction of additional assumptions not belonging to the specified rules of argument.
>
> (p. 308)

(ii) The matter of the institutional bases of communicative ethics raises this question: does Kantian moral theory have a privileged object domain, namely, the domain of legal and juridical relations between individuals, but remain blind to other forms of relationships, familial, erotic, fraternal and the like? This would be so if, where there are conflicting interests, participants could legitimately come to an agreement while simultaneously refusing either (a) to forgo any of their own interests, or (b) to consider changing the form of life which generated those interests in the first place. And this would be so if general interests were defined, Rawlsianly and minimally, as 'not taking an interest in each other's interest' (p. 311). Accepting this has the undesirable consequence of letting our form of life in which the pursuit of happiness is defined in terms of the private consumption of material goods remain unquestioned, and reducing the rules of justice to rules for regulating commercial warfare. In short, if these conditions obtain, then the universalist ethical position is exhausted by a legal/juridical construction. On this matter, Benhabib contends, while Habermas does have a participatory democratic aspect to his thought which would entail the promotion of (a) and (b), that is, an aspect which regards the process of argumentation as capable of transforming given interests and questions the forms of life in which given interests are generated, he fails adequately to appreciate the problem, and hence vacillates between a legal/juridical conception of universalizability, indistinguishable from assorted other such versions, and a radical democratic conception which would see universalizability as procedurally generating radical social transformations.

(iii) Since communicative ethics does not Kantianly distinguish between duty and inclination, Benhabib reformulates the Hegelian objection to Kantian moral psychology through this question: 'does the cognitivist bias of communicative ethics also lead to the *rationalistic fallacy*, namely, to a view of reason as a self-generating faculty, determining both the conditions of its own genesis and application?' (p. 317). Benhabib contends that this question must be answered in the affirmative for three reasons. First, what may be called the Gadamer objection states that the ideal of a rational consensus can only be relevant when it is an ideal consciously striven for in a particular culture. But this culturally concrete ideal assumes, amongst those using it, a reconciled intersubjectivity; after all, rational consensus inscribes part of the integrity of their form of life. However, for those who feel that the reconciled intersubjectivity of the culture has been produced at their expense, it might be morally legitimate to refuse to participate in the rational consensus game until it appears to be materially applicable to them. Hence, either the theory is what I called in the last chapter logically binding but without an affective basis; or the theory has an affective basis, but then it cannot be binding on all.

Second, Habermas insists on distinguishing moral justification from questions of contextualization or application. But this elides the question of moral judgment; and if we consider moral judgment a question of (social) character, then this elision entails a question mark as to what it might mean concretely to embody the virtues of communicative rationality. In short, the question of application cannot be regarded as wholly independent from the question of justification, for until we know what will count as a proper application of the principle we know far too little. The point here is not that we require a formalism to specify its conditions of application; it is rather that the meaning of the formalism itself is only revealed fully through its concrete embodiment. (In response to this objection, Habermas has adopted a new 'discourse of application', which I discuss in detail in Chapter 7.)

These two objections together yield the third objection, namely, that Habermas provides insufficient motivation for pursuing rational argument.

Benhabib states, following Hegel, that reason can become a fact only if it shapes and transforms desire: 'The desirability of reason entails the rationality of desire. Reason that refuses to heed inner nature and the individual's demand for happiness and fulfilment can lose its motivating power' (p. 324). But is not this to say that reason can motivate us to justice only if happiness too is promised? Not for nothing did Hegel regard Kant's 'Postulates of Pure Practical Reason' as the exposed and vulnerable core of the Kantian programme.

DESIRE: PUBLIC OR PRIVATE?

Benhabib summarizes her critique of Habermas's communicative ethic by reiterating the objection encapsulated in the passage quoted above: either Habermas's theory is too empty and/or formal to be morally informative, or it requires additional assumptions that cannot be justified in the theory's own terms. Benhabib relentlessly tracks down the source of this difficulty in Habermas's continuation of the discourse of the philosophy of the subject. This occurs at those points in his theory when the reconstruction of our species competences becomes a 'formative history of the subject of history' (p. 331). Habermas's procedure *assumes* that the standpoint of the reconstruction is the standpoint of mankind as such. Not only does this procedure construct the 'we' of the present theoretically, but in so doing it neutralizes real history into a 'semantic gloss on a structural process which proceeds with necessity and invariably from one sequence to the next' (p. 331).

Further, as already noted, even if we grant that evolutionary argument takes us to the standpoint of a postconventional, universalistic morality, such a theory is useless in arbitrating between competing universalistic theories and positions. Since the future is not theoretically determined, then the application and contextualization of the theory for the sake of the future cannot be worked in theoretical terms; or better, the application of theory cannot be made from the position of the third, the thinker–observer.

Now there is an aspect or moment of Habermas's theory which pushes in this direction, namely, his addition to the Kohlbergian scheme of a stage of universalizable need interpretations. The significance of such a thesis is not far to seek, for it contravenes the privacy of human desire presupposed by most deontological ethical theories. As Benhabib baldly states the issue: 'To want to draw this aspect of a person's life [i.e. their needs, desires, and feelings about things] into public–moral discourse would interfere with their autonomy, i.e. with their right to define the good life as they please as long as this does not impinge on others' rights to do the same' (p. 332).

Habermas backs the requirement for this stage with the relatively uncontentious thought that needs, desires and the like are always already socially mediated, and in that sense not private; and that the grammatical logic of the term 'I' reveals that the use of the term by a unique subject involves a recognition of other such subjects to hold this position. One becomes an 'I' only in a community with other subjects who are also 'I's.

It is at this juncture that Benhabib transforms the Habermasian discourse into her own. Benhabib claims that needs and their interpretations can only be discursively thematized if the cultural traditions and practices, the semantic content of which defines the good life and happiness, are thematized. But this will reveal, and subject to interpretation and critique, that our idea of justice itself rests upon a certain understanding of needs. When such an interpretive search is pressed, it reveals the non-detachability of conceptions of justice and the good life. And while this says something we already knew, namely, that the idea of a public discourse of rights and entitlements as capturing the highest stage of moral development secretes the idea of a good life as something to be sought in private, it goes further. For the insistence that universalizable need interpretations move into the centre of moral discourse is not simply a further evolution of the perspective of rights and entitlements, it entails a 'utopian break' with it; it involves a fundamental transfiguration of the perspective of universalistic moral theory.

This is the 'belated vindication' of early critical theory I mentioned at the outset. I want to argue that Benhabib's brief fleshing out of the politics of transfiguration in fact requires more of the resources of early critical theory than she recognizes, and hence a more sympathetic reading of it than she, under the influence of Habermas, offers. I shall discuss these problems under three rubrics: the question of the separation of the spheres of value; the question of nonidentity; and the question of the political.

ART, OR THE POLITICS OF DESIRE

Habermas labels the forms of discourse in which our need interpretations are thematized, and whose semantic content defines happiness and the good life, 'aesthetic-expressive'. This, of course, coheres with the idea that the good life is a (semi-) private affair, that is non-universalizable and culturally specific, and hence outside the bounds of either truth or morality. In the previous chapter, we saw how Habermas attempted to sustain this privacy through his distinction between moral reason and ethical identity. If at the centre of ethical identity is a fundamental desire or project, who I want to be, then the grammatical distinction between the logic of moral reason and the logic of ethical reason is coextensive with and ultimately dependent on the binding sphere differentiation between the moral and the aesthetic-expressive. Benhabib contends that the distinction between the normative and the aesthetic-expressive does not do justice to the significance of needs and their interpretations in the moral realm. One can only read Habermas's preservation of this distinction as an attempt to protect the purity of the moral realm; and this appears to prohibit Habermas from making good his critique of theories of justice which do not extend to a critique of consumerism, and possessive-individualist modes of life. Benhabib goes on to note that there is a continuing vacillation in Habermas between a model of community as one of rights and entitlements, and a model of community as formed through needs and solidarity.

Benhabib states that Habermas has failed adequately to thematize the idea of a community of needs and solidarity because, following Mead, 'he assumes the standpoint of the "generalized other", of rights and entitlements to represent the moral view par excellence' (p. 339). Now while Benhabib's point has real force, as I shall elaborate in the next section, it moves too quickly past the issue of Habermas's acceptance of Weber's thesis that the separation of spheres of value, the separation between the discourses of truth, right, and beauty, represents an unassailable and irreversible accomplishment of modernity. What is ironic here is that although Benhabib has been brought to the pitch of doubting this thesis because of the now evident lacuna in the post-conventional, universalistic standpoint which traces the idea of a community of rights and entitlements, she fails to draw the obvious conclusion that this standpoint *requires* the prohibition on universalistic need interpretations, and hence requires the autonomy and independence of aesthetic-expressive discourse, i.e. art, for its maintenance. This exclusion of need interpretations, and the consequent marginalization/autonomization of art echoes the substantial exclusion/ marginalization/*domination* of persons (Benhabib herself will evidence the silencing of the voice of women) which conditioned the reconciled intersubjectivity of the bourgeois, liberal state. The shape of liberal justice confers legitimacy on only those desires, those conceptions of ethical identity, hence those fundamental need interpretations that can be pursued by privatized and autonomous subjects, subjects whose conception of the good life is one in principle satisfiable privately and 'authentically' in the sense of that term I provided in the previous chapter. What I there specified in terms of the distinction between autonomy and self-determination is equivalent to keeping need interpretations individual and art autonomous, that is, a domain of semblance and illusion. These exclusions, I am now claiming, are, however obliquely, in the mode of a mutual conditioning, the same exclusion. It was just this thought that led Adorno to regard autonomous art as a privileged object for critique.

Because she has failed to see that the point of Adorno's focus on autonomous art is to critique the extrusion of need interpretations from morality and social understanding – Adorno attempting to draw the question of need interpretation (sensuous particularity) and therefore morality into the scope of direct cognitive consideration – she is led to make three false claims concerning Adorno's theory: firstly, that the theory of nonidentitary reason, a reason which would not (violently) subsume particulars under universals, conceives of such a reason as essentially non-discursive (p. 170); secondly, that in Adorno '*poiesis* becomes not *praxis* but *poietics*' (p. 220); and thirdly, that the destruction of objective reason is irrevocable (p. 215).

Adorno does not claim that either language or conceptuality is intrinsically identitary, and that therefore a relation to the other which does not linguistically or discursively dominate must be non-discursive. On the contrary, he contends that nonidentity is 'opaque only for identity's claim to be total' (*ND*, 153); and in *The Dialectic of Enlightenment* he attempts to reveal how this claim became materially and historically dominant. It is only for us now that nonidentitary truth remains non-discursive, for example, any attempt to discursively cash out the truth claim of a work of art will be subject to the now suppressive logic of identity thinking; autonomous art's resistance to the claims of discursive reason as it now exists and its nonetheless continuing, albeit conditioned and contingent, *claim* on us is its critique of autonomous truth and purified, formal and procedural morality. Benhabib conflates the critical, non-discursive *illusion of nonidentity* (which is the truth claim of a modernist work of art) with the idea of nonidentitary reason itself.

This explains why she thinks that Adorno reduces praxis to poietics. Again, autonomous artistic practice is not itself praxis, any more than it is a realization of nonidentitary reason. Rather, such practice presents the *image* of true praxis, but as an image it is still confined to the illusory world of art; illusory because its practice is neither truly transformative nor truly, fully, cognitively meaningful. Nonetheless, insofar as art works make objective claims on us, then they must be intervening in and interrupting the smoothly functioning discourses of morality and truth. In this respect, Habermas's contention that art cannot be of moral relevance because it cannot convince us of anything on the 'basis of its *own* arguments' (*JA*, 74) simply begs the question about what arguments aesthetic-expressive discourse *could* present if not silenced, and conversely what is distorted by forms of argumentation that necessarily exclude an aesthetic-expressive dimension. Adorno presented this problem in terms of an aporia: philosophy now can only heed the demands of sensuous particularity by offering to art, as aesthetic theory, a voice whose ground would be nothing other than works themselves. Adorno, then, does not think that true praxis would be poietical practice set free into experience, whatever that might mean; true praxis would be transformative activity and cognition practised without the exclusion of aesthetic-expressive considerations. To claim, as Benhabib does, that for Adorno 'non-sacrificial non-identity is not a social ideal, but an aesthetic one' (p. 211) misses the point of the function of aesthetic theory within Adorno's critical programme.

The 'hinge of negative dialectics' (namely, to change [the] direction of conceptuality, to give it a turn toward nonidentity' – *ND*, 12) is embodied in the *social* practice of autonomous art where form, the artistic equivalent of conceptuality, 'mobilizes technology in a different direction than domination does' (*AT*, 80). If the truth claim of autonomous art is valid – and remember Adorno believes that 'Art works are true in the medium of determinate negation only' (*AT*, 187), i.e., the determinate negation of the categorial differentiation of spheres – then, finally, objective reason is possible. Such an objective reason would not have the articulation of truth, beauty and goodness grounded in either nature or some transcendent source. The ground of a new objective reason would have to be the solidarity of its communal carriers. We call such reason objective because of four considerations.

(i) It denies that reason in any of its concrete, worldly employments can be formal, deductive or inductive, or that the truth of some state of affairs can be had through the operation of an algorithm. Reason can only be objective if it is not separable from, capable of being identified independently of, its object. Hence . . .

(ii) In the same way in which we now concede that the social world is value constituted, so we will have to concede that it is aesthetically-expressively constituted as well, i.e., not only are there no concrete value-neutral facts, but equally there are no concrete aesthetic-expressive-neutral facts.

(iii) Truth is holistic, i.e., the truth of a proposition depends on the semantic content of the terms employed as they feed through the totality of the discourses and practices in which they are employed, where those discourses and practices are recognized as being historical through and through, albeit not merely historical and hence not merely conventional.

(iv) What would further make such reason objective is that it would not 'rigidly' juxtapose 'rationality and particularity' (*AT*, 144); and it would equally be ends and not means rational:

> In the eyes of existing rationality, aesthetic behaviour is irrational because it castigates the particularity of this rationality in its pursuit not of ends but of means. Art keeps alive the memory of ends-oriented reason. It keeps alive the memory of a kind of objectivity which lies beyond conceptual frameworks [construed as ways of ordering rather than revealing the world]. That is why art is rational, cognitive. Aesthetic behaviour is the ability to see more in things than they are [in accordance with conceptual frameworks].
>
> (*AT*, 453)

If we tie these points together, what they amount to is some version of the thesis that subjective reason is to be identified with that independence of reason from the shape of the world, and hence the objective reason is entailed directly by the denial of the intelligibility of any form of duality which distinguishes our conceptual scheme from the world. Reason cannot be peeled off from the world and examined and legitimated independently. But this thought, which has in recent years received renewed support, is quite distinct from traditional theological metaphysics.[4] Hence, the idea of objective reason, the idea that the real must be rational and the rational must be real, cannot be quite the pre-modern fiction that Benhabib and Habermas suppose.

THE CONCRETE OTHER AND NONIDENTITY

As noted above, Benhabib regards Habermas's failure to thematize the idea of a community of needs and solidarity as following from his adoption of Mead's conception of the standpoint of the 'generalized other', the standpoint of rights and entitlements, as representing the fulfilment of the moral point of view. Adopting the standpoint of the generalized other involves abstracting from the concrete individuality and identity of the other, which allows us thereby to treat this other, and hence all others, as equal rational beings who are entitled to the same rights and duties as we would wish to ascribe to ourselves. On this account, the moral dignity of individuals derives not from what differentiates them from all others, but from what, as speaking and acting agents, they have in common with all others. Within such a scheme our relations to others are governed, for the most part, by public and institutional rules obeying the norms of formal reciprocity.

In opposition or contrast with this Benhabib proposes the standpoint of the 'concrete other'. This standpoint requires us

> to view each and every rational being as an individual with a concrete history, identity, and affective-emotional constitution. Our relation to the other is governed by the norm of *complementary reciprocity*: each is entitled to expect and to assume from the other forms of behavior through which the other feels recognized and confirmed as a concrete, individual being with specific needs, talents, and capacities. The norms of our interaction are . . . the norms of solidarity, friendship, love and care.
>
> (p. 341)

This standpoint, Benhabib states, has been silenced, even suppressed by the liberal political tradition.

Clearly Benhabib believes that the standpoint of the concrete other corresponds to the general requirement for the universalizability of need interpretations; or better, that we cannot think such a universalizability unless we are willing publicly, as it were, to include the standpoint of the concrete other. Further, however, we have already seen that Benhabib regards the standpoint of universalizable need interpretations as what separates critical theory from other universalistic moralities, i.e., from liberal moral and political theories. From this it would follow that whatever grounds this standpoint grounds critical theory. However, Benhabib *introduces* this standpoint via Habermas's adding of it to the Kohlbergian scheme after having demonstrated that this scheme, as it figures in Habermas's theory, is not, and cannot be, rationally compulsive. At best, the denial of the penultimate stage of the scheme involves a pragmatic contradiction. And this should not be regarded as overly significant since a pragmatic contradiction will ensue from the denial of any 'foundational' belief within a cultural tradition; for example, if all meaning

151

comes from God, then the denial of God's existence pragmatically contradicts itself.

Even granting the pragmatic contradiction, however, does not stretch very far for Benhabib's purposes since within our tradition no pragmatic contradiction is involved in our denying the universalizability of need interpretations. On the contrary, morality subtends need interpretations by requiring that privatized need interpretations be compatible with others satisfying their privatized need interpretations. Hence what presumptively grounds the moral – the performative contradiction invoked by its transgression – *entails* that need interpretations are not universalizable in the same sense. What makes morality for Habermas necessary is thus what makes the programme for universalizable need interpretation contradictory, requiring that some desires and needs be obligatory in just the manner that the moral was thought obligatory. Nor is this surprising since the idea of universalizable need interpretations entails that morality involves more than a critical and negative constraint on what can be rationally willed. But one cannot supplement a procedure whose force with respect to need interpretations is negative and critical with one that is positive and obligating.

This apparently leaves critical theory without a rational, normative foundation; and hence puts Benhabib in a position not significantly different from the position in which Adorno and Horkheimer found themselves. If the formal, universalistic reason of our tradition *excludes* universalizable need interpretations, and the motivation for securing reason relies on the promise of happiness, then we cannot regard the ideal of the formation of communities of need and solidarity as a rational *supplement* to the model of a community of rights and entitlements. That is, if the standpoint of the generalized other stands to the standpoint of the concrete other as third person, observer accounts of our moral-political situation stand to a participatory perspective, and the former perspective has been established and consolidated through its exclusion of the latter, then 'our' position is like those members of a tradition who feel that its reconciled intersubjectivity has been established at their expense. This is not to deny the standpoint of universalistic morality, or the ideal of a community of rights and entitlements; it is only to claim that 'we' can only pursue this ideal on the basis of an alternative perspective. Again, the 'rights', including rights to privacy, security, and the like, of a solidaristic community would not be negative; they would be elements of the communal interpretation of the good life and hence necessary features of the good life of an individual in such a community.[5]

We therefore cannot assume that this alternative perspective can be simply adopted, that there is waiting a standpoint – that of the concrete other alone or somehow synthesized with the generalized other – available such that if we adopted it, then a politics of transfiguration could be pursued without further ado. At one point, Benhabib quotes the following statement from *Negative Dialectics*: 'The concept of the person and its variations, like the I–Thou relationship, have assumed the oily tone of a theology in which one has lost faith' (*ND*, 277). Now Benhabib goes on to claim that in order to reject this claim we must demonstrate that intersubjectivity points to a genuine lacuna in negative dialectical thought. But we can now see that whatever that presumed lacuna is, it is not one that can be filled by the Habermasian account of communication; and further, that the standpoint of the concrete other, at least as Benhabib presents it, surely does have the sound of 'the oily tone of a theology in which one has lost faith'. Benhabib cannot both equate communicative rationality with bourgeois formality, bemoaning it for its formality, claim there has been an exclusion or suppression of the position of the concrete others and universalizable need interpretations (aesthetic-expressive discourse), *and* assert that what has been excluded and dominated is there, well-formed and ready to supplement the perspective of the generalized other. This is simply to ignore all the *categorial* issues, the problems of sphere differentiation, that her analysis implies.

Adorno was not unaware that communication could not be theorized in terms of the labour model of activity; but for this very reason he regarded the 'idea' of communication as harbouring an inexpungible transcendence (a utopian moment) which marked the limit of theoretical reflection.

> If speculation on the state of reconciliation were permitted, neither the undistinguished unity of subject and object, nor their antithetical hostility would be conceivable in it; rather, communication of what was distinguished. Not until then would the concept of communication, as an objective concept, come into its own. The present one is so infamous because the best there is, the potential of an agreement between people and things, is betrayed to an interchange between subjects according to the requirements of subjective reason.[6]

Adorno's complaint here is that the present conception of communication, of which Habermas's is an example, reduces it because in it the goal of agreement between subjects trumps response to *die Sache selbst*, the real thing.[7] In broad terms, communicative reason's trumping is equivalent to displacing truth by communication, which anyway has been a problem for Habermas's theory almost from the outset.[8] Because Adorno does not think that 'objects' are situated other than within the logical space of reasons, then for him because the distinction between subject–subject relations and subject–object relations (which includes objects in everything other than their natural scientific presentation) is not fully discriminable, then an emphatic notion of truth and an objective but non-formal conception of communication would be equivalent. However idiosyncratic this may be, the point here is that the concrete other as Benhabib conceives it is logically more akin to emphatic 'truth' than another layer of communicative rationality itself.

Objective communication signifies reconciliation, about which theory can only respond in the language of *Sollen* (ought); hence Adorno's withdrawal of the image of communication in its positing. Without decrying the virtues of love or sharing, we need to assert that these are not 'universal' virtues that have remained untouched by the formations and deformations of capital expansion and suchlike; and hence, that the 'hard' (difficult/critical/aporetic) political love *required* by the standpoint of the concrete other as transfigured, its notion of communication, is quite unlike the privatized/domesticated/ fetishized love of our present.

As for universalistic need interpretations, as we have seen, they have been systematically relegated to the autonomous domain of art. Adorno never meant to say that nonidentitary reason was restricted to art in modernity; but he did want to assert that only there was it preserved, for the time being, in an intrinsical way; and further, therefore, only there could we begin to appreciate what taking the standpoint of the concrete other *required*, as taking the standpoint of an aesthetic observer makes stern requirements, and as works of art themselves make demands and claims on us.[9] Said otherwise: Benhabib fails to consider what is implied by considering solidarity, friendship, love and care *norms* since the deontological conception of normativity presupposes that it is actions, not feelings and emotions which can be subject to principled ordering and constraint. While the mechanisms through which we consider the appropriateness of maxims for actions legitimate or not, morally worthy or not, will engender transformations of emotions, that concession is not sufficient to answer the complaint of which the concept of the concrete other is an expression.[10]

If the concrete other really does point to a lacuna in Habermasian ethics as Benhabib insists, then the norms applicable to it are not deontological norms. If not, then *universalizable* need interpretations are not anything like universalizable maxims for action. That analogy consistently misleads Benhabib. The meaning of universality in the context of need interpretations will have to shift away from the paradigm of communication altogether since it will have an epistemic component equivalent to whatever is involved in *recognizing* others in their concrete particularity, which, again, is what Adorno employs art in order to interrogate; and hence an alternative conception of what universality means for ethical theory if need interpretation is nonetheless going to be an element of a universalistic moral theory.

The whole point, then, about the standpoint of the concrete other, about, that is, nonidentitary reason, is that within our tradition it is 'beyond' reason, beyond the claim of reason and beyond what reason requires. Only critique can reveal that this is not a criticism of the standpoint of the concrete other, but a categorial fault in the constitution of reason itself in modernity.

RISK: PRAXIS WITHOUT FOUNDATIONS

Earlier I noted Benhabib's criticisms of Habermas for committing what she termed the 'rationalistic fallacy', the view of reason as a self-generating faculty. Now I want to suggest here that Benhabib commits just this fallacy twice over. First, nowhere does she overtly concede what she needs to concede if the standpoint of the concrete other is to be adopted, namely, that the grounds for autonomous action are themselves heteronomous. This, I take it, is *the* point of Hegel's *Phenomenology*. The whole course of that work is a search for recognition and self-possession (autonomy), which continues to fail either through taking the wrong sort of object, or through committing some form of the rationalistic fallacy. While recognizing its inadequacy, Hegel uses the theological term 'forgiveness' in establishing the moment of reconciliation between self and other, the recognition of self in otherness, precisely in order to reveal that such a recognition does not conform to the dictates of categorial reason (God's forgiveness of evil is excessive); and further, that categorial reason can gather itself only if it first dispossesses itself of what we call its autonomy. 'Our aim', Adorno says, 'is total self-relinquishment' (*ND*, 13).

This is a somewhat oblique way of pointing to the fact that in adopting the standpoint of the concrete other we must, perforce, acknowledge our dependence on the other; but this ethico-ontological dependence is not something that can be established from 'within', by what we call autonomous reason, by adopting the standpoint of the spectator, observer, or theorist. It is no accident, I think, that Benhabib so misreads Hegel and Adorno, for she reads them as theorists, while their programmes of 'phenomenology' and 'critique' are avoidances of theory.

Secondly, although Benhabib notes, and indeed urges the thought, that the neglect of a radical, participatory, and pluralist conception of politics has been a central blind spot in the development and history of critical theory, she conceives of this neglect as a 'theoretical' fault. But surely this 'fault' is itself an exemplar of the rationalistic fallacy? Since Plato, western metaphysics has attempted to ground politics, a just political order, on a secure theoretical, normative foundation. A good political order was to be the instantiation, the application of the 'Rational Idea' of such an order as it was theoretically established; in short, the tradition subordinated politics to theory. Does not the theoretical inadequacy of the standpoint of the concrete other follow from the attempt to ground it theoretically, while its very character seems to entail that it is *it* that founds theory and makes it possible? And isn't this what Adornesque critical theory was pointing to in its refusal of theory? And isn't this what makes critique as practised by Adorno a form of political discourse in circumstances where the so-called political realm had disposed of the truly political?

At one point Benhabib criticizes Habermas's theoretical construction of the 'we' of the present postconventional, universalistic moral standpoint in these terms: Habermas's 'shift to the language of an anonymous species-subject preempts the experience of moral and political activity as a consequence of which alone a genuine "we" can emerge. A collectivity is not constituted theoretically but is formed out of the moral and political struggles of fighting

155

actors' (p. 331). But if collectivities are themselves the source of the discourses through which their experience can be rendered theoretically intelligible, then one can only found critical theory by struggling for the community of needs and solidarity it critically images. Such a project, however, is both paradoxical and risky: paradoxical because the ground of such a 'self-transforming', 'self-grounding' project is beyond the self in the nonidentical other; and risky, therefore, because pursuing such a project requires surrendering the self which has made the undertaking of the project 'necessary' – Adorno's project of self-dispossession again. Self-dispossession, however, is only pretended if it amounts to no more than obeying impersonal rules of argumentation, a principle of universality. Alternatively, we cannot simply or immediately abandon ourselves to the other. To release what is suppressed in the other is only possible by a stringent process of self-overcoming. But if this stringency is not to descend into another methodology, another practice of the self, then it cannot avoid a moment of excess, of radical indeterminacy. With good reason, Hegel made 'risk' the master trope of the entire phenomenological programme.

Finally, however, this risky and paradoxical project cannot be pursued blindly; theory must be 'risked', both attempted and subordinated to the political. Or better: dialectic is the acknowledgement of philosophy's non-identity with itself which is acknowledged and then suppressed by conceiving of that relation in terms of fallibilism. Philosophy, theory, can remain self-same and universalistic in Habermas's sense only through the repression of the nonidentical other. Dialectical phenomenology or negative dialectics is the presentation of the misrepresentations of subject and substance, of subject as substance. In Adorno's words, dialectics is 'the ontology of the wrong state of things' (*ND*, 11). It is 'the self-consciousness of the objective context of delusion [which] does not mean to have escaped from that context' (*ND*, 406).

RECONCILIATION

Benhabib closes her book with a beautiful vision of communities of need and solidarity united into 'polities' governed by the ideal of a community of rights and entitlements (p. 351). There are two quite natural ways of reading this vision: firstly, as an imaginative account of what we desire; and secondly, as an account of how things 'ought' to be. Neither of these readings is plausible. The first contravenes the critique of privatized desire, while the second would be a morally legislated blueprint detached from the subjectivities of those whose actions it was to guide and govern. How else are we to read this vision than as an identity, a reconciliation, of identity (rights) and nonidentity (solidarity)?

For Benhabib the ideal of a community of rights and entitlements is both what is and what ought to be. As what is, it is deformed by its exclusion of particularity, need, happiness, solidarity. Its concept images the equality and liberty of all, which in practice, because of what it excludes, becomes a form of domination. Communities of need and solidarity equally both are and are not;

they are but only as deformed by their grounding in the contingent overlap of privatized desires. Each form of sociation, dialectically comprehended, comprehended in its historical determination and in its concept, presses towards the other, its other as that which it historically requires and refuses.

Something more needs saying here, for, thus far, the idea of the perspective of the concrete other as it operates in Benhabib's work sounds as if it were a pure theoretical construct. Such is not the case. In footnoting her claim that the standpoint of the concrete other 'has been silenced . . . even suppressed' by the tradition of universalistic moral and political theory, she says that this suppression is, without doubt, 'also a consequence of the epistemic and social exclusion of women's voice and activity from the public sphere and their denigration' (p. 409). The claim of the perspective of the concrete other as a theoretical figure is parasitic upon the claim of woman, women (and doubtless other peoples whose exclusion is equally a condition of the reconciled subjectivity of the liberal state). It is, however, because Benhabib has been unwilling to problematize this claim, to note the contradictions *in* that silence and *in* that suppression, that she can so easily dismiss the claims of the aesthetic with the calm brush-off that the perspective of the concrete other cannot be accommodated by aesthetic-expressive discourse because 'relations of solidarity, friendship, and love are not aesthetic but profoundly moral ones' (p. 342) – as if for us what is moral or love or friendship has not become deeply problematic, aporetic; as if we knew what we do not: that the moral is different from the aesthetic, and the aesthetic indifferent to questions of morality or love. Benhabib's appropriation of the silence and silencing of women is too direct, it is made without anxiety, without the anxiety which would mark that appropriation as a repetition whose excess 'beyond', whose nonidentity with that silence alone gives it voice: makes it the claim of the nonidentical other.

The relation between concrete other and generalized other, fulfilment and transfiguration, ought and is, in Benhabib repeats Adorno's speculative identification of autonomous art and philosophy. Must we not say here that the figures of art and woman are equivalents, that they translate one another with respect to their third: the dominion of subjective reason? As figures of nonidentity autonomous art and feminism critically install the remembrance and anticipation of an other reason, of reason as for the other, of reason transfigured. The historical experience informing Benhabib's dialectic simply blinds her to the historical experience informing Adorno's dialectic. Both dialectics, however, are dialectical only through their speculative constructions of an identity of identity and nonidentity, through their recognition of the possibility of overcoming the duality of particularity (solidarity) and universality (justice) without positing that overcoming.

Benhabib's dialectic, often despite itself, articulates the speculative sentence that 'the standpoint of the generalized other and the perspective of the concrete other are one', just as much as Adorno's writing is governed by the unacknowledged speculative sentence that 'philosophy and art are one'.[11]

These statements of identity are equally statements of nonidentity. Since the speculative thinking of the state of reconciliation, absolute *Sittlichkeit*, which both sentences evoke – the first ethico-politically, the second cognitive-rationality – is neither a statement of fact nor a deontological prescription of what ought to be (conceptually coming to perceive a diremption is not equivalent to the legislation of a principle of action), then we must acknowledge that speculative thinking is, as such, a form of political insight, political wisdom, *phronesis*, theory mediated self-reflection. In acknowledging this we are not following an inference or obeying an obligation (from a principle); rather, such an acknowledgement would be aporetic, difficult, an anxious act of political love.

6

THE CAUSALITY OF FATE
On modernity and modernism

A SUPPRESSED DIALECTIC

In *The Philosophical Discourse of Modernity*[1] Habermas argues that the rationalization processes of modernity are essentially ambiguous: rationalization involves
both a real increment in rationality and a distortion of reason. The real
increment in rationality can only be comprehended from the perspective of
communicative rationality; while the distortions of rationality are best comprehended as illegitimate extensions of subject-centred reason into an intersubjectively constituted lifeworld. In engaging with the distortions of reason
and rationality the philosophical discourses of modernity that are the target of
Habermas's critical history – the writings of Heidegger, Bataille, Derrida,
Foucault, Adorno and Horkheimer – commit a metonymic fallacy, taking
subject-centred reason as the whole of reason. Such totalizing critiques of
enlightened reason involve an inevitable recoil, leaving them without any
possible rational foundation or ground, any place from which their critique can
be lodged. As a consequence, these writers are forced to generate an 'extraordinary discourse' that 'claims to operate *outside* the horizon of reason without
being utterly irrational' (p. 308).

Because the writing of these philosophers is distinctive, 'extraordinary', and
because the claims of this writing are to be sustained by specific practices of
writing, the object of Habermas's critique can be denominated as 'philosophical modernism', its practitioners 'philosophical modernists'. This is a
presumptive, and partial, classification; its raison d'être is to provoke a consideration of the connection between artistic modernism and a self-conscious
philosophical discourse that has become extraordinary.

Philosophical modernism cannot be said to be unaware of the communicative rationality that Habermas contends provides the sole basis for enlightening
reason about itself. On the contrary, Habermas's strategy in *The Philosophical
Discourse of Modernity* turns on revealing communicative rationality as the road
not taken by Hegel (pp. 27–30, 37–40), Marx (pp. 62–5), Heidegger (pp.
136–7), and Derrida in his discussion of Husserl (pp. 168–72). And because
the road of communicative reason was not taken, because the difference

159

between the dominating reason of the philosophy of consciousness and the reason of communicative actions oriented toward establishing intersubjective agreement was not heeded, then either subject-centred reason comes to aporetically invade, recoil upon, the very discourses lodging a critique of it (pp. 151, 274), or the force of critique is voided (pp. 183–4, 237). Manifestly, this same point cuts the other way; if Hegel, Heidegger, Derrida and Adorno had the option of communicative rationality and refused it, then perhaps what Habermas claims for it is not truly available, or available in the way he thinks it to be.[2] And this supposition would gain force if it were discovered that the duality between subject-centred reason and communicative reason was neither unambiguous, nor absolute or exhaustive. What if communicative rationality, *as* Habermas conceives of it, is itself a product of subject-centred reason, is itself a distortion of reason? What if the social logics of subject-centred reason (systems integration) and communicative reason (social integration) are never pure; the espousal of their purity a mask for their (constitutive) interdependence? What if there is more to reason and rationality, a form of reason and rationality, that is neither subject-centred nor communicative as Habermas understands these terms?[3]

Habermas contends that 'we need a *theoretically constituted perspective* to be able to treat communicative action as the medium through which the lifeworld is reproduced' (p. 299). The theoretically constituted perspective is that of the ideal speech situation (p. 323), which corresponds to, is a theoretical articulation of, 'the capacity of responsible participants in interaction to orient themselves in relation to validity claims geared to intersubjective recognition' (p. 314). This theoretical articulation is not the consequence of transcendental reflection seeking intuitive insight into self-consciousness – the form of analysis consonant with subject-centred reason – but rather a product of the reconstructive sciences that bring to light the implicit rule-knowledge actually exercised in the generation of utterances (pp. 297–8). It is nonetheless the case that the perspective attained allows, for validity claims, a moment of absolute transcendence that ' "blots out" space and time' (p. 323). In *PDM*, more than previously, Habermas gestures at the social and historical embedding, the contextual constraints, that form the other side of validity claims. Despite these gestures, it remains the case that the theoretical perspective articulated through the deployment of the reconstructive sciences is of an ideal speech situation; and it is through the consideration of claims in terms of the ideal speech situation that their putative validity is one that transcends spaces and times. It is this universality, ideality and transcendence which have consistently been the target of Habermas's critics.[4]

Philosophical modernism's totalizing critique eschews procedural rationality and universality, conceiving them as figures of domination; its extraordinary discourses presumptively[5] leaving behind the claim of enlightened rationality for the sake of an apparently blind, normless particularism. Habermas, in contrast, wants to salvage the claims of enlightenment through the reconstructive sciences, operating as analogues of transcendental reflection and legislation. A choice between these extremes – philosophical modernism's immanence and particularism, and Habermas's transcendence and universalism – is less than inviting. Can we not recognize in these extremes of universal and particular a fateful dialectic at work? A sundering of the very comprehensive reason for which Habermas takes himself to be spokesman? Can we not recognize in philosophical modernism's particularity a substantiality that has forgotten that it is also subject? Can we not recognize in Habermas's ideal speech situation a subjectivity that has forgotten its substantiality? Are not these two extremes but two halves of an integral freedom to which, however, they do not add up? Can we not recognize ourselves in the dialectical belonging and separation of these conflicting positions?

In what follows I want to pursue this suggestion through an examination of the truth claims of philosophical modernism and Habermasian modernity independently of their reflective comprehension of their respective projects. In concrete terms, this means following through the suggestion that the philosophical discourses of modernity are modernist, their claims discursive analogues of one aspect of artistic modernism's claim of being the 'other' of reason (p. 96). The appropriateness of such a focus derives directly from the oft-noted disanalogy between the cognitive status of aesthetic judgments, and the validity claims of truth and rightness within Habermas's tripartite scheme;[6] and, the fact that this tripartite scheme only comes into view through the abandonment of the perspective (level) of judgment (p. 312). The claims of art and aesthetic judgment signify within the tripartite scheme the claims of what is abandoned when the level of judgment, the ontic fundament, the life-world is abandoned. These claims return in philosophical modernism. The latter, then, come to stand to Habermas's account of truth and normative rightness as Kant's third *Critique*, which was to bridge the gulf between knowledge and moral worth, stands to his first and second *Critiques*.[7] What is abandoned and excluded from, marginalized within, philosophical modernism is the claim of comprehensive reason. This claim comes into view, it claims us, through the operation of the causality of fate.

FROM FALLIBILISM TO MODERNISM

In a long and nervous footnote (pp. 408–9) to his excursus 'On levelling the genre distinction between philosophy and literature', Habermas addresses the question of philosophical modernism from a diagnostic angle; not, that is, in terms of its aporetic comprehension of reason and modernity, but rather in terms of its rhetoric and writing. The footnote appears as an 'after-worry', a worry that in his systematic critique he had not quite come to terms with the motives underlying the extraordinary discourse of philosophical modernism.

Habermas chides the philosophical modernists for their naivety in thinking that a special sort of writing is necessary to avoid metaphysics – the systematic gathering of foundations, presence, self-presence and certainty. Systematic philosophy, with its claims for closure, completeness, determinacy and uniqueness, which together would make the world fully present to self, and the self fully present to itself, is, Habermas contends, a straw man. Philosophy has long since followed the path of the sciences and given up the ideal of systematic closure, thereby acknowledging the fallibilistic character of its pursuits. Nowadays 'we reckon upon the trivial *possibility* that they [our truth claims] will be revised tomorrow or someplace else'. It is because they have failed to see that this is the case, because 'they still defend themselves as if they were living in the shadow of the "last" philosopher', that the philosophical modernists get caught in the paradox of self-referentiality – since the tools they employ in order to lodge their critique is the same as its object, the dissolution of the object devours critique at the same time; this is the aporia of totalizing critique.

Now it would be odd if the philosophical modernists had been twisting and contorting their discourse because they had failed to notice that philosophy had become fallibilistic. Odder still to adopt complex strategies of writing to avoid the claims of closure, completeness and certainty if these claims are, as the modernists contend them to be, non-satisfiable. Why struggle to avoid what you acknowledge as impossible to achieve either in fact or in principle? Habermas's contention that Heidegger, Adorno and Derrida (three writers who offer to art and aesthetic discourse a form of prioritizing and attempt, in some sense, to render philosophical discourse 'aesthetic') confuse the universalist problematics that remain in a fallibilist context with long-since 'abandoned status claims' rings hollow against the background of *acknowledged* aporia and a concern for alterity that marks all three writers' discourses. Does fallibilism really capture what philosophical modernism resists of modernity? Or does fallibilistic self-consciousness repress the problematics of aporia and alterity motivating philosophical modernism?

No help in answering this will come from the excursus to which the footnote in question is appended. There Habermas defends a thesis, namely, that from the perspective of ordinary usage the genre distinction between philosophy and literature cannot be levelled, a thesis that, so far as I am aware, Derrida never denies.[8] What Derrida suggests is rather that dominant philosophical understandings of the distinction misconstrue it, fixing it and purifying it in ways that belie the connectedness and interdependency of the items distinguished.[9] And what better way of demonstrating this could there be than revealing the feint, trope, excess underpinning presumptive demonstrations of purity? That this might matter, in general, is something that Derrida cannot demonstrate, nor would he want to; mattering being strictly parasitic upon the mattering, the claims, of the text being deconstructed.

However, some headway can be made here if we examine briefly some of Habermas's comments on Foucault. Habermas avers that if one attempts to elicit the norms tacitly appealed to in Foucault's indictment of disciplinary power 'one encounters familiar determinations from the normativistic language games that he has explicitly rejected' (p. 284). So we rediscover in Foucault the 'asymmetric relationship between powerholders and those subject to power, as well as the reifying effect of technologies of power, which violate the moral and bodily integrity of subjects capable of speech and action' (p. 284). If we but rediscover in Foucault a reaffirmation of what we already believe, why does he bother to reject the language game of norms? And how are we to understand the appeal, the demand of his writing?

Habermas elegantly, and better than self-proclaimed Foucauldians, answers these questions for us, without, however, quite seeing the consequences of his own points. In Foucault, he claims, 'power'

> preserves a literally aesthetic relation to the perception of the body, to the painful experience of the mistreated body. . . . The asymmetry (replete with normative content) that Foucault sees embedded in power complexes does not hold primarily between powerful wills and coerced subjugation, but between processes of power and the bodies that are crushed within them. It is always the body that is maltreated in torture and made into a showpiece of sovereign revenge; that is taken hold of in drill, resolved into a field of mechanical forces and manipulated; that is objectified and monitored by the human sciences, even as it is stimulated in its desire and stripped naked. If Foucault's concept of power preserves for itself some remnant of aesthetic content, then it owes this to his vitalistic, *Lebensphilosophie* way of reading the body's experience of itself.
> (p. 285)

After quoting the closing peroration of *The History of Sexuality* in which the dream of another economy of the body and its pleasures is offered, Habermas comments that this

> *other* economy of the body and of pleasures, about which in the meantime – with Bataille – we can only dream, would not be another economy of power, but a postmodern theory that would also give an account of the standards of critique already laid claim to implicitly. Until then, resistance can draw its motivation, if not its justification, only from the signals of body language, from that nonverbalizable language of the body on which pain has been inflicted, which refuses to be sublated into discourse.
> (pp. 285–6)

One might well ask after the evidence for the thesis that in the realization of the dreamed-of new *economy* of the body and its pleasure Foucault believes that employed but unstated norms of critique will suddenly become available. Put this query aside. What needs illuminating first is the force and significance of the thesis that the relation between power and the experience of the body in Foucault is 'literally aesthetic'. How does this thesis connect with Foucault's overt rejection of the language game of norms in a context where his writing continues to affirm the 'content' of those norms? And are these connections really best understood in terms of a *Lebensphilosophie* way of reading the body's experience?

If we are to follow through on the aesthetic connection between power and the perception of the body, then we need first to remind ourselves of an inner connection between reflective judgment in general, aesthetic reflective judgment and modernist art. In the first *Critique* Kant opens the space in which the problem of judgment arises when he notes that the understanding, as the faculty of rules, cannot be self-sufficient since it is impossible to give general instructions of how we are to subsume particular cases under those rules: 'to distinguish whether something does or does not come under them, that could only be by means of another rule. This, in turn, for the very reason that it is a rule, again demands guidance from judgment' (B171). Judgment cannot itself be a rule-governed activity since the 'fit' between concept (a rule) and an intuition cannot, without generating an infinite regress, make reference to another rule. It is this space, the mediation of concept and intuition, that Kant interrogates in the third *Critique*.

There he distinguishes between determinant judgment and reflective judgment. While determinant or subsumptive judgment is the bringing of intuitions or particulars under concepts, reflective judgment is the cognitive appraising and discerning of particulars in anticipation of any concepts under which they might be subsumed. Making determinate judgments is equivalent to the raising of a validity claim. What Kant came to recognize in the third *Critique*, however belatedly and obliquely, is that even determinant judging must give way to reflective judging, since in order to apply a concept one must first be oriented toward the features of the particular case. So subsumptive *judgments* presuppose reflective *judging*, while reflective judgments are themselves those that deploy the activity of reflective judging without taking the step of subsuming the reflectively articulated particular under any particular concept. Aesthetic reflective judgments, where the suitability of an object for subsumption is interrogated, are thus best regarded as species of reflective judgment in general. Hence what aesthetic reflective judgments do is to thematize the pre-reflexive attunement between mind and world that makes subsumptive cognitions possible. If there is such an attunement, it follows that intuitions are not 'blind', sheer raw matter which conceptuality can carve up in any way it pleases. Reflective judging reveals the worldly constraints on knowing that make subsumption more than a sheer subjective projection of a concept of an object onto a wholly featureless material flow.

Aesthetic reflective judgments begin with a consideration of the presentation of a particular; the consideration is 'autonomous' and disinterested in that it is made apart from epistemic, practical (moral) and sensible interests one may have in the object or state of affairs presented. Disinterested reflection renders the presentation autonomous from the network of cognitive, practical and sensible ends or purposes in which it is otherwise implicated. Judgments issuing from disinterested reflection are themselves 'autonomous' because although the presentation judged is reflectively articulated, the judgment itself is not the subsumption of the object under any normative or epistemic concept.

Analogously, we describe a work of art as 'autonomous' just in case its forms, and hence the integrity of the work itself, are not derived from concepts and forms – religious, cultic, moral, political, etc. – external to the work itself. A work's intelligibility is a product of its internal working, without this working being beholden to purposes or ends external to the work. The self-conscious pursuance of autonomy, the awareness that the aesthetic sense-making cannot rely on anything external to the work itself, informs the practice of artistic modernism. It is this awareness that underlies the more typical reflective characterization of modernism as the interrogation of art concerning its own nature.

What Habermas fails to notice, or take sufficient account of, in Foucault is the close inner connection between the body and writing, between the non-verbalizable language of the body inflicted with pain, which refuses to be sublated in discourse, and a writing of that body, a discourse that refuses the language game of norms. However skewed Foucault's own comprehension of his amnesiac objectivity, his happy positivism, against the background of the project of artistic modernism, of his deployment of power, power complexes, the play of differential forces and the like, becomes intelligible as the genera-tion of counter-concepts, non-logical (albeit economic) forms whose acon-ceptuality allows for the possibility of a sense-making resistant to given regimes of sense-making, for a kind of purposefulness (of writing) without (external) purpose, and hence for a kind of non-teleological history. Power, as an aconceptual concept which operates like the moment of dissonance in modernist works of art, permits a writing that still harbours 'an archaic unity of logic and causality' (AT, 199). In brief, the claim of Foucault's discourse must be comprehended as a philosophical internalization of whatever we take the claim of artistic modernism to be.

Before taking up the claim invoked by this idea of sense-making, to be elaborated in the next section, three comments are in order. It is no accident that Foucault should take the body as a recurring focus of his investigations. The role of the body in Foucault, as in Nietzsche, must be understood both substantively and strategically. The body signifies, as writing does in Derrida, the suppressed other of reason, language, logos, universality. As such, it further signifies the claim of particularity against universality; a particularity that would hence be further violated if its history and suffering were inscribed in a history generated in the very terms responsible for its suppression. The body can be given voice, its suffering made visible, only if its articulated par-ticularity and integrity are, in some sense, respected.

This helps explain two distinct if interconnected features of Foucault's writing: its strong reliance on images and set pieces (the grand confinement, the panopticon, the scene of torture, the confession, the surgical body, etc.), and a writing that continually disclaims itself, refusing the discursive consequences (the implied norms, for example) of its analyses. Foucault is implying that if one cannot judge that *here* is subjugation and domination, that *this* is a violation of the integrity of the body, the person, then there can be no claim worth heeding; or better, any further heeding must acknowledge *this* if that heeding is not going to be a brute refusal of the claims of individuals and their bodies. This is not a defence of intuitionism or decisionism; on the contrary, those gestures of the tradition are themselves products of looking elsewhere for justification for judgment, of not recognizing the other in their concrete particularity, as if it were the concept (law, rule, universal) that made the violation a violation rather than being an expression of it. In order to flatly accuse Foucault of falling back into intuitionism one would equally have to charge all judgments of beauty with falling into mere taste. But if Kant is right in thinking that aesthetic reflective judgments can be objective, speak with a universal voice, without being subsumptive, then it becomes plausible to consider Foucault's project as the attempt to free reflective judgment from its confines in aesthetics by showing it as a general ethical and cognitive strategy. Whether or not Foucault understood himself in this way is irrelevant. His books are meant to be *judged* as one would judge a work of art rather than raising a validity claim which could be vindicated by the force of better argument and outside the context of its inscription. Foucault's set pieces are no more detachable from the history they expose than that history is intelligible apart from the scenarios in which the relation between a regime and an object becomes perspicuous.

All this is to say that Foucault's work is not cryptonormative (pp. 282–4), but just normative otherwise, 'internally' normative perhaps. The charge of cryptonormativism presupposes that normativity is the deriving of judgments from universal premises or procedures, and hence that the force of normative judgments is derived from the general (the Categorical Imperative, or the Utilitarian Calculus, or the Ideal Speech Situation); but of course it is this subsumption model of the force of norms that Foucault's 'aesthetic' discourse is challenging. Hence a concept of power that definitionally built the judgment of domination into it would defeat the point of employing it as a non-concept. One aspect of domination is revealed by the aesthetic presentation of vulnerable, injurable bodies whose integrity is violated by this or that complex of power. The validity of rules and norms that are to protect those injurable particulars must make essential reference to them if they are not to betray the claim of injurability. Injurability in the relevant sense is what is reflectively presented and judged. For the same reason that we cannot discursively vindicate why the deep luminosity of the blue of the sky in 'this' painting is essential to the beauty of the whole, although we can art-critically point to it, so the injurability of the body (which negatively reveals the body's 'integrity') cannot be wholly vindicated as morally relevant in discursive-subsumptive terms.

Finally it follows from all this that the aesthetic content of Foucault's relating of the body and power does not derive from any *Lebensphilosophie* way of reading the body's experience of itself. Aesthetic content is the content of artistic modernism with respect to both autonomous judgment and autonomous work. Each of Habermas's three charges against Foucault – presentism, relativism, and cryptonormativism – whatever their validity from the perspective of discursive reason and the universalist problematics still maintained by philosophy, dissimulate and disengage the actual validity claims of Foucault's discourse. Foucault's presentistic procedure is the attempt to render his discourse, in the relevant sense, 'autonomous', to sustain the preponderance of intuition (which is not blind) against concept, and hence make his writing a work to be judged rather than a discourse to be logically assessed. It is the discursive, philosophical analogue of 'aesthetic' autonomy and not value-freedom or empiricist purity that is at issue here. Hence, Foucault's work cannot claim the status it seeks for itself without undermining that status; like the modernist work of art it can say what it wants to say only by not saying it (*AT*, 107).

If the discursive but non-demonstrable judgment of the body inflicted with pain provides motivation for resisting domination, this can be no idle point for Habermas, since a perpetual difficulty for his theory has been the absence of a motivational base for taking up the claims of communicative reason. And what better evidence could we want for the existence of an aporia concerning the relation of particular and universal than the division between a discourse perpetually refusing itself, and a reflective theory without a motivational base?

MODERNISM AND LOCAL REASON

It is usually argued that a break in Foucault's trajectory occurs after *The Order of Things*, that he moves from a conception of language informed by a modernist thematics of writing which operates a refusal of representation and an acknowledgement of the non-discursive sources of meaning, to a theory of power. Prior to his writing on power Foucault had let the significance of his work be governed by the modernist idea of writing, such that it, and not philosophy, was the repository for our understanding of modernity. Hence art and literature generally, and modernist writing in particular, were conceived as meta-epistemic, 'allegories of the deep arrangements which make knowledge possible'.[10] The continuity in Foucault becomes visible if we read the significance of modernist art, against Foucault, in the manner of Adorno; treat power in the double register of a force of social structuration and an aconceptual form for writing; and notice the coincidence of Foucault's turning away from literature with the drying up of the critical force of artistic modernism in the 1960s. Philosophy, then, could no longer be parasitic on modernist art, be the self-effacing saying of art's saying by not saying, as Adorno had attempted it; but had, as it were, to make those claims, those sayings through not saying, its own, make them come from it. Philosophical modernism, the extraordinary writing of Foucault (and Derrida) had to attempt to secure for itself the kind of autonomy that had previously been the prerogative of modernist art. For categorial reasons this project is even more fraught, more difficult, more aporetic than the project of critical artistic modernism.

Before limning these categorial restrictions, we need first to ask after the substance of the project. Earlier I suggested the thesis that the writing of modernist philosophy was geared toward producing a form of sense-making that remained at a distance from the Enlightenment conception of discursive reason, reason as subsumption, entailment, inference, system, and so on; that is, reasoning as governed by forms whose force is indifferent to content. In fact, most concepts we employ are non-topic-neutral (unlike the logical constants and such terms as 'several', 'most', 'although', etc.), and therefore are not and can not be governed by pure (logical) forms. Most concepts 'have their own informal logical powers which can only be understood from coming to know their own distinctive uses and employments'.[11] While topic-neutral constraints might be conceived of as providing the outer boundaries of rationality, actual inferences, and hence patterns of inference, are dependent on the practices in which concepts are employed. To use a well-known example, it is not the law of non-contradiction that makes the statement 'All bachelors are married' self-contradictory and so false, but our practices. If our practices change, then so can the meaning of the words in the statement. So, nowadays there are many unmarried men who are not bachelors, and equally many married men who are. Hence if I said, 'Although he is married, he is still a bachelor', for the present one might say I was speaking metaphorically, my comment ironic or a joke of sorts; but further changes in patterns of marriage could make the metaphorical use of 'bachelor' into a simple ambiguity between its legal and lifestyle sense. In which case, my original textbook logical contradiction could become an emprical truth.

Now the kind of connection between social practices and meaning evinced in the above case provides an image of how meaning and practice support one another. This kind of integration of meaning and practice is, I presume, a good deal of what Habermas means by his notion of the lifeworld, what is 'always already intuitively present to all of us as a totality that is unproblematized, nonobjectified, and pretheoretical (*PT*, 38). Hence a useful way for considering what Habermas means by the rationalization of the lifeworld and the substitution of systems integration for social integration is that rationalization tendentially brings the operative force of the central concepts of particular domains within the orbit of a procedural governance that weakens, to the point of disappearance, their reliance on intersubjective practice for their sense. And this has the consequence of making the sense (the logical powers) of indefinitely more expressions dependent on forms whose functioning is a material equivalent of the functioning of syntactical and logical forms, and so becoming topic-neutral terms. Money could hence be viewed as a logical connective in economic exchanges, and the idea of the exchange value dominating use-value would be equivalent to saying that economic exchanges are subject to logical laws operating independently of intersubjective sense. Hence, what comes within the orbit of this process is deprived or drained of its intersubjective sense or meaning. In other words, one way of reading rationalization would be to claim that it renders increasingly more terms *effectively* topic neutral, which is equivalent to saying that it is a process rendering various objects and practices effectively intersubjectively meaningless.

Although analogous to what Habermas intends in labelling money and power 'media', the idea of construing power and money as tendentially syntactical operators which practically trump intersubjective meaning constitution is quite distinctive. With the notion of, let us call it, syntactical trumping, empirical predicates are subsumed within a structure that detaches their potential for meaning from both intersubjective practices and their referential objects. So, although coats still possess the quality of 'keeping warm', the 'value' of the coat is determined by the syntax of the market that makes no reference to its qualitative characteristics. Hence, the coat comes to have another value than its use-value, one beholden to an abstract or topic-neutral syntax. Now we can look at this either from the side of the syntax or from the empirical-practical angle of the syntactical trumping. From the perspective of the syntax itself the coat and our economic practice simply disappear. Yet, the reality of economic practices is a bifocal engagement with an object as both use-value (semantically meaningful) and exchange value (syntactically trumping). Hence, the account of media as mechanisms for the domination of pragmatic semantics by syntax is a version of systematically distorted communication, something occurring *in* lifeworld practices, in the sense elaborated in Chapter 3, with the idea of topic-neutral meaning picking up just the kind of rigidification and loss of connectedness to *context* Habermas first analyses through the idea of ritualized linguistic usage.

In *The Theory of Communicative Action*, Habermas fails to follow his own lead on this matter. Rather than considering media as syntactical operators within language, he comes to conceive of them as a replacement for linguistic action altogether, hence generating a dualism between lifeworld and system.

> The transfer of action coordination from language over to steering media means an uncoupling of interaction from lifeworld contexts. Media such as money and power attach to empirical [not rational] ties; they encode a purposive rational attitude toward calculable amounts of value and make it possible to exert a generalized, strategic influence on the decisions of other participants which *bypass* processes of consensus-oriented communication. Inasmuch as they do not merely simplify

169

linguistic communication, but *replace* it with a symbolic generalization of rewards and punishments [profit and loss], the lifeworld contexts in which processes of reaching an understanding are always embedded are devalued in favour of media-steered interactions; the lifeworld is no longer needed for the coordination of action.

(TCA, II, 183)

The distortion wrought by the media for Habermas is the shift from communicative rational to purposive rational. But the idea of lifeworld contexts becoming 'devalued' or 'bypassed' is a misleading analysis of what occurs, above all because economic exchanges and power-political actions are lifeworld practices. Hence, what is necessary is to explicate the logical connection between different aspects of practices. In considering media as syntax for the semantics of economic action just such a connection is elicited. Methodologically, this keeps issues of action determination, empirical motivation and participants' calculations fully bound up with the processes in which steering media are employed. More to the point for our purposes, it explains the distortions of money and power as logical-procedural, subsumption and trumping, rather than as simply marking a shift from one orientation (communication) to another (strategic and purposive). What is *wrong* with strategic-purposive calculation is that it devalues particular qualities of objects, use-values, and thereby rigidifies the potential for meaningfulness (epistemic and axiological) of routine empirical predicates. It is that potentiality for meaningfulness, the genie in the bottle, that critique means to set free.

However dangerous analogies are, if an analogy is what is at issue here, then it looks plausible to say that the rationalization of the lifeworld is the process whereby determinant judgments become independent of their reliance on reflective judgments, for example, what an object is worth is determined by the mechanism of the market rather than judgments which match qualities of the objects with needs of the subject. Of course, it is equally true that the mechanism of the market takes over from, 'colonizes', the communicative infrastructure of the lifeworld. Further, it is true that the displacement of communicatively established meaning by impersonal mechanisms like money and power will itself make what is so displaced tendentially meaningless. But the reason why this displacement has that effect is because the particular sensuous features of things and persons, the match between qualities and needs, are being withdrawn as components of the 'value' of things. Hence, the mechanisms of meaning destruction is best explained in terms of a process of abstraction where meaning ('value') is determined independently of sensuous particularity, and hence by a process that renders particulars 'blind' by subsuming them into a procedure indifferent to them as particulars. Conversely, part of the rationality of *ordinary* communicative interaction derives from the fact that in it reflective and determinant judgment remain entwined and mutually dependent. Hence communicative action remains meaningful

170

just in case it maintains that mutuality between reflective judging, openness to the object, and determinant judging, the raising of validity claims.

Aesthetical sense-making in its modern guise, the drive for autonomy, is centrally concerned with the possibility of making the coherence, intelligibility and claim of a work remaining irrefrangibly local, a product of the internal connections among the elements of the work, and hence inexponible – *incapable* of being subsumed. In Kant, the possibility of aesthetic 'provincialism' was dependent on aesthetic ideas, inexponible products of the imagination which induce 'much thought, yet without the possibility of any definite thought whatever, i.e. *concept*, being adequate to it, and which language, consequently, can never quite get on level terms with or render intelligible'.[12] As aesthetic ideas (which for Kant were the non-phenomenal predicates belonging to morality) were increasingly drawn within the governance of enlightened reason, their capacity to inhibit interpretation and conceptual articulation weakened; traditional works, including pre-modernist autonomous works, were drawn level with language by an increasingly self-confident critical community. Modernist art hence had to disabuse art of its reliance on these ideas and turn inward onto its own productive forms: narrativity itself, words and their associations, paint on canvas, the material inscription of space, bodies in motion. Even without their attachment to (moral) ideas, and even without reliance on extrinsic notions of unity and harmony, these works made 'sense', were compelling objects of attention inducing much thought, without, again, language getting on *level* terms with them. These were *pure* use-values, non-exchangeable against anything else (and hence, as Adorno would have it, pure commodities since not truly useful at all). Hence, they announced the possibility of non-exchangeability without realizing that possibility. The demand for universality led in time to an expert culture of art criticism that, perhaps despite itself, placed these innovations on a level with language. Hence the search for more radical forms that effectively would reduce comprehension to the local demands of the context of meaning produced by the work itself. And these forms, again, were not purely logical forms, but still harboured 'an archaic unity of logic and causality', that is, they demanded that conceptual understanding be bound to perceptual experience. Power, difference, and so on, are non-concepts in just this way; they are for the sake of localizing discourse, which can, thus, 'induce much thought' without any concept being able to subsume the discourse and hence generate conceptual closure.

Philosophy was late in absorbing the lessons of modernism; which is perhaps why it receives denominations – 'post-structuralism', 'postmodernism' – drawn from different histories, different temporalities; and equally why it has proved so difficult to perceive that the claims of philosophical modernism, however its practitioners understand them, are best understood as the progeny and continuers of the project of critical artistic modernism, the project of revealing a *rationality*, which must itself be construed as coextensive with what is

171

meaningful, which is neither subsumptive (deductive) nor procedural in character.

This project involves the elaboration of the interconnection of three elements: local reason and rationality, sensuous particularity (nonidentity, alterity, otherness, the body), and judgment. Roughly, the logic at work here is that nonidentity (of object with concept) is threatened by rationalization, which is metaphysics come of age, metaphysics become modern. Methodologism is to scientific discourse what proceduralism is to philosophy, and system is to the lifeworld. In each case constitutive concepts and meanings are rendered effectively topic neutral. So, in the case of morality for Habermas, instead of moral norms receiving their validity in part through reference to injurable bodies, they become *worthy* of recognition only in virtue of having survived the procedure of argumentation (*MCCA*, 126). From the angle of the moralist (Habermas), the procedure does indeed appear as that which will protect morality against further sceptical incursions by a reason loosened from its ties to tradition, history and community; from the perspective of the modernist, however, the claim that only the procedure of argumentation can provide norms with worth is itself what makes them appears as the 'rubble of devalued traditions', 'merely conventional' (*MCCA*, 126). By requiring that the worth of norms be attached to what is unlike them, communication, the presumptively only negative criterion for worth empties the original empirical orientation of the norm of its original sense. *Communicative rationality thus appears to be an example of syntactical trumping.* For the modernist, then, the gaze of procedural morality is itself sceptical and nihilistic. The claims of practice and the other can only be rendered visible through the instauration of a local reason working against the claims of abstract, procedural reason; for only within the ambit of a local reason is discriminatory judgment necessary and unavoidable, judgment which, while supported by context, is nonetheless, because context dependent, resolutely particular. As in modernist art, the creation of a certain type of context reveals an objectivity internal to what is being thereby objectivated. Hence, the goal of modernist philosophical writing is best defined as the attempt to make itself an object demanding reflective judgment, attempting by its practice to disallow the disassociation of reflective and subsumptive judgment.

Without relying on the employment of non-concepts, but with a strong claim for the place of rhetoric in writing, the 'Introduction' to *Negative Dialectics* provides a defence of philosophical modernism as the interweaving of these three elements, an interweaving that describes well Foucault's actual practice of writing. Philosophy now, Adorno maintains, must concern itself with what philosophy has traditionally shunned, 'nonconceptuality, individuality, and particularity – things which ever since Plato used to be dismissed as transitory and insignificant, and which Hegel labeled "lazy Existenz" ' (*ND*, 8). The goal of negative dialectics is to change the direction of conceptuality, to block the movement of subsumption, the 'rationalized rage at nonidentity' (*ND*, 23)

implicit in idealism as the *summa* of the history of philosophy, and give conceptuality 'a turn toward nonidentity' (*ND*, 12). To release the 'coherence of
the nonidentical, the very thing infringed by deductive systematics' (*ND*, 26)
is possible only through a reliance on writing and language, a writing, then,
that refuses to halt, stop, name: 'The determinable flaw in every concept
makes it necessary to cite others; this is the font of the only constellations
which inherited some of the hope of the name' (*ND*, 53). 'Constellation' is
Adorno's name for the entwinement of particular and context in philosophical
thought (*ND*, 162–3). Constellations are philosophical 'compositions' (*ND*,
165), philosophical 'works'. Because not governed by abstract reason, logic,
foundations, first principles, such philosophizing must rely on 'the consistency
of its performance, the density of its texture' (*ND*, 35) as its guarantor. Such
writing requires and leads to judgment, discrimination, 'that which escapes
the concept' (*ND*, 45). Only in judgment is the (rational) 'elective affinity
between knower and known' (*ND*, 45) realized and sustained.

If philosophy is to go in the direction of nonidentity, it must refuse closure;
and that does not mean merely certainty (as the contrary of fallibilism), but
more centrally, full conceptual articulation.

> . . . instead of reducing philosophy to categories, one would in a sense
> have to compose it first. Its course must be a ceaseless self-renewal, by its
> own strength as well as in friction with whatever standard it may have.
> The crux is *what happens in it, not a thesis or a position* – the texture, not the
> deductive or inductive course of one-track mind. Essentially, therefore,
> philosophy is not expoundable. If it were, it would be superfluous; the
> fact that most of it can be expounded speaks against it.
>
> (*ND*, 33–4, emphasis mine)[13]

The 'what happens' in a discourse as opposed to a 'thesis or a position' (a
validity claim argumentatively vindicated) specifies the space separating the
judgment of local reason from the discursive redemption of claims. In *Aesthetic
Theory* Adorno goes on to acknowledge, and, indeed, insist upon, the fragility
of the truth of modernist works; their capacity to resist the effort of interpretation and criticism is under present conditions only ever temporary:
'Neutralization is the social price art pays for its autonomy' (*AT*, 325).
Neutralization, I take it, flows from the demand that the object meet context-
independent standards of objectivity; these standards themselves are just the
idealizations that Habermas contends are what makes objectivity possible.
Thus, equally, neutralization must be the social price that modernist philosophical works pay for their autonomy. Local reason is powerless to resist
indefinitely the claims of universality; its claims depend on context, on the
fine-grained texture of the non-topic-neutral logical powers of its concepts,
powers generated and released by the contextualization provided by the
density and texture of writing. Once its claims are removed from that context,
they evaporate: its writing becomes presentism; its localism aporetic and

self-defeating; its immanent standards pseudo-normative. Their 'temporal substance' makes the truths of philosophical modernism 'suspended and frail' (*ND*, 34), ever subject to neutralization. 'The transcendent moment of *universal* validity [that] bursts every provinciality asunder' (p. 322), that ' "blots out" space and time' (p. 323), is their *death*.[14]

REASON: DIVIDED AND DISTORTED

The claims of local reason cannot be heard by Habermas for the very precise reason that his communication theory becomes visible and operative only when the analytic level of judgment is abandoned (p. 312); and worse, once the level at which communicative rationality manifests itself is attained, its form of transcendence entails a virtual silencing of the claims of local reason and its objects, the others of universalist reason: nature, the human body, desire, the feelings, sensuous particularity. Nonetheless, Habermas might still argue that this rationality and intelligibility has been placed so far outside what we now recognize as reason that its claims do not just appear as muted, silent; they are non-claims because there is no possible, non-utopian way in which local reason and universalist reason can be reconciled. From Habermas's perspective, the claims of local reason are the claims for a still-enchanted reason which 'we' moderns can only see as mere conventions, trashed tradition.

This thesis, that there can be no reconciliation between local reason and the insights of universalistic morality procedurally understood, depends on Habermas's contention that local reason operates on the basis of an 'exclusion model' (p. 306) whereby what has been suppressed and denied by instrumental rationality is the sheer other of reason and not a form of latent rationality. In opposition to this he supports a 'diremption model' of reason in which the other of subject-centred reason is 'the dirempted totality, which makes itself felt primarily in the avenging power of destroyed reciprocities and in the fateful causality of distorted communicative relationships' (p. 306). In order, then, to resist Habermas's silencing of local reason it is first necessary to demonstrate that the diremption model and the exclusion model are not themselves exclusionary; that the dirempting of (comprehensive) reason can at the same time be an excluding and a silencing.

The difficulty facing us here is that Habermas distinguishes between what he regards as a legitimate disarticulation of substantial reason from the diremption of reason. This distinction leads to an overburdened conception of modernity in which the comprehension of the ambiguity of rationalization processes is partially constituted by the non-diremptive disarticulation of reason. Hence, what would need to be shown in order to demonstrate the compatibility of the diremptive and exclusionary models is that there is diremption where Habermas perceives disarticulation; that the overcoming of diremption, and with it the claims of comprehensive reason, occurs – slightly – elsewhere than Habermas avers; and that the positive claims of modernity can be detached from Habermas's strong theory of communicative rationality. While the demonstration of all these theses would be an elaborate and extensive affair, the central markers for such a set of propositions are readily available.

Habermas contends that latent within Kant's conception of formal, differentiated reason is a theory of modernity. Roughly, Habermas reads the Kantian disarticulation of substantive rationality into the three procedurally legislated domains of objective knowledge, moral-practical insight, and aesthetic judgment to be the philosophical crystallization of the Weberian theory of rationalization whereby, through value intensification, there develop the differentiated value spheres of science, morality and art.[15] Habermas gives this account a further twist in contending that the three value spheres that are philosophically written in terms of the trisection of reason represented by the three *Critiques* are just the three primordial functions of language that come into view when we abandon the level of judgment (p. 312). The components representing the three fundamental linguistic functions – the propositional component for representing states of affairs; the illocutionary component for taking up personal relationships; and the components that express the speaker's intentions – are mutually combined and interwoven in elementary speech acts (p. 312).

It is the binding of the Kantian–Weberian account of modernity to speech act theory that overburdens the former. The thrust of my argument to here has been that philosophical modernism is best understood in terms of the claims and aporia of Kantian aesthetic judgment; claims and aporia that are equally those of modernist art. What these aporetic claims amount to is the thesis that one branch of trisected reason, namely, aesthetic judgment, when realized in the value sphere of art discovered its autonomy, its separation from cognition and moral rightness, to be a distortion of it which, a fortiori, entailed the distortion of reason in its non-aesthetic forms. From the perspective of philosophical modernism the trisection of reason is the *exclusion* of reflective judgment and its form of object-relatedness (and so its objects) from practical rationality and cognitive claiming. Habermas thinks that modernist writers are speaking about the other of reason as such because he has already constituted reason as fully cognitive only when it adopts the standpoint of procedural rationality communicatively understood.

It is difficult to see what the dirempting of aesthetic judgment and its objects from considerations of truth and rightness could be if not a silencing of it and them: if art works are not making epistemic and evaluative claims, what are they doing? 'Providing pleasure' hardly fits our actual experience of works. Yet, if more than pleasure is involved, then a difficulty emerges since even Adorno concedes that art works are now trapped in a domain of semblance and illusion. In order to *be* a work of art now means abiding by modes of sense making that are essentially not those of epistemic and evaluative claiming. This is the silencing of art. How could this silencing make its experience of

175

diremption speak if it has been constituted through the silencing of its claims; and procedural reason in its cognitive and moral forms has been constituted as procedural and universalistic through the exclusion of judgment, through the reduction of reflective judgment to aesthetic judgment and art to autonomy? Hence, when aesthetic judgment does try to speak, as it does in philosophical modernism, its speech is paradoxical and aporetic. Still, there are claims being made in such discourse; cognitive, moral and reflective claims; and we can only begin to come to a comprehension of the diremption of reason by heeding those claims.

RECOGNITION AND COMMUNICATION

In engaging with claims similar to the ones I have been forwarding, Habermas has been content to concede the thesis that works of art have a 'truth potential' which does not correlate with any one of the three validity claims constitutive of communicative rationality; but goes on to follow Wellmer in thinking of this potential as something to be released *into* the lifeworld, and not as a (proto-) cognitive challenge to the trisection of reason which, if successful in its claiming, would amount to a (temporary) dismantling of the division of reason. But a dismantling of the trisection is tentatively broached in the passage from Wellmer that Habermas quotes:

> We can explain the way in which truth and truthfulness – and even normative correctness – are metaphorically interlaced in works of art only by appealing to the fact that the work of art, as a symbolic formation with an aesthetic validity claim, is *at the same time an object of life-world experience, in which the three validity domains are unmetaphorically intermeshed.*[16]

(emphasis mine)

Having conceded art's silencing, it follows that claims for truth and moral rightness can enter into art works, as art works, only metaphorically. What happens to these very same claims when they issue from a work of philosophy? Are they still just metaphorical? Is philosophical modernism's work of undoing the purified categorial distinction between literal and metaphorical discourse itself literal or metaphorical? Might it be neither as a claim of local reason, but become neutralized and so become a 'merely' metaphorical, albeit categorial, denial of the distinction between literal and metaphorical when taken up by universal (trisected) rationality? What if, to paraphrase Habermas (p. 199), the presupposed idealizations that transcend any particular language game are what deform reason because they are idealizations that transcend the particularities that constitute the meaningfulness of concrete items, because they press local reason into saying what it does not want to say (breaking its entwining of reflective and determinate judgment), silencing its (categorially) transgressive movement? How is categorial transgression possible? How can philosophy eschew its own categorial placement without contradicting itself? What might the lifeworld's unmetaphorical intermeshing of validity claims token for philosophy? Can philosophy judge?

Wellmer's statement attempts to blunt the sting of aporia while acknowledging its force. If art works are 'at the same time' objects of the lifeworld, then either the silencing of judgment and local reason has not really occurred; or, it has occurred, and cannot be undone, but the effects can be mitigated through the transmissions of mediators and interpreters. In opting for the latter alternative Habermas now appears to have conceded that diremption and exclusion are compatible models; without, however, seeing how his theory of communicative rationality colludes with the very diremption of reason it now seeks to undo by taking up the position of interpreter on behalf of the lifeworld.[17] Of course, the adoption of the position of an interpreter on behalf of the lifeworld is paradoxical since it assumes *both* the position of comprehensive reason, now understood as the claims of the lifeworld; *and* the position of enlightened reason that regards the trisection of reason as the cognitive achievement of modernity. Habermas avoids contradicting himself only by refusing to examine his competing accounts at the same time.

Wellmer states, and Habermas by implication appears to concede, that the three validity domains are unmetaphorically intermeshed in the lifeworld. This is a systematically ambiguous claim; how ambiguous it is becomes apparent, however, only in the light of an examination of what I believe to be the unacknowledged constitutive theme of Habermas's thought: the fate of the causality of fate.

From 'Labour and interaction' to the Freud chapters of *Knowledge and Human Interests* through to *The Philosophical Discourse of Modernity* (pp. 26–30, 306, 316, 324–5), Habermas has been attempting to preserve what he regards as the fundamental validity of Hegel's model of the causality of fate. Using Hegel's example of a criminal and his punishment in 'The spirit of Christianity and its fate', Habermas depicts the operation of the causality of fate in these terms.

> A criminal who disturbs such ethical [*sittlich*] relationships by encroaching upon and oppressing the life of another experiences the power of the life alienated by his deed as a hostile fate. He must perceive as the historical necessity of fate what is actually only the reactive force of a life that has been suppressed and separated off. This force causes the one at fault to suffer until he recognizes in the annihiliation of the life of the other the lack in his own self, and in the act of repudiating another's life the estrangement from himself. In this causality of fate the ruptured bond of the ethical totality is brought to consciousness. This diremped totality can become reconciled only when there arises from the experience of negativity of divided life a longing for the life that has been lost – and when this experience forces those involved to recognize the denial of their own nature in the split-off existence of the other. Then both parties

see through their hardened positions in relation to one another as the result of detachment, of abstraction from their common life-context – and in this context they recognize the basis of their existence.

(pp. 28–9)

As I suggested in Chapter 3, the problematic of modernity, and with it the force of the diremptive model and the critique of subject-centred reason, are together best understood in terms of a heightening of the operation of the causality of fate to the historical and collective level. The individual act that sets the operation of the causality of fate into motion in antiquity becomes the categorial deformation of the ethical totality in modernity: 'This act of tearing loose from an intersubjectively shared lifeworld is what first *generates* a subject–object relationship' (pp. 29, 315).

According to Habermas, because Hegel 'indissolubly' associated the force of the ethical totality with popular religion, on the one hand; and on the other hand came to recognize in civil society a new form of social organization which fundamentally breaks with the models of antiquity (and underlines the achievement of self-consciousness in modernity), he could not sustain the full movement of the causality of fate as an analysis and comprehension of the modern predicament (pp. 30–1). If one could separate the force of ethical totality from the claims of popular religion, then it would become possible to use the model of the causality of fate as the early Hegel had done. This detachment of ethical totality from popular religion would count as a detachment, and not as a transplantation, if it could acknowledge reason's altered – self-grounding, time-conscious – status. These two desiderata – holding onto the model of the causality of fate while acknowledging the claims of disenchanted reason – define Habermas's project exactly: the comprehension of language as communicatively structured is to take up the burden of the intersubjective and hence social mediation of the subject; while the establishment of communicative rationality, with its quasi-transcendental status, is there to acknowledge the 'reflective concept of reason developed in the philosophy of the subject' (p. 30).

Stated in this way, it appears evident that the *force* of ethical totality, whose unifying power Hegel collected under the titles of love, life, recognition, Spirit, and, more complexly, faith, has, as it were, been divided, dirempted, in Habermas into the claims of the lifeworld itself, without which there would be no causality of fate, no 'world', for example, for money to 'de-world' when it is introduced as a universal medium of exchange (p. 350); and into the claims of communicative rationality, without which the achievements of reflective reason would remain unacknowledged. And this severing into two of the force of ethical totality correlates with a noted systematic ambiguity in Habermas's use of communicative action: firstly, as signifying actions that operate through explicit or implicit intersubjective consensus about norms, values and practices; and secondly, as signifying actions which are geared explicitly to establishing norms, truths, and the like, through dialogically achieved consensus.[18]

This duality is further underwritten by Habermas in his claim that there are two heritages of self-reflection that go beyond the limits of the philosophy of consciousness: rational reconstruction, which is directed toward anonymous rule systems; and methodologically carried out self-critique, which is related to totalities as deformed by the operation of quasi-causal mechanisms (pp. 298–300). These two programmes respond to starkly different needs. The project of the rationally reconstructed sciences is a replacement programme for transcendental reflection, securing for communicative reason, however fallibilistically, a quasi-transcendental right; methodologically carried out self-critique responds to the fact that in modernity the force of the causality of fate is experienced in symptomatic and displaced ways, ways that correspond to the fact that the act of diremption that sets the causality of fate into motion is a collective act, 'an involuntary product of an entanglement that . . . communicative agents would have to ascribe to communal responsibility' (p. 316).

What Habermas's argument reveals, despite itself, is that the model of the causality of fate can, and indeed must, be operative independently of communicative rationality as strongly (transcendentally) interpreted. The modern subject, enlightened subjectivity, and hence subject-centred reason, are the *fate* of substance. The becoming subject of substance does not entail the disappearance of the latter, but only, and precisely, its deformation and occultation. While the occultation of substance allows for the indubitable cognitive achievements of modernity, those achievements are misrecognized if not recognized as products of deformation and occultation. Habermas misidentifies the precise nature of the achievement, and hence fails to attend to the incommensurability between communicative reason and the logic of the fate. The governing rationale behind the causality of fate as a philosophical trope is to suggest that it is only in virtue of its workings, its avenging forcing (even, especially, when muted, occluded) that we come to recognize that 'any violation of the structures of rational life together, to which all lay claim, affects everyone equally . . . [that] "betrayal of another is simultaneously betrayal of oneself; and every protest against betrayal is not just protest in one's own name, but in the name of the other at the same time" ' (pp. 324–5).[19]

To concede this is to make the lifeworld, ethical totality, into a 'comprehensive reason', an unmetaphorical intermeshing of the three validity claims. But this argument does not, nor am I claiming that it does, do all that is necessary to resurrect the claims of the causality of fate. For what is perspicuously absent is the *force* of the claim of the lifeworld; the force which was located in (the faith in) popular religion, which Hegel thematized in terms of recognition, love and life; and which Habermas himself acknowledged the need for in his writing on Freud under the headings of transference and 'a passion for critique'. But the best analysis of the disappearance of this force from the

179

lifeworld, the revelation that the very lifeworld which is the ground and repository of our collective life has been as lifeworld systematically 'de-worlded', suggests that rationalization has distorted and deformed reason *intrinsically* by trisecting it, by categorially disallowing where needed an unmetaphorical intermeshing of validity claims. More precisely, the structures of the lifeworld have been distorted such that they appear, almost always and nearly everywhere, to accord with the claims of subject-centred reason. Which is to say, communicative action, in the weak sense, has been constituted by power relations that render invisible the operation of the causality of fate; and thereby defuses the claims of reciprocity that its avenging power is said to reveal.

Habermas's strong analysis of communicative reason is there not only to take up the claims of subject-centred, reflective reason; but equally, it is there to make up, albeit in rationalist terms, the affective deficit left by the systematic rationalization of the lifeworld. But this, of course, it cannot do. The ground for our orienting ourselves toward establishing validity claims through intersubjective recognition is intersubjective recognition. The claims of others register as claims only insofar as we already recognize them as other selves (persons). It is only in virtue of recognizing that the refusal of the other is equally a refusal and betrayal of oneself that leads one to orient oneself to establishing validity claims through consensus and intersubjective recognition. Communicative reason can *express* this recognition once made, but cannot ground it. If the force of ethical totality could be grounded, in universal norms, say, becoming thus an obligation deriving from such a norm, then there would be no avenging force acting back upon the subject. That there is such a force, no matter how displaced and defused, marks the entwinement of passion and (re-)cognition, the very entwinement foreclosed by the duality between philosophical modernism and enlightened modernity.

Habermas would respond to this claim by insisting that there is a force that acts back on the transgressing subject: it is the force of the constraints of communicative reason itself that is revealed by those who would deny it, thus coming to find their performances existentially self-defeating. It is hence to that issue we must turn.

PERFORMATIVE CONTRADICTIONS, LIFEWORLD SOLIDARITIES

Not only has the idea of the causality of fate served Habermas as a model to be vindicated at a higher level, but both the actual operation of his argumentation in defence of discourse ethics and his increasingly sensitive gestures toward the solidarities of the lifeworld and ethical life as *necessary* complements to universalistic morality all but restore Hegel's doctrine to its original state. To the extent this is true the actual status of communicative rationality becomes proportionately problematic.

Looking again at the description of the operation of the causality of fate we notice that its fundamental operation can be captured through the idea of a performative self-contradiction: the criminal's action is existentially self-defeating since the strategic attempt to suppress the other in fact ruins (in the form of suffering) the life of the criminal; the trespasser intended to do away with another's life but instead destroys his own. The explanation of this is that in acting against the other the criminal attempts to deny the unavoidable presuppositions of his own action. This in itself does not justify the ethical totality on which the criminal attempts to encroach, but instead reveals ethical life as something for which there are no alternatives.

Analogously, in 'Discourse ethics: notes on a program of philosophical justification', Habermas defends his argumentative version of the principle of universalization against the sceptic and moral fallibilist who claims that there are no universal moral principles, by demonstrating that as soon as the sceptic attempts to argue for his position he *must*, on pain of performative contradiction, accept the rules of argumentation that prohibit all internal and external coercion other than the force of better argument. The demonstration of a performative self-contradiction does not justify the rules of argumentation (*MCCA*, 95), it reveals them as 'inescapable presuppositions' (*MCCA*, 89) of argument, pragmatic universals for which there are 'no alternatives' (*MCCA*, 95). The construction of the full set of rules of argumentation is a negative procedure generated through the negation or transgression of its pretheoretical but intuitively known equivalents in argument. It is the sceptical challenge of the argumentative criminal then that first reveals the pretheoretical constraints on argumentation that the reconstructive science of discourse ethics descriptively elaborates. Habermas's use of performative contradiction is hence not quite the formal or logical procedure he presents it as, nor is it simply a heuristic matter that it is the philosophical sceptic who is the interlocutor of the reconstructive scientist. The philosophical sceptic, like the Hegelian criminal, represents the moment of negativity that first dirempts the ethical totality of communicative action oriented to reaching an understanding from itself, thereby revealing it, with its fundamental structures, as the actual ground on which both sceptic and scientist must base themselves. In fine, the construction of discourse ethics is itself ethical, repeating at the level of argumentation the dialectic of moral life first surveyed in 'Labour and interaction'.

That argumentative struggle recapitulates the dialectic of moral life at the level of discourse forms the rational core of its ethical claim. But as a repetition at a higher level, it must face the challenge that in attempting to secure the necessity of reciprocal recognition as a constraint on discourse only, it abstracts so far from the concrete dynamics of ethical life itself, the actual dependencies of self on other and the actual recognitions and misrecognitions of self in otherness, that its claim to have found the existential ground of the moral constitution of the subject, which is also the rational ground of the subject, becomes insupportable. Or better: because what is revealed are the transcendental constraints on discourse, then the question arises as to how they relate to ethical substance itself. These questions concerning the proximity or remoteness of discourse to ethical substantiality are coextensive with Habermas's linguistic turn in general, and specifically his contention that action oriented to reaching an understanding forms not just *a* but *the* pivotal structure of communicative interaction as the medium of coordination for social action. In Chapter 3, I suggested that the perspective of action coordination was, as it were, too functionalist a conception of morality, a point I shall return to below, and that as a consequence Habermas illegitimately separated moral (constraint) from ethical (identity). In perceiving the construction of discourse ethics as a recapitulation of the dialectic of moral life, we perforce face that issue again. In testing this claim, however, we are simultaneously testing the presumptive structural centrality of action oriented to reaching an understanding itself. In challenging Habermas on these matters it is not necessary to question the thesis that communicative rationality recapitulates at the level of discourse the dialectic of moral life. The claim is rather that discourse ethics is only or at most a recapitulation, but that in *substituting* discourse ethics for the dialectic of moral life, which is just what the linguistic turn entails, Habermas empties morality of its ethical substance. If the dialectic of moral life transpires only at the level of argumentation under conditions of modernity, if self-recognition in otherness transpires only as a commitment to rational argumentation, then one may well wonder how substantial the moral really is for Habermas. Conversely, if Habermas does not intend to substitute discourse ethics for the dialectic of moral life, and we shall see that there is room to doubt that he does intend a full-scale substitution, then what is the status of the claim that the rationality of morality is only available at this level?

Habermas's example (*MCCA*, 90ff.) of how his argument works is illuminating for our purposes. Say I am attempting to convince H that *p*. If I am truly wishing to convince H that *p*, then the claim 'Using lies I convinced H that *p*' would defeat itself since being convinced means (for us, now) accepting a belief without force or coercion; deceit is a form of linguistic coercion since the withholding of information entails bypassing the rational powers of the other. If the other cannot agree (or disagree) to *p* because I bypass her rational powers, then my relation to her will is strategic, a use of force, rather than rational. What makes this plausible derives wholly from my original intention of wanting to *convince* H that *p*; if I had had the weaker desire, say, for H to act on the basis of *p*, then the argument would have failed since only the result, H's behaviour, and not the reasons for it would have been relevant. The deceit works, however, because H presupposes that in addressing her intentionally, through linguistic action, I am trying to convince her. If so, then the non-self-defeating, straight manipulation also only works because H presupposes that our interaction is intentional and not strategic and causal. Hence, the same logic which shows that attempting to convince through lying is self-defeating equally shows that explicit manipulation, attempting to get H to act on the basis of p, itself presupposes non-strategic, convincing argumentation.

The explicit pattern of argumentation Habermas adopts here should strike us as familiar: it is the structure of Hegel's dialectic of master and slave. Arguments for Habermas are equivalent to struggles for recognition. In the same way in which the master defeats his desire for recognition by coercing it from the slave, so being recognized only by one whom he does not recognize, hence cancelling the recognition received, so the lying arguer defeats his desire for recognition of the truth of the belief that p by lying. Argumentation itself is the Habermasian, discourse equivalent of struggles for recognition.

This is telling *against* the force of using performative contradiction as a distinctive strategy for vindicating the discourse theoretical version of the principle of universalization. Two disanalogies between Hegel's master/slave dialectic and the dialectic of argumentation begin to show why. Firstly, Hegel's account is set within a deeper metaphysical setting; he is seeking to demonstrate that intersubjectivity is a necessary condition for subjectivity, self-consciousness in its Kantian sense. Self-consciousness in this sense, that is, awareness that my actions and cognitions are *mine* and that nothing could count as a cognition or an action unless accompanied by such self-ascription, is constitutive of the very idea of being a self. Since the resolution of conflict by argumentation cannot be regarded as a necessary condition for the possibility of linguistic practice, nor is argumentation necessary for those within a linguistic community to act on the basis of true beliefs, it follows that what is to be demonstrated is too remote from what is basic to individual and collective life as such to receive defence through the idea of performance contradiction. The demonstration presupposes that we seek to justify and vindicate our beliefs through argumentation, and hence that we possess the practice of rational argumentation, for us this practice is ineliminable, and further that our possessing it represents an inescapable characteristic of the human form of life, albeit one which is only revealed in our form of life. Clearly, the attachment of argumentation to our form of life is the source of the difficulty since, as argued earlier, any fundamental practice of any historical community will be sufficient to generate a performative contradiction. Any complex set of beliefs will presuppose other beliefs, and for any complex set of beliefs, a conceptual scheme, there will be some presupposed basic beliefs. Hence any sufficiently rich and wide set of beliefs will yield performative contradictions from those that attempt to step outside that belief structure, the conceptual scheme in which we live and breathe. In order for performative contradictions to be revelatory of more than our basic beliefs they must approach something deeper than basic beliefs. That is what makes Descartes's Cogito forceful: I cannot actively doubt that I *exist*. Hence, the very idea of existentially self-defeating performances needs to touch something like the conditions for being a self (a thinking being, self-consciousness) as such. But this looks impossible since all we ever have to deal with is a conception of what it is to be a self or self-conscious or a person; hence, the most that can ever be revealed by pre-suppositional arguments that use performative self-contradictions of the Habermasian sort is *our* fundamental beliefs. And how good those arguments are will turn on how basic the presuppositional set is in relation to our form of life; even for us, some presuppositional sets, basic beliefs, do not appear very basic because we can conceive of the practices they ground disappearing. Argumentation may be like that.

Habermas both does and does not concede this. So in responding to an objection of Karl-Otto Apel's he argues:

> This demonstration of the factual inescapability of substantive normative presuppositions of a practice *internally interwoven with our socio-cultural form of life* is indeed conditional on the constancy of this life-form. We cannot exclude a priori the possibility of its undergoing changes. But that remains an empty possibility since – science fiction scenarios that transform human beings into zombies aside – we cannot even imagine a fundamental alteration of our form of life. The weak transcendental proof . . . suffices to ground the universalistic validity claim (valid for all subjects of speech and action) of a moral principle conceived in procedural terms.
>
> (JA, 83–4; emphasis mine)

The puzzle here is between the concession in the first half of this passage and its withdrawal as relevant in the second half.

This brings up the second disanalogy with Hegel. The master/slave dialectic is not the endpoint of Hegel's argument, but occurs close to its beginning. Hegel realized that performative self-contradictions derived all their logical strength from ends set by the individuals undergoing the experience; only the ends of seeking recognition, or freedom or salvation, to somehow ground one's fundamental being in the world could *practically* yield a performative self-contradiction if that end was pursued consistently. This led Hegel to regiment his use of performative self-contradiction in three ways: (i) performative contradiction as a philosophical procedure must be used phenomenologically, that is, only a form of (natural) consciousness testing itself could yield compelling performative contradictions since only by permitting each form of consciousness to stipulate its own criterion for ultimate grounding prevents the demonstration from being question-begging. (ii) But this is equivalent to saying that there cannot be direct transcendental arguments for fundamental beliefs since the philosopher is always dependent on natural consciousness's stipulation of basic elements of the conceptual scheme. Hence it is only a whole series of performative contradictions (coupled with the philosopher's recognition of determinate negation: conceptual schemes displacing one another in order to overcome the inadequacies of the previous scheme) that can show that there are no alternatives to the philosopher's favoured belief set. (iii) Performative self-contradictions therefore are idle against the philosophical sceptic since he or she has already refused to posit any criterion of what is to count as a fundamental ground of experience and therefore is immune to the force of what a performative contradiction brings about in any particular context. Only with respect to life-practices do self-defeating performances matter. Hence for Hegel the core of the force of the employments of performative contradictions is that they permit the possibility of tracing a series of fundamental *ethical experiences* (*Erfahrung*), the repeated forms of despair (not doubt) that consciousness suffers at its own hands when it attempts to ground itself otherwise than through recognition of the life it gains through sharing and participating in a sociocultural life with other (free and equal) selves.

All that goes wrong in Habermas's defence of argumentation does so because he wishes to abstract from the concrete ethical experiences of defeat and the consequent transformations of consciousness, its conversion to new forms of ethical orientation. For Hegel theoretical or philosophical insight is logically dependent upon the ethical standpoint of the subject. That is the significance of Hegel shifting from the model of the criminal or sceptic in his earliest writings to natural consciousness in the *Phenomenology*. Rather than avoiding competing conceptual frameworks, presupposing our own and eliciting the services of the sceptic, we must, as it were, begin with those alternatives. (This, of course, is closer to the practice of *Knowledge and Human Interests*.) Hence what Habermas casually acknowledges with the phrase 'with our sociocultural form of life' is for Hegel the question: how are we to identify and describe the essential components of our sociocultural form of life as a non-reversible achievement? The phrase 'our sociocultural form of life' cannot reasonably be contrasted with us becoming zombies; rather, it must refer to our substantive ethical identity as constituted by an elaborate set of values and ideals – who we want to be. Hegel infers from this that no theoretical or neutral account of who we are can be compelling; hence, his recourse to an account of the history of self-consciousness described phenomenologically.

In a sense, Habermas reverses Hegel's procedure: where Habermas uses the idea of the reconstructive sciences, including developmental moral psychology, Hegel presents the performative self-contradictions of the ethical forms of life that precipitated and led to our own; where Habermas uses performative self-contradictions to defeat the sceptic, Hegel has the philosophical comprehension of the previously given ethical history. In this respect, Hegel's philosophical procedure operates a generalization of the causality of fate structure, keeping the entire argumentation bound to the demands of any concrete ethical life: every previous form of life will be shown to be transgressive or negative to the extent that it grounds its possibility of being the form of life it is on something other than its own life-practices and the mutual recognitions and (misrecognitions) it involves. Habermas's inversion of Hegel's procedure amounts to the abstraction of his claims from the ethical history of the subjects for whom those claims *can* be seen as true. If the force of performative self-contradiction is itself ethical, a crystallization of the movement of the causality of fate, then abstracting it as a procedure to a merely formal or logical use involves a suppression of the ground which makes it function; the existential concretion of ethical life cannot be distilled to its logical underpinning without bypassing the subjects who carry it out. Habermas's use of 'our sociocultural form of life' in setting up his transcendental argument operates precisely this acknowledgement and suppression of ethical substantiality.

Of course, in concrete terms the presuppositions of argumentation are avoidable even in our sociocultural form of life. I can quite consistently regard myself and others as autonomous, and further acknowledge our reciprocal dependency on one another and nonetheless believe that the best way to vindicate disputed validity claims over moral norms is by means of, for example, self-expressive forms of action, writing novels, designing alternative experiments in living that exemplify the adoption of different moral norms, etc. (NB: all these counter-examples displace rational argumentation with a dialectic of presentation and judgment.) Accountability does necessarily entail rational argumentation; and alternative forms of being accountable do not necessarily involve coercion or force. Hence, it is false to claim, as Habermas routinely does (*MCCA*, 102), that our choice is between acting communicatively in order to reach an understanding and acting strategically. Indeed, where fundamental moral values are at issue, it could be claimed that expressive, symbolic and aesthetic presentations (e.g. draft card and bra burning, war photographs, etc.), all of which combine the strategic and the communicative but do not seek to force or coerce, are more rational forms of interaction than rational argumentation itself. And this raises deep questions about moral argument itself that Habermas, overly focused on expert cultures and institutions of argumentation, simply slips past. Habermas's riposte to counter-examples of this kind, namely, that we cannot always avoid communicative interactions may be true, but leaves unanswered the question of where within our practices his version of moral argumentation fits. Even to admit that it simply has a role along with other practices displaces it from being fundamental in some morally significant sense. As I shall argue in the next chapter, what makes his either/or of either communicative or strategic look compulsive is an overextension of the place of communication itself in his philosophy of language.

The ethical goodness of argumentation is bound to particular practices – democratic citizenship, expert cultures, and the like – that are particular realizations of autonomy and reciprocity. But this is only to say that discourse rules, whose factual validity and moral worth are not in dispute, are merely *a* historically specific expression of the notions of autonomy and reciprocity that are non-detachable from the concrete practices in which they play a constitutive role. This concession does not entail autonomy and reciprocal recognition being merely historical values; only that there are no a priori forms or procedures that are unique and unavoidable articulations of them, although it may be the case that we cannot now sustain those values without affirming the rational core of some of those concrete ethical practices. This is Hegel's method: to justify highly abstract notions – broadly: self-recognition in absolute otherness – in relation to historically specific concrete practices.

The force of performative self-contradiction in Habermas depends upon its structure exemplifying the logical movement of the causality of fate. His use of it fails in the task assigned because in substituting the philosophical sceptic for the criminal (the master, the unhappy consciousness, Antigone or Creon, the hard heart, etc.), he abstracts from the concrete dependencies of self on other that make encroachments on the life of the other *existentially* self-defeating, and hence something that matters to the ethical individual herself. Her despair is what keeps the dialectic in movement. As Habermas has acknowledged (*MCCA*, 99), the attempt to make the moral sceptic exemplary has the decisive drawback of leaving open the possibility of the sceptic simply refusing to play the argumentation game. Habermas's argument against the principled sceptic uses the causality of fate again, but equally in a misleading way: '. . . the sceptic may reject morality, but he cannot reject the ethical substance (*Sittlichkeit*) of the life circumstances in which he spends his waking hours, not unless he is willing to take refuge in suicide or serious mental illness' (*MCCA*, 100). The refusal to participate in social practices may have these consequences, and for good phenomenological, causality of fate reasons; but this is beside the point since a different sceptic may engage in the communicative practices of ethical life but deny that those practices possess any moral or ethical validity: ethical life can be acknowledged as de facto necessary without that giving it any de jure validity. Performative self-contradiction remains idle unless related to the possibility of ethical insight. In this, Habermas's detachment of the inescapable from the justifiable looks too absolute.

Habermas's allegiance to Hegel's conceptions of ethical life and the causality of fate is more extensive than his use of performative self-contradiction might indicate. At the end of his long defence of discourse ethics we find the following strange passage:

> The *moral* intuitions of everyday life are not in need of clarification by the philosopher. In this case the therapeutic self-understanding of philosophy initiated by Wittgenstein is for once, I think, appropriate. Moral philosophy does have an enlightening or clarificatory role to play vis-à-vis the confusions that it has created in the minds of the educated, that is, to the extent to which value scepticism and legal positivism have established themselves as professional ideologies and have infiltrated everyday consciousness by way of the educational system.
>
> (*MCCA*, 98)

At one level this passage is not quite as odd as it may first appear. Habermas is insisting here that morality does not require fundamental grounding or ultimate justification because the universalistic intuitions that are a component of everyday moral practice are themselves correct. And indeed, Habermas must believe this if he is going to regard the argumentative defence of discourse ethics as a reconstructive science explicating the intuitions and pretheoretical knowledge found in everyday practice. The function of philosophical theories is to combat other philosophical theories, but it cannot justify or ground its insights in a non-circular fashion without supposing that there is some ground other than the mutual recognitions of lifeworld practices that give morality its meaning and possibility.

Insofar as Habermas is thus claiming that moral norms are grounded in the reciprocities of everyday life, which is self-grounding, transcendental and empirical at once, he is operating within standard Hegelian parameters. How the empirical and the transcendental, the real and the rational are connected does, however, make a difference. Habermas agrees with Foucault that the idealist version of the connection is inherently unstable: 'Because these hybrid enterprises chase after the utopia of complete self-knowledge, they flip-flop again and again into positivism' (p. 262). The notion of complete self-knowledge here is misleading, a cartoon version of Fichte. What the Hegelian claims is not complete self-knowledge, but that our self-knowledge is non-detachable from the conditions that made it possible; to affirm itself it must affirm them, and hence negativity (what denies ethical life) in general. This knowledge is 'absolute' in Hegel's sense because what is absolute or unconditioned, knowledge of ethical life as ground, includes the conditions that made it possible. Thus there is no logical duality between the empirical (the conditions) and the transcendental (the unconditioned): both are ethical life.

Habermas, in contrast, does conceive of the conditioned and unconditioned, transcendental and empirical, as lying on logically different levels, which is what makes his Wittgenstein comment disingenuous. From the perspective of discourse ethics 'there are no shared structures preceding the individual except the universals of language use' (*MCCA*, 203). Moral argumentation is a distillation of lifeworld communications; but from the perspective of the participant in discourse the 'lifeworld totality has lost its quality of naive acceptance, and the normative power of the factual has weakened. . . . Under this gaze the store of traditional norms has disintegrated into those norms that can be justified in terms of principles and those that operate only de facto' (*MCCA*, 108). (How, one might ask, does this 'gaze' differ in its reifying power from the 'stoical gaze' (p. 253) that precipitates or marks the archaeologist's descent into positivism?) It is here that the philosophical modernist re-enters the debate since she disputes the thesis that moral intuitions of the lifeworld, the way it blends empirical and normative features of discourse, are recaptured when we move to the higher level of argumentation. Again, although designed merely as a negative or critical test of the validity of moral norms, the discourse ethical procedure in fact transforms *forms* of mutual recognition into *abstract rules* for the coordination of action. Said otherwise: for everyday moral practice, principles, norms, value predicates and the like are more than contingent empirical items whose worth is dependent upon their compatibility with the universals of language use. If only the negative test provided by principle U reveals the rational core of moral norms, then the positive moral content of norms is irrational: blind intuitions receiving their sense from the moral form of argumentation.

In this respect, Apel was correct in being 'shocked and mystified' by Habermas's Wittgensteinian passage.[20] Habermas cannot say both that everyday moral intuitions of the lifeworld are in good order and that the universals of language use are the only shared structures preceding the individual; for Wittgenstein it is the whole complex and conceptually irretrievable motley of the human form of life that precedes the individual. Yet, Habermas cannot follow Apel's notion of an ultimate grounding without at the same time accepting the Peircean idea of an ultimate communication community which will possess ultimate moral truth. This would make history only a passageway to a point beyond it.[21] Ethical life and lifeworld practices have no such telos for Habermas, which is why he consistently says that the norms of argumentation are only critical constraints, hence negative tests for validity. Proceduralism intends and looks to keep lifeworld practices intact as historically substantial. It can do this, however, only by making communicative rationality ethically exemplary; but it is only exemplary, a *presentation* of the movement of the ethical, then its claims to universality is undermined. Hence, Habermas attempts to provide for communicative rationality the status of a universal of linguistic usage. But that empties lifeworld practices of their moral substance – the true force of the gaze of modernity – as surely as Apel's foundational teleology (*MCCA*, 125).

This level of emptying and abstraction is built into Habermas's theory twice over. In the first instance it derives from his agreement with Adorno and Horkheimer that traditional philosophies of history, like Marx's, in which the dynamic and the normative are fully integrated, are no longer available. As a consequence, two 'abstractions' are required: '(i) abstracting the development of cognitive structures from the historical dynamic of events, and (ii) abstracting the evolution of society from this historical concretion of forms of life' (*TCA*, II, 383). While Habermas is correct to demur from an account of history which reduces it to an unfolding a priori structure, his way of disentangling developmental dynamics (phenomenology) from developmental logic is to provide a logic without a phenomenology. The price Habermas pays for this way of distinguishing and then relating history and logic, objective and absolute spirit, is to leave him with no way back to historical concretion, the very fragile lifeworld practices his critical theory means to foster and protect.

Secondly, Habermas fails to see how deracinating his conception of morality is because, in the final analysis, his definition of morality is *functional*:

'In anthropological terms, morality is a safety device compensating for a vulnerability built into the sociocultural form of life' (*MCCA*, 199). This defines morality naturalistically and externally, from the observer's point of view. In contrast, Foucault's dramatizations of vulnerable and injurable bodies bind moral intuitions to ethical perception. With some irony, a writer who appears to Habermas to be taking the position of the ethnologist (*MCCA*, 99) in fact is attempting to slip between the either/or of abstract moral rationalism or complacent traditionalism, while Habermas himself has already integrated a wholly externalist perspective into his account of what participating in communicative interaction implies.

Habermas believes that the only alternative to universal moral norms deracinated from their place in the lifeworld and validated discursively would be a return to blind traditionalism – the critical move which prevents him from integrating the rational and the real. As a consequence, he accepts the thought that argumentatively validated moral norms 'retain only the rationally motivating force of insights' and lose 'the thrust and efficacy of empirical motives for action' (*MCCA*, 109). In order to compensate for this lack of efficacy and loss of ethical substance, Habermas must appeal again to concrete ethical life, a form of life that would 'meet universalist moralities halfway [and] in this sense fulfil the conditions necessary to *reverse the abstractive achievements of decontextualization and demotivation*' (p. 109; emphasis mine). If it is necessary to reverse the achievements of abstract morality, and if decontextualization and demotivation are necessary implications of adopting proceduralism, then in what sense is Habermas's version of universalism a cognitive achievement? Consistently, Habermas's anxiety about relativism (the universalism question) leads him to accept decontextualization and demotivation (the nihilism problem) as the flip side of moral truth. To his credit, he sees nihilism as a problem, but believes only luck and good will answer it. In this way he flatly ignores the philosophical problems to which the Nietzschean tradition directs itself.

The notion of a form of life that would meet procedural universalism halfway equates to stipulating solidarity as the reciprocally required complement of justice: 'every requirement of universalization must remain powerless unless there also arises, from membership in an ideal communication community, a consciousness of irrevocable solidarity, the certainty of intimate relatedness in a shared life context'.[22] With this 'intimate relatedness' re-enters all the concretion left behind by the required abstractions and the functionalization of morality; yet, this ethical substantiality is in a sense entering blindly, without cognitive sense or rational meaning, since Habermas has already deprived such intimacies (feelings, affects, concerns) of any but de facto sense by handing over to communicative interactions hegemony over questions of rationality and truth. It is impossible from where we have arrived not to see in these blind intimacies, regulated from above by universalistic moral norms, the very vulnerable bodies and nonidentical objects that Foucault and Adorno lamented. Indeed, one can almost hear in Habermas's call for solidarity 'a longing for the life that has been lost', a plea for forgiveness from the lifeworld that has been dirempted into the moral and the solidaristic.

UNIVERSALITY: PROCEDURAL, CRITICAL AND SUBSTANTIAL

If the trisection of reason silences local reasons, the claims of sensuous particularity and the public acknowledgement of individual needs, it equally empties universality of substantiality, either reifying it into a transcendental form or, what is nearly the same thing, transforming it into an abstract procedure presumptively expressive of reason itself. In Kant's moral philosophy transcendental form and procedural rationality become indissolubly entwined. Habermas follows Kant down this path. From what has been said thus far it may appear that in siding with the modernists against Habermas a stand against universalistic morality and the moral ideals of the Enlightenment is being taken. Yet, standardly philosophical modernists do not doubt the worth of those ideals, and certainly Adorno does not.

What makes Habermas's response to this issue appealing is that he can acknowledge the collapse of tradition as a force of reason, acknowledge the innovative character of social life and yet hold firm to the commitment to universalism by placing the pragmatic constraints on argumentation in the place of substantive norms and values. Even Seyla Benhabib, who shares the scepticism of Habermas's critics who claim that at most his universalization principle provides legitimation for norms rather than validity, believes that proceduralism possesses a moral insight into the meaning of universalism. Her strategy is to drop U, the rule for argumentation, and opt directly for the principle of discourse ethics itself, D: 'Only those norms can claim to be valid that meet (or could meet) with the approval of all affected in their capacity as participants in a practical discourse.' Her reason for adopting D without U is that the latter emphasizes the result while the former focuses on the process by which that result is generated. Hence, even if not all can or could agree to a norm, if it is adopted in accordance with argumentative procedures that are themselves reasonable and fair, then that procedure goes toward underwriting the 'moral worth' of the norm.[23]

Benhabib's suggestion is peculiar. Firstly, it is unclear how proposing D without U answers the charge that there is a conflation between legitimacy and validity in the original proposal. Secondly, in detaching D from U Benhabib cuts D off from what is supposed to ground it, namely, the unavoidability of the constraints on argumentation. Benhabib is certainly correct in pointing out how part of the appeal of the original proposal, its emphasis on processes having a certain character, can stand apart from the strong idealizations that Habermas imports into the procedure in order to tie procedure and validity together in a Peircean manner. But once the Peircean way of connecting procedure and result is broken in two, then the connection between

191

procedure and universality or moral worth equally collapses; rational procedures can form a constraint on what is of moral worth, but how can correspondence with those constraints be thought of as somehow constituting an item as morally worthy? Nothing Benhabib says, to use a Rousseauian analogy, permits a distinction between the will of all and the general will. Peirce's idealization, the *unlimited* communication community, is meant to explicate precisely how the separation between those two can be critically sustained. Benhabib's intuition about the significance of procedures thus remains only an intuition.

Put these points aside. The problem remains: if tradition is not per se binding, then how can the ethical perceptions of a local reason capture our universalist moral commitments? Why doesn't the combination of universalistic procedures plus historical contents represent the ideal synthesis of competing allegiances to universality and historicality? If elsewhere Habermas separates what needs uniting, here he identifies what needs separating. In the communicative retrieval of the claims of subject-centred reason, in the communicative transformation of procedural reason, Habermas runs together two quite distinct features of reason in modernity: universality and rational reflection. The rights of reason, as it were, are recognized when implicit claims become subject to the demands of discourse oriented toward reaching agreement. The claims of universality, however, can never be read off from the procedural forms through which claims are validated. On the contrary, to steal a trope from Marx, it seems more correct to say that there is a conflict between the substantive content of universalistic claims and the procedural inscription of them, between, that is, the forces and relations of universality.

While a full defence of universalism would be an extended affair, its central elements are readily accessible. As the title to this section indicates, moral universalism possesses a variety of senses which require coordination. The primary sense of moral universalism is substantial; we count a moral norm as universal if and only if it possesses unrestricted scope in its applicability. This is substantive rather than formal because it repeats a certain history of moral progress, namely, the path through which we discovered that various restrictions on the scope of *application* of moral predicates could not be sustained. Sedimented in our moral norms is the history, the struggles for recognition, through which the restrictions of colour, race, gender, religion and language were discovered to be morally irrelevant to whether or not a particular moral predicate (including the 'rights' that were thought to ground legal entitlements) could be applied to any one or group of individuals.

Transformations in the scope of application of moral predicates and norms are bound to a complex dialectic in which restrictive moral schemes were immanently challenged as to their internal coherence. In each case a similar challenge was put: does the actual practice of applying a moral predicate make essential reference to its objects possessing particular empirical features (being white, male, Protestant and English speaking, say)? What characteristics do the class of objects to which the predicate is said to apply possess that is not possessed by the class of objects to which the predicate is said not to apply? Typically, pressing these questions was made possible by some members of the oppressed group already possessing and demonstrating the complete set of intersubjective capacities and abilities that constituted the possibility for inter-subjective practices within the dominant group (capacities to read or write, speak the native tongue, take on complex responsibilities in organizing others, demonstrate affection or concern or loyalty to the oppressor, etc.). In such cases, exclusion became stark and visible in its arbitrariness, especially to the oppressed themselves.

While the progressive increase in the scope of application of moral norms and predicates was in part dependent upon the insights of the monotheistic religions and Greek rationalism, both of which provide criteria for being a 'man' that abstract from straightforward material predicates and point to capacities and qualities of agency, its fundamental movement would appear to follow the lineaments of the causality of fate, with scope restrictions acting as the dirempting moment. Further, and important, the dynamic movement of this process continued despite, and separately from debates and arguments concerning the grounds of morality. Actual practices of recognition and mis-recognition formed the bedrock of struggle within which no conspicuous distinctions between considerations of justice and considerations of solidarity (empathy or sympathy) were drawn; questions of dignity, integrity and respect (autonomous selves) were indissolubly entwined with considerations of benevolence, concern and care (injurable and vulnerable bodies).[24] This is the history inscribed *within* our moral predicates and norms, the history through which first one, then some, then all were recognized as free. Hence part of the meaning and content of those norms and predicates is bound to their material inscription in that history, their rational force bound to the memory of the violations and sufferings that their restrictive applications wrought and the *prise de conscience* invoked with the overcoming of those restrictions. In this process there is an internal relation between moral insight and moral experience (*Erfahrung*). It is this internal connection that communicative rationality prohibits.

This, of course, is not an argument, but a reminder about a fundamental meaning of moral universalism. Universalism opposes the restriction on the scope of the application of moral predicates and not, fundamentally, their acceptability. Conversely, no matter how grounded, it is scope restrictions that constitute the core of domination and oppression. The history of moral universalism thus coheres with Habermas's own views about the generation of moral intuitions:

We learn what moral, and in particular immoral, action involves *prior* to all philosophizing; it impresses itself upon us no less insistently in feelings of sympathy with the violated integrity of others than in the experience of violation or fear of violation of our own integrity. The inarticulate, socially integrating experiences of considerateness, solidarity, and fairness shape our intuitions and provides us with better instruction about morality than arguments ever could.

(*JA*, 76)

Habermas continues his argument here by insisting, again, that moral theories only oppose other moral theories that tend to alienate us from our better moral intuitions. But in making the moral point of view turn on acceptability to all rather than applicability to all, does not Habermas's theory alienate us from just the intuitions and processes that he announces as constitutive of the moral? And does not his critique of philosophical modernism further read out from moral consideration experiences of violation and fear of violation?

In suggesting that moral universalism turns on the removing of strictures from the application of moral predicates, that this process of the widening scope of application occurs independently of debates about grounding, and that when criteria for acceptability are interpreted procedurally they disable the very intuitions (I would prefer to say: practices and experiences) that make moral progress possible, I am calling into question the way in which Habermas conceives of the relation between discourses of justification and discourses of application. This large issue is the topic of 'Rational transfigurations' in the next chapter (pp. 221–28).

Very quickly now, the critical conception of universality reinforces and complements the substantial conception. Universality is in each case substantive, responsive to the particular requirements of a situation. Which is to say that claims to universality can be understood as having the force of a critical reminder, and hence that the appearance of 'bursting every provinciality asunder' (p. 322) derives from its critical operation. Universality always works against a provincialism, a restriction on the scope of validity claims, an exclusion; that is why the claim is raised, the point of raising it. In being raised in this way the appearance is given out that local restrictions have been surpassed, and hence a real, absolute universality achieved; a universality free from the charge of provincialism. But the force of the claim of universality derives not from its utter universalism, its speaking to the unlimited communication community, but rather from the fact that it acknowledges claims which existing universality suppresses; the new universality reveals past universality to be the non-acknowledgement of implicit claims, the reification of an inessential particularity. What is thus entwined in such a movement is not the real communication community with an ideal one (p. 323); but, as before, the present community with a potential future community.[25]

In order to substantiate a thesis of this kind one would need to point to the variety of 'provincialisms' against which universality claims have been raised, for example, religious authority in early modern science; restrictions of class, gender, race, and so on in political life; restrictedly meaning- or participant-oriented conceptions of the understanding of social life, and so on. And then continue to reveal how the reification of the universalist critical claim led to difficulties and disasters whose correction involved the acknowledgement of new provincialisms, for example, the local laws of a natural habitat or ecological system, or the role of local and non-rationalized paradigms in scientific research; the claims of particular groups and communities against the bias of neutral equality ('all rights are rights to inequality'); the interpretive perspective from which 'objective' features of social life come into prominence, and so on. This dialectic is quite different from Habermas's dialectic of contexts of justification and contexts of discovery (pp. 323–4); that dialectic looks to the material interests in which validity claims are raised, and leads to ideology critique. The dialectic I am pointing to is not for the purpose of unmasking, however relevant that might be; but for the purpose of revealing the actual material content and local inscription of universalist claims.[26] The temptation to secure universality from the threat of substantiality by making it formal and procedural does not alter the dialectic, but only makes its operation more difficult to detect.

There are grounding difficulties here. But these grounding difficulties, what makes claims whose origin and ground are local *appear* relativistic, turn on worries about atemporal conceptions of truth and rationality – discourse-theoretical idealizations and the unlimited communication community – that philosophical modernism has brought to the fore. It is the problem of this appearance that Adorno has in mind when he states that the nonidentical, the local, the particular, the apparent other of reason itself, 'is opaque only for identity's claim to be total' (*ND*, 163). Habermas's version of proceduralism keeps the others of reason other *to* reason and hence opaque. In so doing, arguably, he squanders his own best insights into the value of communicative reason procedurally understood.

In moral matters, proceduralism, Benhabib's appeal to process, is parasitic upon substantive and critical universalism. Communicative rationality is substantive, a counter to restrictions and silencings in particular contexts and circumstances. Its force is, again, the claim of a radical and participatory democratic polity against the silencing and neutralization of democratic ideals consequent upon the rationalization of the economy together with the cutting of ethical life into public and private spheres that reiterate the trisection of reason. As we saw in Chapter 1, Habermas began his critical career in attempting to demonstrate how the bourgeois norms of personhood, reciprocity, justice and equality expressed in the conception of a juridically constituted state were not mere ideological protections for an exploitive economy, as Marxists were wont to argue. Rather, the force of those norms and ideals was tied to their capacity to protect and nourish a public sphere in which truly public opinions could be formed. Only in the absence of such a sphere do those norms take on ideological colouring, do they become mere ideals, abstract norms whose very abstractness and universality serve to reinforce rather than inhibit or diminish domination and exploitation.[27]

Autonomous public spheres, however, are the voice and the claim of the lifeworld against the demands of system (p. 364). It is not only money and power which cannot buy or compel solidarity and meaning (p. 363); procedural reason philosophically understood cannot obligate solidarity and meaning either. Solidarity and meaning are the claims of the lifeworld, claims which precede whatever mechanisms are deployed in order to *acknowledge* those claims. Autonomous public spheres would be the precipitates of a political love which both felt the suffering of the lifeworld through acknowledging the movement of the causality of fate; and simultaneously took up the standpoint of modernity by allowing us to adopt the perspective of a participant in a radicalized democratic polity whose norms and rights were applicable to all. But this is to say that the claims of the lifeworld, the claims of philosophical modernism (local reason), and the claims of modernity are, in distorted form, the same claim. That the debate between modernity and modernism remains a theoretical or philosophical debate over the fate of reason in modernity represses the absent politics of which both the local reason of philosophical modernism and the universalist reason of philosophical modernity are distorted recognitions.

No reader of *The Philosophical Discourse of Modernity* can fail to be struck by the marginalization of the political in both Habermas and his adversaries. Discussion of politics, the fate of politics, the fate of the public sphere, does not enter centrally into Habermas's discussion of philosophical modernism, but arises only in the context of his analysis of relations between lifeworld and system in the final chapter. This marginalization, this absence of the political *is* the *philosophical* discourse of modernity, not, as it were, wilfully or by avoidance, but fatefully. 'Philosophy, which once seemed obsolete, lives on because the moment to realize it was missed' (*ND*, 3). Living on, which is neither the realization of philosophy nor its overcoming, is the ambiguous state, the aporia, of a philosophy which can neither be itself nor fail to be itself; which sustains itself through its relation to non-philosophy, through, say, its relation to art or sociology; or by being non-philosophy, by attempting to occupy the space of its other, to hold it as its own. The figure of living on falters, however, when it forgets that that is what it is doing, that living on is, perhaps always, the realization and non-realization of philosophy. And we understand both living on and its faltering when we see, in the trisection of reason and the postures of philosophy identifying itself with one of its broken moments, the inscription of an absent politics.

7

LANGUAGE, WORLD-DISCLOSURE AND JUDGMENT

MEANING OR VALIDITY? ROMANTICISM OR LIBERALISM?

At the end of Lecture XI of his *The Philosophical Discourse of Modernity*, entitled 'An alternative way out of the philosophy of the subject: communicative versus subject-centered reason', Jürgen Habermas presents an 'Excursus' on Cornelius Castoriadis's *The Imaginary Institution of Society*. Lecture XI attempts an exposition of the thesis that the proper object of critique of modernity is not reason as identified by the philosophical discourses of modernity, that is, reason in terms of logocentrism (Derrida) or the metaphysics of presence (Heidegger) or Platonism (Nietzsche) or instrumental reason (Adorno and Horkheimer), but is rather subject-centred reason. By taking subject-centred reason as the whole of reason the practitioners of totalizing critique deprive their critiques of modernity of any possible rational foundation; worse, because their critiques are totalizing they recoil upon themselves, vitiating the very terms in which their critiques are articulated.

Subject-centred reason is the reason and rationality of the transcendental subject; it is the reflexive reason of the philosophies of consciousness of Kant, Fichte and Hegel. Habermas's philosophical wager is that the cognitive achievements of these universalistic philosophies can be preserved, and their deficiences overcome, if those achievements are translated into the theoretical language of intersubjectivity and communicative action. Habermas's theoretical procedure for analysing modernity in this way, and the theoretical gains which follow from the adoption of this procedure, are threefold. Firstly, he can sociologically explain the deformations of reason and society in modernity through a unified analysis of the illegitimate extension of subject-centred reason into an intersubjectively constituted lifeworld. Such an extension involves, on the one hand, a weakening of the requirements for social integration in favour of the demands for system integration; and on the other, a concomitant displacement of communicative, intersubjective rationality by instrumental rationality. Together these effects of societal rationalization engender a tendential 'de-worlding' (*PDM*, 350) of the lifeworld. Secondly, Habermas can nonetheless sustain the claims of universalistic reason by demonstrating that not only is subject-centred reason a product of division and usurpation whereby a subordinated moment assumes the place of the whole without the power to assimilate the structure of the whole; but that, further,

> the communicative potential of reason had to be released in the patterns of modern lifeworlds before the unfettered imperatives of the economic and administrative subsystems could react back on the vulnerable practice of everyday life and could thereby promote the cognitive-instrumental dimension to domination over the suppressed moments of practical reason.
>
> (*PDM*, 315)

Finally, then, with these analyses in place, Habermas's critique of modernity can be seen as sustained by the normative authority of communicative rationality, understood as the presupposed norm requiring responsible participants in interaction to orient themselves to validity claims geared to inter-subjective recognition.

Both in Lecture XI (*PDM*, 318–21) and in the 'Excursus' following it, Habermas takes Castoriadis's development of the philosophy of praxis as the version of it most deserving of independent discussion. This is not surprising since it is sufficiently close to the philosophical discourse of modernity under attack while, at the same time, participating in the linguistic turn away from the philosophy of consciousness that Habermas himself promotes to make it a particularly unique challenge to Habermas's dissolution of praxis into communicative action.[1] The precise character of this challenge will be examined below. Nonetheless, there is a fairly explicit set of reasons why it is appropriate for me to consider Castoriadis's challenge to Habermas's theory at this juncture. Firstly, a central argument of Chapter 1 turned on the refutation of the idea that an adequate conception of human praxis required a theoretical grounding in virtue of which the potentialities of the present could be unlocked in a manner that provided a transparent projection of the present into the future. A politics of fulfilment of this sort displaced creative or transfigurative praxis with a philosophy of history in which human praxis repeats an unfolding historical logic. While the detachment of praxis from theory was certainly a suppressed element in Georg Lukács's philosophy of praxis, there can be little doubt that it has been Castoriadis's singular ambition and achievement to separate out Marx's implicit theory of praxis from his theory of history.

Secondly, a persistent element in my critique of Habermas has been the attempt to free the transfigurative dimension of human activity from any form of transcendental grounding, including the quasi-transcendental claims of the ideal speech situation. Here too Castoriadis's work has led the way, consistently urging that human creations make possible the more mundane rational practices of speaking and doing. For Castoriadis, it is not intersubjectivity and communicative rationality that have been suppressed by traditional theory,

198

what Habermas labels subject-centred reason or the philosophy of consciousness, but the creative dimension of human action. Stating the matter this way
is too sharp but still illuminating: if you believe that the problem of modernity,
the incompleted project of the Enlightenment, is the problem of justice, then
you might consider an intersubjective turn toward grounding human interactions in reciprocity and mutuality the most important. This is one road out
of Marx, where the phenomena of domination, exploitation and the like are
the most salient. If however, with Nietzsche and Heidegger, you believe that
alienation, loss of meaning, demotivation, and the like are the really trouble-
some phenomena of our time, then a project that explicates these in terms of a
suppressed creative dimension to human activity will appear the most salient.
It is even tempting to consider the justice road as yielding a liberal Marxism
and the nihilism road as yielding a romantic Marxism.[2] So Johann Arnason
has defined romanticism as 'the defence of meaningfulness against subsumption under the meaning-destroying mechanisms of an Enlightenment geared
towards the expansion and rationalization of power and embodied in the
reified economic and political structures of the modern world'.[3]

Retrospectively, we can now identify the main thesis of the last three
chapters as stating that, despite himself, in his conception of an unlimited
communication community and the associated principles U and D, Habermas
is contributing to and underwriting the meaning-destroying mechanisms of
the Enlightenment – that is the consequence of letting considerations of
validity trump questions of meaning. Further, Habermas appears to be aware
that this is the case: 'The horizons of our life histories and forms of life, in
which we always already find ourselves, form a porous whole of familiarities
that are prereflexively present but retreat in the face of reflexive incursions'
(JA, 16). The question Habermas side-steps is whether reflexive incursions
are essentially destructive of meaning in its substantive sense, or whether only
a certain form of reflection, one set within a trisection of reason and pursued
in accordance with only procedural norms as reliable, entails that consequence. Because Habermas does not see the difference between these two
possibilities, he assumes that with the arrival of reflexive modernity ideas of
substantive meaning must give way to rational consensus over validity claims.
In this he assumes too much.

As we saw previously in the discussion of Mead on conventions, Enlightenment modernity is a reflexive incursion into the lifeworld that alters norms
into cases of problematic justice or 'social norms' into 'possibilities for regulation that can be accepted as valid or rejected as invalid' (MCCA, 126). The difference between an accustomed social norm and a regulation is just the
difference between pre-reflexive cognition and formal rule, with the movement from the former to the latter marking a shift from intersubjective
performance to a monological engagement with an abstract entity, even if
communicatively validated. The process of validation may determine how we
regard the abstract rule (as just or unjust), but makes no difference to the fact

that the procedure itself alters its form. While this alteration in the form of social norms has certainly occurred, the neo-Durkheimian analysis denied that cultural reflexivity itself is sufficient to explain it. On the contrary, it is rather the shift from a cognitive conception of social integration to one based on will-formation through rational consensus that explicates the drying up or dissolution of substantive social meaning. But the model of will-formation and consensus, it was argued, presupposes and corresponds to an image of self-interested individualism where only agreements that accord with individual interests can unite us. For the neo-Durkheimian, this image is itself a complex cognition of our ethical life. In order to support the cognitive conception of social integration, what is required is a cognitive moment distinct from communicative interactions. The idea of linguistic world-disclosure is precisely such a form of cognition.

As my handling of the separation of moral discourse from evaluative discourse in Chapter 4 also attempted to show, it is a mistake to believe that we can satisfactorily prise apart justice from meaning. In this respect the debate between Habermas and Castoriadis is partial, as if we need to and can choose between solving one problem or the other but not both. Nonetheless, there is a heuristic purpose served in taking the Habermas–Castoriadis debate literally: it permits us to focus on the items mentioned in the title of this chapter in their own right, and thus to become a little clearer about the possibilities of rational critique. After rehearsing the basic elements of the debate, I shall turn toward an elucidation of its central features: the role of meaning-creation in relation to questions of justification and application, and the rationality of practices that partake of extensions to meaning. In considering the problem of the status of world-disclosure, I will take up Habermas's critique of that idea in an essay of Charles Taylor's; in tackling the problem of the rational extension of meaning I will focus on Habermas's late acceptance of the idea of a separate discourse of application for moral norms. I shall have to leave to another occasion the answer to the question of how Castoriadis's and Adorno's romantic critiques of modernity can be fused. Both critiques point to the same negative phenomenon – broadly: rationality as subsumption or the reduction to identity – but their positive emphases are quite distinct. Adorno looks to a domain of particular truths, and so of difference and contingency, beyond standard propositional truth, while Castoriadis looks to the creation of new horizons of meaning, and hence some version of truth as disclosure. Adorno, we might say, asks after the possibility of truth without subsuming particulars under universals, while Castoriadis asks after the possibility of creating the universals under which we do our subsuming. Adorno's emphasis is intransigently micrological, while Castoriadis's is adamantly macrological. Since their negative theses draw on the same sources, it can be hypothesized that truth as nonidentity and truth as disclosure can converge. Nothing said here, however, demonstrates that belief.

Let me begin with the central elements of Habermas's critique of

200

Castoriadis. Unsurprisingly, Habermas's fundamental objection to Castoriadis's position is that it lacks a normative foundation; more precisely, his fundamental ontology leaves no room 'for an intersubjective praxis for which socialized individuals are *accountable*' (*PDM*, 330). Typically, Habermas modulates this criticism through a variety of registers oriented by his own conception of communicative action and rationality.

Habermas's first line of criticism suggests that Castoriadis's emphasis on ontological novelty, on the production of new forms, allows for only a 'rhetorical difference' between his 'voluntaristic' conception of 'institution' and Heidegger's fatalistic conception of new epochs as 'dispensations' of Being (*PDM*, 318). Habermas concedes that Castoriadis intends the revolutionary project to be a self-consciously intended practice of autonomous and self-realizing individuals; and further, that this practice is to be done out of and for the sake of autonomy, without the historically unavoidable pretence of pre-modern societies that hid their origin in imaginary significations beneath extra-societal projections, for example, the God of the Christians and Jews. (Needless to say, at this juncture there are no grounds available to distinguish Castoriadis's analysis of pre-modern societies from Durkheim's.) Even granting these points, Habermas denies that on Castoriadis's account we have any rational *grounds* for undertaking the revolutionary project other than the existential resolve: 'because we will it'. But Castoriadis's 'we' cannot rationally will its own self-transformation since it is itself an 'instituted' product of the social imaginary. Hence the production of new social forms is as rationally uncontrolled and ungrounded as the dispensations of Being, and Castoriadis's gestures toward autonomy are self-cancelling; all that remain are the historically mutating forms of social imaginary significations themselves.

Habermas identifies the reason for this lapse of praxis into forms more consonant with Heideggerian dispensations of Being as necessitated by Castoriadis's philosophy of language's inability to sustain a viable distinction between meaning and validity (*PDM*, 331). However much Castoriadis insists upon the unsurpassability of identitarian-ensemblist thinking, what Adorno would call simply identity thinking, in everyday speech and action, in *legein* and *teukhein*, that level of activity is always conditioned and instituted by the social imaginary significations of the society in question as a whole, significations that make it the very society it is. And this does entail that for Castoriadis there is a tight inner connection between the horizons of meaning for social practice as a whole on the one hand, and the quite concrete practices and accomplishments of everyday speaking and doing on the other. As a consequence, Castoriadis is committed to upholding a discontinuist account of socio-historical change. Habermas reads off this conclusion a very strong incommensurability thesis between socio-historical formations, such that 'intramundane praxis cannot get learning processes going' (*PDM*, 331), even in the domains of the natural sciences and the forces of production. If social formations possess constitutive horizons of meaning, each society a 'paradigm' as it were of what a society can be, then how can we 'learn' from history? What would count as historical learning on this account? I take this question to be directly analogous with rationalist responses to the philosophies of science of Kuhn and Lakatos.

For Habermas the fact that the social imaginary significations institute the horizons for intelligibility in general entails that the question as to why 'this' set of significations should be chosen in opposition to any others is unanswerable; indeed, it is a question that for Castoriadis is incapable of even being properly framed and asked. But, Habermas continues, this has the consequence of reversing the direction of Castoriadis's analysis. He 'can no longer conceive of autonomous action as intramundane praxis; instead, Castoriadis has to assimilate it to the language-creating, world-projecting, world-devouring praxis of the social demiurge itself' (*PDM*, 332). If the finitude of praxis is traceable to resistant nature and the constraints of local horizons of meaning, then that which brings the horizons of meaning into being is not finite, not intramundane, and not therefore truly socio-historical in character.

This result leads to a refined reiteration of the question of Castoriadis's 'we'. Through the assimilation of intramundane praxis to linguistic world-disclosure Castoriadis loses the capacity to localize the political struggle for an autonomous way of life; and this because, again, there is no meaning to the local apart from its installation within the social imaginary significations of society as a whole. Hence, either Castoriadis follows the path of the young Heidegger and takes revolutionary praxis as the call releasing subjects from their lostness and entanglement in their everyday *legein* and *teukhein*, what the early Heidegger identified as the they-self and the later Heidegger as the call of the essence of technology, into 'the primordial happening of a self-instituting society' (*PDM*, 333), a happening that is, as a happening, heteronomous. Or autonomy is salvaged, not for any individual agents, but only for the 'absolute ego', the world-disclosing social demiurge itself.[4]

Structurally, Habermas's criticism works to position Castoriadis between the Scylla of the Heideggerian happening of the event of disclosure, thereby squandering human autonomy; and the Charybdis of a Fichtean absolute ego that returns praxis to a speculative philosophy of consciousness. Only communicative rationality itself can steer a clear path between these alternatives.

COMMUNICATIVE REASON AS INHERITED THOUGHT

Because Habermas positions Castoriadis in a manner that makes the theory of communicative rationality the only plausible alternative, a defence of Castoriadis can but begin with a counter-critique. Nor is this step avoidable since the persuasiveness of Habermas's argument depends upon assumptions and positions which are the direct critical objects of Castoriadis's programme.

Unlike Habermas, Castoriadis is not attempting to provide a *theory* of social reality, a theory in principle capable of guiding social praxis. Castoriadis terms the form of theoretical activity in which he engages 'elucidation'. Elucidation is the piecemeal work of clarifying from *within* history an understanding of what being in history means. Elucidation possesses neither a grounding origin nor a determinate telos; its activity is consonant with the fluctuating and indeterminate work of history itself. Elucidation seeks lucidity about our situation, a situation that is misrecognized because of the sway of the claims of theory throughout history. Elucidation is the historically conditioned response to the intransigence of our predicament when surveyed against the background of inherited thought: 'Our project of elucidating past forms of humanity's existence takes on its full sense only as a moment of the project of elucidating our existence, which, in its turn, is inseparable from our current *doing*' (*IIS*, 164).

Lucidity is equivalent to neither transparency nor mastery. On the contrary, according to Castoriadis it is inherited thought, what Heidegger conceived of as the metaphysics of presence, that seeks transparency and mastery. However, although the desire for transparency and mastery are consequences of the constitutive presupposition governing inherited thought, they are not identical with that presupposition. Rather, it is the drive for determinacy that forms the primal impulse of inherited thought and ontology: to be means to be determined and determinate: self-identical. Of course, indeterminacy is a recurring fact of historical existence; but that is why determinacy comes to be identified either with the telos of history, the end of history as a resolution of the internal antagonisms that have driven history forward; or with the formal categories, procedures or methodologies that measure, cognitively or normatively, the contingencies of empirical life and practice while remaining distinct from it. Indeterminacy is the Castoriadian thought. His theory of social imaginary significations is for the sake of thinking, elucidating, that thought.

Lucidity is the form of cognitive accountability appropriate to subjects whose thinking is entwined with doing, whose thinking is an endlessly reiterated moment within social doing. It is the form of thinking that acknowledges indeterminacy. Like *phronesis*, of which it is clearly a historicized variant, elucidation, and its contextualized goal – lucidity, is an intellectual virtue that is also an ethical virtue; it operates without first principles, and it is unable to justify its results in accordance with determinate norms. While for Aristotle *phronesis* was the form of intellection appropriate to ethical life only, when ethical life comes to be recognized as the only life there is, then a variant of *phronesis* must come to be acknowledged as all that philosophy, theory, can be. Castoriadian elucidation is such an acknowledgement.

Habermas's austerely posed either/or to Castoriadis – either participation in the heteronomous happening of the event of institution of the social imaginary or the autonomous positing of a social demiurge – repeats exactly the either/or of inherited thought that refuses indeterminacy. What is shared by the Hegelian thought of absolute knowledge (= autonomy) and Gorgias's claim for absolute non-knowledge (= heteronomy) is the premise of complete determinability. For Hegel this premise is satisfied, while for Gorgias it is forever unsatisfied (*IIS*, 176). The measure and power of Habermas's either/or is the measure and power of inherited thought: the presupposition of determinacy.

Determinacy is overtly implied, within a fallibilistic context and as, perhaps, only a regulative ideal, by the obligatory normativity of communicative rationality itself. That normativity is provided with a quasi-transcendental status by Habermas through demonstrations that, relying on the results of the quasi-empirical reconstructive sciences of cognitive psychology, genetic epistemology and generative linguistics, reveal communicative rationality as the product of the rational reconstruction of the anonymous rule systems or deep structures underlying cognition and action. Moreover, Habermas conceives the criteria of communicative rationality to be the consequences of a non-reversible or developmental process of social learning or evolution whose compelling logic is underwritten by those same reconstructive sciences – sciences whose quasi-empirical work is the heir to the work of transcendental reflection.

Habermas's conception of the ideal speech situation stipulates the criteria, presupposed in, and therefore binding for, all actual communicative exchanges, in accordance with which validity claims concerning truth, truthfulness and moral rightness can be raised and argumentatively assessed. The goal of the exercise is uncoerced, and therefore rational, agreement. Agreement through rational argumentation thereby becomes the new conception of determinate truth. What makes this ideal of determinacy possible is Habermas's weak prising apart of validity and meaning. Validity now comes to refer to the procedural norms governing the argumentative assessment of claims raised within the three validity domains or 'worlds' (*PDM*, 313) of truth, truthfulness and moral rightness. The categorial separation of these three worlds, each now regulated by the norms of communicative rationality, isolates validity from the meaning-horizon of world-disclosure, thereby licensing the possibility of intramundane learning processes that are relatively autonomous from macroscopic socio-historical change.

Looking at Habermas's project from the perspective of the social imaginary, his account appears as an attempt to immunize reason against the fatalities of history, from the indeterminacy and lack of grounds that make history history and not an anonymous unfolding of a developmental logic that itself represses human doing and attempts to offer to reason a status safe from the claims of praxis. In fine, communicative rationality, and the developmental history underwriting its authority, is but another avatar of inherited thought, another projection of instituting praxis into a formal world outside the flux of history.

In saying this we are not just counterpointing Castoriadis to Habermas.

Rather, the positioning of Habermas within inherited thought, within theory, directs attention to the most vulnerable aspect of Habermas's project. Having separated out the three validity domains of truth, truthfulness and moral rightness, making each answerable to the procedural claims of communicative rationality, Habermas is left with the question of how these three domains are to be harmonized and re-articulated: what would make *a* world of the disparate truths emanating from the three worlds in which validity claims arise? Habermas sees the question here – 'In place of false consciousness there today appears a fragmented consciousness which, thanks to the mechanism of reification, is prevented from achieving enlightenment' (*TCA*, II, 342) – but fails to acknowledge the way in which his trisection of reason underlines and reifies the very fragmentation against which he is protesting.

When Habermas does confront the issue of fragmentation he necessarily has recourse to a holistic perspective.

> It would be senseless to want to judge such a conglomeration as a whole, *the totality of a form of life*, under individual aspects of rationality. If we do not want altogether to relinquish standards by which a form of life might be judged to be more or less failed, deformed, unhappy, or alienated, we can look if need be to the model of sickness and health. . . . Perhaps we should talk instead of a balance among non-self-sufficient moments, an equilibrated interplay of the cognitive with the moral and the aesthetic-rational. But the attempt to provide an equivalent for what was once intended by the idea of the good life should not mislead us into deriving this idea from the formal concept of reason which modernity's decentered understanding of the world has left us.
>
> (*TCA*, I, 73–4)

Communicative rationality provides for the whole span of human activity the equivalent of a conception of 'right'. But no account of the right can operate in independence from a matching conception of the good. Procedural rightness is only ever a sedimented and disguised presentation of a substantial conception of the good, that is, a sedimented and disguised set of social imaginary significations.[5] In Chapter 4, I suggested that the notion of democratic citizenship was one such imaginary signification for us. Now at the precise moment that Habermas perceives the overlap between the fragmentation of modernity he wishes to overcome and the trisection of rationality he wishes to support he must separate himself from liberal social imaginary significations and proleptically hint at an alternative set. These he specifies in terms of, first, sickness and health; only then to suggest the holistic model of harmony and integration derived from aesthetic rationality. At the moment when the problem of modernity as a whole is raised and the thought of an alternative to it is broached, Habermas's weak distinction between meaning and validity must give way to an account of an alternative entwinement. If Castoriadis is right, he could hardly do otherwise.

As commentators on Habermas have been quick to note, when the issue of a holistic perspective does come to the fore so does the treatment and placing of art and aesthetic rationality.[6] Aesthetic reflective judgment, we might say, represents just the sort of reflection which could supplement rational argumentation by providing the excess of meanings that would allow fragmentation to be perceived as fragmentation, and new syntheses of domains of activity projected. Habermas himself acknowledges that 'the potency to create meaning, which in our day has largely retreated into aesthetic precincts, retains the contingency of genuinely innovative forces' (*PDM*, 321). Because philosophy is a cognitive discipline, it must remain remote from these meaning-creating practices. But then the question arises, how can philosophy *interpret* these innovations and offer them to the lifeworld if neither innovation nor interpretation are themselves fundamentally *cognitive* (truth bearing or goodness disclosing) activities? Bizarrely, Habermas sees no connection between this retreat of the creation of meaning into aesthetic precincts, the privatization of meaning creation, and his own weak prising apart of validity and meaning. For him art becomes the repository of new meanings and new forms that can be channelled into the lifeworld and then validated through argumentative procedures. This involves a compromise formation whereby what is to suture the wounds of social fragmentation gets legitimated, validated, through the fragmented forms of reason that insulate modernity against meaning in this elaborated sense. Castoriadis's project, alternatively, looks to the productive imagination as what has always been displaced by its own products. Within secularized modernity that displacement takes the form of the restriction of the production of new meanings to an autonomous domain: institutionally the art world, and formally aesthetic rationality.

If there are 'truths' in artistic productions, then they are truths only to the degree to which they exceed the confines of the art world and aesthetic criticism, that is, to the degree to which they illuminate social experience. As one of Habermas's ablest defenders, Albrecht Wellmer, has put the point: artistic truths (metaphorically? illusorily?) interlace truth, truthfulness and moral rightness which are at the same time objects of 'lifeworld experience in which the three validity domains are unmetaphorically intermeshed'.[7] This intermeshing reveals two things: firstly, that the three validity domains are abstractions from a lifeworld whose reality denies and defies their separation; and secondly, that it is only truths exceeding the rationalized spheres of validity that can inform the lifeworld as a world. What makes the lifeworld a world, and not a mere cluster of disjointed practices, is the articulating work of social imaginary significations. Under capital those significations generate the unity of non-unity, the unity of fragmented and autonomized spheres of activity (*IIS*, 115ff.).

CREATION, WORLD-DISCLOSURE AND JUSTIFICATION

If our counter-critique of Habermas has undermined the presuppositions on the basis of which he lodged his critique, it has not, for all that, answered his criticisms of Castoriadis. On the contrary, one might still feel that Habermas's either/or points to or locates the vulnerable nerve of Castoriadis's project. But if the force of Habermas's either/or depends upon the ideal of determinacy, then how is our sense of his specification of the place of difficulty in Castoriadis to be understood?

The answer to this question depends upon our comprehending that place of difficulty *as* difficult, as, I want to say, aporetic. Castoriadis's social ontology is an aporetic ontology; it poses the being of the social-historical as neither act nor product, neither instituting nor instituted, but as the continual passage from one to the other without rest or resolution. At its most extreme point, this is to say that we can attempt to think the being of the social-historical *as* instituting praxis – the perspective of agency and autonomy; or *as* instituted – the third person perspective of the always already produced, and so of heteronomy; what we cannot think through or get behind is the *as* itself that is the place of exchange between instituting and instituted. The instituting/instituted *as*, which cannot be got behind, is what forever, so long as there are social doings at all, prescinds reason from determinacy.

Castoriadis marks the double regressive *as* of the social imaginary, that is the fact that the instituting/instituted *as* itself cannot *literally* appear and be determined, in his contention that 'every expression is essentially tropic' (*IIS*, 348). To say this is just to say that there is no literal meaning, and therefore no determinately valid truths, whose sense or truth could not be infringed upon through further determination. But it is also to say that the *as* of the social-historical itself can be elucidated but not determined.

The *as* marks the place of ontological genesis. For Castoriadis each product is a created *eidos*, a new social type; as is each word, practice, institution and society.

> Society establishes itself as a mode and a type of coexistence: as a mode and type of coexistence in general, with no analogue or precedent in another region of being and as *this* particular mode and type of coexistence, the specific creation of the society considered.
>
> (*IIS*, 181)

The enigma, aporia, of auto-production arises because social creation fails to accord with what can be comprehended from the perspective of inherited thought: social creation is neither a part of a natural process of generation and corruption – which would reduce it to heteronomy; nor is it, however, an act of absolute freedom proceeding from a fully self-transparent, self-possessed self-consciousness (absolute ego) – which would make it asocial and ahistorical. In accordance with the dictates of inherited logic and ontology creation, autonomous action can truly occur only once, after which time all else is a conditioned unfolding. Of course, no one actually believes this to be the case, but the demands of identity and determinacy continually press inherited thought in this direction; which explains at least part of the appeal of compatibilist accounts of human freedom.

It is because ontological genesis is incompatible with the demands of inherited logic and ontology, because social creation 'brings about beings as *eidos*, and as the *ousia* of *eidos*, another manner and another type of being and of being-a-being', it may well be the case that it is, at most, 'recognizable but not thinkable' (*IIS*, 181). Although Castoriadis's descriptions and accounts of societal self-creation often sound as if it proceeded from a social demiurge, an absolute ego, precisely because created forms are without explanatory antecedents, this misidentifies the logic of creation, a logic requiring not transparency or absolute opacity, but indeterminacy. However, if this indeterminacy is pervasive and therefore not a block or obstruction to truth and reason, if elucidation is a form of cognition, then we require a wider comprehension of the cognitive domain, one which can acknowledge the whole range of human innovative practices as having cognitive reach, where cognitive reach itself had better mean: within the bounds of reason. In order to move ahead on this topic, we need to leave Castoriadis behind.

Habermas now concedes that there is an essential place for the activity of interpretation within philosophy, namely, mediating between the different validity spheres for the sake of lifeworld interactions in which those spheres are non-metaphorically woven together (*MCCA*, 18–19). Yet, at the very moment he raises the possibility of philosophical interpretation, he immediately takes the rational core of those interactions to be their raising of validity claims procedurally capable of being grounded and justified within, again, the three separate spheres (*MCCA*, 19–20). Interpretation thus gets pressed aside almost as soon as it enters the picture. Why? At least in part because he believes the line must be drawn between what we believe here and now, what is acceptable to us, and what can be justified as a valid claim. On the side of the here and now we find forces of habit and convention, on the side of justification we find the force of better reasons. But this is as much as to say that *rationality belongs solely to the discourses of justification* which themselves now reside primarily within the three validity spheres. Although, then, Habermas grants that there exist ethical discourses and discourses of application (of norms), these are only discourses in a honorific or metaphorical sense since without the idealizing assumptions governing justificatory discourses proper they cannot really attain to full cognitivity. How, Habermas might ask, can a practice be cognitive and rational if there is no reasonable hope for convergence and consensus? Since there is no such hope in ethical discourse and discourses of application, then a fortiori those discourses are not fully rational.

In order that what follows is not misunderstood, let me recall some theses already forwarded. Firstly, strong idealizing procedures are applicable to

208

truths concerning the natural world because it is constituted as indifferent to human ideals and concerns. Because strong idealizing assumptions are tied to nature's indifference to human mattering, they are inapplicable in ethics and morals. In questions of ethics and morals, therefore, discourses appeal to our community as it is extended in space and time, but not beyond. Our idealizations are here, so to speak, substantive and weak rather than formal and strong. Secondly, the rational core of universalist claims in morals is not procedural, but is rather equivalent to the recognition that ethical predicates cannot rationally be restricted in the scope of their application by reference to race, colour, creed, sex or, we might add, property ownership. It has been these and like scope restrictions that formed the direct grounds for most institutionally reproduced forms of domination, and it has been struggles for recognition that have raised innovative claims in relation to existing ethical identities that has led to the removal of such restrictions. Thirdly, we sustain that universalistic moment in political life through the promotion of the idea of civic citizenship and democratic practice, which practice itself can plausibly be regarded as having as one of its ethical ideals the procedures implicit in the ideal speech situation. The procedural moment of democratic will-formation tracks our commitment to the ethical ideals of civic citizenship. In making these three points, the suggestion is that the more contextualist approach to rationality and cognition that follows need not be deaf to idealizations concerning truth, universalism in morals or the rationality of procedures. It is the unrestricted concatenation of these in the idea of Enlightenment rationality that is objected to.

In the way that Habermas offers priority to justificatory discourse I hear the old positivist contention that there can be no logic of creation or discovery, and therefore only practices of justification can be fully cognitive and rational. It is prescinding from practices that themselves extend our existing conceptual framework title to rationality and cognitivity that grounds Habermas's exclusion of interpretative discourses from being full and equal citizens with justificatory discourses in the domain of reason. In order to demonstrate the illegitimacy of this exclusion, two things need to be shown: (i) that we must conceive of innovative discourses as themselves rationally governed; and (ii) that the best characterization of the difference Habermas sees between justificatory and other discourses is not in terms of an absolute difference in kind but a difference in degree with respect to the ease or difficulty of there being convergence and consensus. (I take this ease or difficulty to map onto the continuum I noted in Chapter 3 between discovery and creation.) Just as Habermas admits that not all truths are subject to deductive demonstration and justification, so it is with some truths that they cannot be justified in accordance with the strong idealizing assumptions of communicative reason. This should not impugn their rationality. Aristotle's statement in the *Nicomachean Ethics* (1094b, 12ff.) that we should only look for as much precision in each class of things just so far as the nature of the subject permits applies with equal force to the question of justification (which in fact is what Aristotle's notion of precision is referring to). For Habermas, the strong idealizing assumptions of the unlimited communication community, his procedural turn, has taken over from classical deductive requirements as the moment of unconditionality that distinguishes justificatory discourse from all else. But the replacement of one paradigm with strong idealizing assumptions (perfect deductive demonstratability) with another equally strong does not depart from the presumption of a uniform criterion of rationality irrespective of its object. Compare Aristotle's thought that in some cases we must be content with 'speaking about things which are only for the most part true and with premises of the same kind to reach conclusions that are no better' with Habermas's: 'Grounds have a special property: they force us into yes or no positions. Thus, built into the structure of action oriented to reaching an understanding is an element of unconditionality' (*MCCA*, 19). The *force* of grounds (what better reasons show) is thus interpreted as unconditional, and this unconditionality is then turned back onto reason as criterial for it.

In order to unpick this claim we need to begin with the model of truth-only cognition as employed in the natural sciences. Again, if we interpret the natural world as subject transcendent, then the creation of theories must be bracketed as relevant to their rationality since the goal of science is to withdraw the projection of the figure of the human onto the natural world. Because what we want from science is a conception of a nature as it *is* (because we regard it as a timeless object), then the *becoming* of the conceptual framework of natural science is only of interest to the degree to which it fosters or prohibits that end. Reason here tracks the unconditionality of its object. Viewed from the perspective of truth-only cognition, creation is reduced to being a psychological prelude to cognition proper – the making of bold conjectures: only the logic of justification, the logic guiding the evaluation of existing theories against the facts, is amenable to cognitive handling, while the logic of discovery, the creation of ideas or theories, belongs to the arational background against which scientific thought emerges. Regarding creation as being of only psychological significance directly entails all the central elements which distinguish the grammar of truth-only cognition from the grammar of interpretation while handing priority over to the former.

If the activity of creation is withdrawn from consideration, then in each case types or universals (i.e., scientific theories) will come to be regarded as logically prior to tokens or particulars. It is this priority which leads to the joint beliefs that truth is timeless or non-historical, and that being true involves a correspondence with always already given facts. The dark question left unanswered by these two beliefs is: independently of the created item, what explains the accessibility of facts to cognitive inspection? If the accessibility of facts to cognitive inspection only becomes available through created items, then either cognitive space is made possible by what is itself non-cognitive, entailing scepticism, or created items are themselves cognitive. Backing for the sceptical limb of this either/or will begin from the assumption that the object of natural science is posited as subject transcendent. By definition then, it exists outside the circle of reasons. If the process of creating new theories to account for past failure is also posited as outside the circle of reasons, then the circle of reasons itself is plunged into darkness at both ends. If reasoning to novel ideas lacks rational governance, then their retrospective vindication is indefinitely subject to the charge of mere rationalization. Our tendency to be sanguine about this in the case of natural science derives from a combination of two sources: firstly, we have sufficient internal criteria for progress (problem solving, discovery of new entities, etc.), and secondly, since the object is posited as subject transcendent, the demand for convergence and consensus will remain whatever theories are proposed.

These two features of natural science make the debate between realism and anti-realism with respect to natural science irresolvable, both views possessing the strength of a corrective. The realist reminding us that truth here must remain subject transcendent, the anti-realist reminding us that subject-transcendent truth can only be pursued within a human practice with internal criteria for progress and learning. If, as argued in Chapter 3, human beings are self-interpreting creatures, then both sets of constraints that operate in relation to natural science drop away and the full sceptical force of submerging interpretation in the darkness of psychological life emerges. In order to maintain the non-sceptical limb of the either/or one must depart from the correspondence theory of truth since the relevant facts only become available through what is created. The notion of truth at issue here is that of truth as disclosure.

Through the history of artistic modernism, we have become accustomed to the thought that art cannot be defined in a priori terms, that there is no general essence or universal which can define what it is for a thing to be a work of art. Rather, what art *is*, what music or painting or literature *is*, is reconfigured and disclosed through artistic practice, through what art *becomes*. Artistic performance, so to speak, the token, brings into being and reveals the essence. Once we come to acknowledge this logic, it can be applied to the natural sciences – scientific paradigms disclose what nature is or means – without that disclosive moment entailing that natural science merely imposes a human grid on the natural world; the combination of what we have come to understand as the object of science and our tailoring of the methods of science to that understanding *keep* the object from being unconditionally reduced. What science discloses nature to be generates the idealizations that keep the temporal movement of science oriented toward it.

Both the force and the content of the argumentative methodologies operative in the natural sciences are dependent upon recognition of the disclosure of the natural world as subject transcendent. Without this conception of the natural world – already implicitly operative in pre-modern cosmologies, thus driving them beyond themselves – neither the unconditionality of

211

propositional claims nor the necessity for taking a yes or no stance toward such claims would be intelligible. It is in virtue of the disclosed meaning of the natural domain, including the disclosing of it as natural (subject to natural laws) and not social (subject to reason and meaning), that a certain type of validity claim comes into being as appropriate.

The idea of a yes or no stance to validity claims only makes sense if the object itself is conceived to be utterly determinate. If an object is so conceived, then it makes sense to claim that a truth claim is unconditional. But what if the object cannot be conceived to be determinate in this way? In order to examine this possibility, let me briefly turn to Kant's analysis of the work of art which focuses on the idea of creation, activity that is productive rather than merely reproductive. This will anticipate some of what will need to be said about both the notion of truth as disclosure and the problem of judgment. Since art works are for Habermas paradigms of disclosure truth, then this analysis is apt here.

An original work of art must, by definition, make original sense as opposed to original non-sense. To make original sense it must distort, deform, or destroy existent rules governing what is and what is not intelligible, what is or what is not a work of art, for example. Rule breaking, at some level, is a constitutive moment of the process of creation. But how are we to distinguish original sense from original non-sense, since not every breaking of rules institutes new meaning? Kant contends that original works are *exemplary*. An exemplar is not an example, for examples are examples of already existing types. Exemplars are original models; what makes works exemplary, however, has nothing to do with the clarity and/or distinctness or the ideas (intentions) of their producers. A work is exemplary only if it can serve as a model for succession. But that a work can serve as a model for succession, that we can 'go on' with the practice in accordance with the new exemplar, is never demonstrable except through succession itself. Products of genius are items for which no rule can be given but which nonetheless themselves serve 'as a standard or rule for estimating'.[8] When modern artists became aware of this fact, when they became aware that succession was the litmus test for exemplarity, they began self-consciously to produce series of works, series whose point was to reveal the new painterly *eidos* as informing its multiple possible exemplifications.

Although art works are somewhat radical cases for innovative practice, especially when novelty or originality is sought after for its own sake, taking account of the logic of exemplarity will prove helpful. A work makes a claim to validity: to be beautiful or simply a work of art. Rather than focusing on the argumentative discourse that might be used to vindicate or refute that claim, Kant focuses on the distinctive feature of an innovative claim, namely, that it outruns the terms of reference which had constituted the domain in which it appears. The work means to transfigure that domain. But a domain can only be transfigured in this way if the necessarily indeterminate instance represented by the exemplary item projects itself into a possible future. The test of the disclosure is being able to continue with the practice in accordance with the exemplary item, being able to map a path forwards and backwards between the exemplary item and what follows it.

If this is the correct way to conceive of radically innovative claims, then they are not unconditional and do not require us to take a yes or no stance. Or better: a yes or no stance with respect to an innovative claim is pointless, whatever artists or critics might think. Their 'truth' is that of an indeterminate possibility, of conceiving of the practice continuing on differently. Despite the fact that we conceive of art works as objects of contemplation, and hence consider aesthetic judgments ones that assess them as given entities, if Kant is right it cannot be an unequivocal actuality that is at issue here. The judgment of validity must claim for the actually given that it reveals a possibility. Because the disclosure of a possibility refers to actual future cases, where nothing short of the realization of those cases can (indeterminately) confirm that potentiality, then the validity of the exemplary case is radically conditioned. One way of stating this point would be to say that in such cases possibility remains prior to actuality because they are implicitly *action* oriented. Claims making an essential reference to action are oriented horizontally rather than vertically because they are liable in the face of their future fate. Conversely, if we attempt to imagine a claim which was unconditional for such an item, for example, a judgment of beauty with respect to particular work is true if and only if the work corresponds to the Platonic idea of beauty, then the condition for determinacy and unconditionality would equally rule out the thought that the work made a claim to original meaning. Nonetheless, only on the presumption of an atemporal standard against which the judgment of beauty might itself be judged does it make sense to regard the judgment and so the validity of the claim of the work as unconditional.

Part of what is meant by the thesis that meaning is prior to validity and not reducible to it, at least for art works, is that the essential reference of a work is to a possible future, that it reveals a horizon of possibility, and that this possibility is essentially connected to future actions. For this to be intelligible, it must further be the case that even where we construe innovative practices as oriented to some end, that end itself is conceived of as necessarily and thereby essentially indeterminate, and hence what constitutes that end is to be in part constituted by creative praxis.

In response to a paper by Charles Taylor, Habermas has agreed that *The Theory of Communicative Action* unfairly treated the world-disclosing function of language. Habermas elegantly summarizes Taylor's view in these terms:

[He] demonstrates how every language opens up a grammatically pre-structured space, how it permits what is in-the-world to appear there is a certain manner and, at the same time, enables interpersonal relations to be regulated legitimately as well as making possible the spontaneous self-presentation of creative-expressive subjects. 'World disclosure' means for Taylor . . . that language is the constitutive organ not only of thought, but also of both social practice and experience, of the formation of ego and group identities.

(R, 221)

Taylor's point in emphasizing as he does the world-disclosive function of language is to urge upon Habermas a generalization of the thesis I made with respect to natural science: the force and form of human reasoning are bound to an appreciation, recognition or acknowledgement of a disclosed object domain. For Taylor, the very idea of language oriented to reaching an understanding as a normative structure is bound to a substantive perception of how we perceive ourselves in relation to others and how that perception relates to our other purposes:

> I must be able to show why it is I attach value to rational understanding so great that it *should* be preferred to all other purposes. In which case, reaching an understanding comprises one *purpose* among others, one which can lay claim to primacy only owing to a substantialist concept of human life.[9]

Habermas's fundamental objection to Taylor, said in a variety of ways, is that he falls into the philosophy of consciousness by treating 'the whole of language as a *self-referential subject* which holds the living process of language together by means of its synthesizing achievements' rather than perceiving this 'synthesis accomplished solely within those forms taken by the diffracted inter-subjectivity of dialogue' (*R*, 216; emphasis mine). A few pages later, explicitly answering Taylor's charge about rationality, Habermas states that according to the theory of intersubjectivity 'the moments of the universal, the particular and the individual are no longer tied into the ongoing process of *self-relation of a higher level subjectivity*' (*R*, 219; emphasis mine). This is exactly the objection Habermas made against Castoriadis, whether in the form of a social demiurge or the social as a Fichtean absolute ego. Roughly, Habermas makes this objection against any conception of language and so of the 'we' that holds them to have some legitimacy and independence from a consensus rationally formed through argumentative procedures. First-person-plural ascriptions are problematic, and our intuitions with respect to them vary. But what is at issue here is not directly the appropriate uses of 'we', but the relation between the disclosive function of language and speech acts that necessarily raise validity claims subject to procedural criteria for rational argumentation oriented to reaching an understanding. In this light, assertions about a self-referential subject or a social demiurge look distinctly out of place.

However bizarre the characterization of Taylor's (or Humboldt's or Gadamer's or Wittgenstein's) philosophy of language as making reference to a self-referential subject, it is important to see how Habermas is forced into this critical strategy once he has conceded that language does possess a world-

214

disclosing function. The idea of world-disclosure is meant by Taylor to be a characterization of an aspect of language that cannot be subsumed under any of the dimensions of validity raised in communicative acts, including explicitly truth-functional discourse, but must be conceived of as *logically* prior to all of them. On this account world-disclosure (what Adorno and Dummett both call the expressive dimension of language) and communication are coordinate but distinct axes of language. To employ a somewhat artificial locution, it is as if language was designed to answer to two distinct and irreducible purposes: revealing the world and communication. For thinkers who conceive of language in this way there is a dynamic dialectic between the demands of expression, revealing the object, and the demands of communication without the presumption that there is some ideal or harmonic relation between these two demands. The illusion that these two demands can be 'solved' simultaneously, so to speak, is once again dependent upon the only domain which ontologically lays claim to being language independent: the natural world.

In his assessment of this issue, Habermas first states what he takes to be Humboldtian common ground with Taylor: 'The language system makes speech acts possible which, in turn, reproduce the language and in so doing, make innovative changes in it, however imperceptible these may be' (*R*, 216). Only a sentence later, however, Habermas forces onto this model an either/or interpretation which it prima facie prohibits: 'Is the whole of language a self-referential subject which holds the living process of language together by means of its synthesizing achievements – or is this synthesis accomplished solely within those forms taken by the diffracted intersubjectivity of dialogue?' In accordance with the model implicit in the first sentence, both forms of synthesis occur, where linguistic synthesis refers to the idea of semantic fields (the language system) themselves formed, de-formed and re-formed through speech, and the second type of synthesis to the regulation or critical reflection on syntheses of the first type through argumentation. For example, the semantic field of epistemology which was once completely beholden to the idea of correspondence (the mirror) is shifted by the introduction of the romantic idea of disclosive truth (the lamp), irrespective of whether or not we can agree to or justify either model. Hence, in talking about knowledge we are first oriented with respect to it through the semantic field constituting it, and in raising claims about it we are simultaneously attempting to reconfigure and control the semantic potentials sedimented in that field. Communicative actions, on this model, are made possible by the indeterminate horizon(s) disclosed by the language system; in raising and argumentatively resolving particular validity claims, for example, can a novel provide us with knowledge?, they re-order future possibilities by shifting possible relations of inference among the terms in a segment of the system. Which is what Habermas is doing when he converts the both/and of Humboldt's picture (the first sentence) into his either/or. His argumentative ploy is also thus an interpretation of the Humboldtian conception of language, transforming its inference structures. In accordance with

215

the Kantian notion of exemplarity, we might say that Humboldt's philosophy of language is the exemplary item, and that Taylor offers it a both/and interpretation and Habermas an either/or interpretation, and hence that both attempt to realize and provide determinacy for the original idea.

Only against the background of the imposition of Habermas's either/or can what I am calling linguistic synthesis be construed as the work of a self-referential subject. Once we acknowledge that in argumentative discourse we are attempting to reach an agreement through, in part, the reinterpretation of particular semantic fields – which is often the point and the achievement of argument in domains where deductive argument is impossible – Habermas's loaded description of linguistic synthesis begins to look implausible. What Habermas may be referring to through the idea of a self-referential subject is the idea that agreements reached in discourses are not and cannot be determinate for the language system as a whole or even for a significant segment of it. Because the meanings and potentialities of inference available within the language system are indefinitely complex and interlacing, then particular regimentations of this system – consider what I have been saying about the conceiving of nature as subject transcendent – will have unintended and unpredictable consequences for the system as a whole. And some of these consequences can be sufficiently radical as to call into question the original determination of validity no matter how well grounded. In this respect the semantic potentialities of the system always exceed determinate claims. But this consequence is benign once we concede that with respect to all matters social discourse claims are directed at future possibilities of action rather than given actualities. Habermas, I suspect, is uneasy about this because he wishes (or wished) to regard some features of the social as themselves akin to natural objects. For example, he once conceived of the reconstructive sciences in this way. If there is no given and determinate actuality against which validity claims can be judged, at least in principle, then it follows that such claims will have as their primary effect a reorientation or transformation of the system, and hence the system, as meaning, will continue to outrun claims made within it. This does not entail that no learning is possible here, or that learning is arbitrary; it means that what learning amounts to here is not learning about some given domain but learning about how we can, and must, conceive of ourselves and our possibilities for acting. If, for example, we learn that nothing in our actual practice of applying certain predicates depends upon race or colour, if what makes those predicates applicable are features that are race or gender indifferent or rely only on their objects having the capacity for speech or self-determined action or suffering, then we have learned something about what our conceptual scheme and its related practices entail and thus something about ourselves.

The language system is not an utterly self-referential subject because what we do and can conceive of doing matters to the shapes the linguistic system takes; it is like a self-referential subject because there is no determinate object

or end to which the system as a whole is beholden. But this is just a consequence of the fact that we are self-determining beings who lack a determinate end to our collective doings. From our anterior thrownness into the
field of language (which is also our thrownness into the world) it follows that
the first person plural does have a weightier sense for Taylor than for
Habermas, and it is doubtless that weightier sense that encourages Habermas
to construe linguistic synthesis as he does. If our intersubjective exchanges are
made possible by the prior 'agreement' disclosed by shared access to a
language, then a communication between you and me substantively presupposes a 'we': the common space *within* which we communicate. This 'we'
is equivalent to neither the aggregation of the users of a particular language
nor Durkheim's *sui generis* society; both of which uses would be legitimate
targets for Habermas's scepticism. Rather the 'we' perspective is a direct
corollary of disclosive truth in that it simply bespeaks our inability to appropriate to ourselves and dispose of individually (or collectively – Hegel's worry
about the terror of the French Revolution) the semantic fields that give us a
world in the first instance.

When you and I are arguing over some empirical matter, whether or not
there are any cookies in the cookie jar for example, we have already 'agreed',
without ever having come to an agreement, about what 'cookie' and 'jar' and
'being in' mean, about the grammatical use of nouns, probably about what
counts as good evidence for there being cookies in the jar; but these agreements about meaning are equally agreements about cookies and jars, those
very wordly items, themselves. Learning the language and learning what and
how the world is are bound together. To say that we agree about how the
world is or that there is a consensus over the meaning of particular terms
presents the wrong image of how language and world are related. We can
argue about how many cookies are in the jar because our world, the very idea
of us having a world at all, is already populated with cookies and jars with
words designating them.[10]

In some cases our arguments are ambiguous, say in arguing over whether
or not to end our marriage we may be argung about whether or not, as a
matter of fact, one or other of us has failed to live up to what we take for
granted a marriage is; but equally we may disagree over the very idea of
marriage, of what being married and so being a husband or wife and so a man
or woman now means. The vehemence and despair associated with the latter
interpretive argument is enjoined by the realization that future possibilities of
this or another marriage are in part determined by how we resolve or fail to
resolve this argument. The resolution of the argument, if resolved, becomes
exemplary. Thus the argument itself is about possible meanings and their
potentialities for being reinterpreted. Interpretive arguments contest ethical
spaces, attempting to shift patterns of inference and hence belief, even when,
as is the case in our culture, some concepts designate a variety of spaces, as
perhaps there are now a certain variety of ways of being married. Still, in

etching out those spaces we must nonetheless employ somewhere disclosures that will not be contested here and now; and what is not contested here and now is much: all the psychology of love, need, pain, visions of togetherness, the history of marriage, the distinct powers of men and women in this society, and so forth. Those temporary resting places within language are presupposed by every discourse; these are places where I and the other are joined prior to agreeing or disagreeing, and thus where what is said is what 'we' say, not because I or my other arrogate to ourselves authority to speak for the collective, but rather because it has already spoken for us, deposited us here and now in this unhappy place.

But this idea of 'resting places' might give on to the wrong impression. In agreeing that we can and do disagree, and that disagreements can be resolved through argumentation, it does not follow that the fallible remainder of world and language, those resting places, are themselves items to which we have agreed. We cannot bring about, through individual or collective efforts, a coordination of language as such and world as such. There cannot be a world that is not already revealed as meaningful, and hence there cannot be a language that is not itself already a disclosing of that world. The image presented by the pattern of disagreement, argument and resolution thus presents an illusory account of what is involved in language–world coordination. Again, I suspect that what is occurring in Habermas's theory is a generalization from a defective case (the fallibilistic character of lifeworld beliefs). Because there are instances where disagreements can be resolved through mutual consent, it does not follow, and, if our having a world is anything like as intransigent a phenomenon as it appears to be, it cannot follow that having a world is constituted from consent so conceived. It thus becomes difficult to see how Habermas's communication theory does not presuppose, however implicitly, some strong version of there being a fundamental gap between conceptual scheme (language) and world.

Habermas, in objecting to Taylor's understanding of the 'we', is objecting to the logical anteriority of language (as world-disclosing) over communication. In order to do this he must fold the world-disclosive aspect of language into communicative interaction. So he contends that in the relation of an ego and an alter-ego '*the space opens up* for an intersubjectively shared life world'; or, he states that the communication-theoretical concept of society depends upon a conception of a lifeworld 'inhabited in common that *emerges in the course of dialogue*' (*R*, 218; emphases mine). The italicized phrases are Habermas's notion of world disclosure. Could it really be the case that the common emerges in the course of dialogue? That only in the relation of an ego and an alter-ego the space opens up for an intersubjectively shared lifeworld? Of course, unless there were concrete, intersubjective speech acts there would be neither semantic fields nor a disclosed world. That is why speech is one of the two ineliminable dimensions of language. What is being contested is only the thought that the disclosed world in some sense depends on *this* speech act.

Individual speech acts cannot be habitually disclosive in the sense suggested by Habermas's two sentences; particular speech acts *orient* us to an aspect of the world already disclosed, or bring to the foreground what has been up till now in the background, or bring a portion of the experienced world to our attention. The point of demanding space for disclosive truth is that we could not begin to orient ourselves in the world unless there was always already operative a correlation between us and the world in order that our actions could thereby be responsive to what already had meaning and salience for us. Habermas's curious locutions are not arbitrary: only if world-disclosure can be shown to be a direct function of infinitely many, singular communicative actions, each one itself a mini- world-disclosure, can he deny that disclosure or expression is an independent dimension of language and hence subsume truth, rightness, and so on under communicative rationality. Humboldt's original doctrine fully acknowledges the factual dependency of language on its performed repro- duction (say: no langue without parole); Habermas's strong claim, langue is a dimension of parole, leaves us without anything to reproduce.

The assimilation of meaning to validity is what makes the idealizations of communica- tive reason a meaning-destroying mechanism. The meanings destroyed are those that belong to language as system. Habermas's procedural reinscription of the equation of rationality with determinacy (unconditionality and yes or no), although designed for the sake of repairing broken intersubjective relations, restoring them at a higher level, by making the higher-level restoration exclusive vanquishes from experience the legitimacy of intersubjective bonds that are incapable of being rationalized in that way. As we saw in the previous chapter, Habermas needs such bonds, forms of life that would meet communicative rationality halfway, in order for his notion of rationality to matter – which was just what Taylor was originally claiming. If that mattering is not going to be an irrational surd in his account, then the anterior coordination of world and language, and hence lifeworld solidarities, require a legitimacy and 'validity' not derivable from communicative interactions.

It is not here necessary to defend any particular dual-axis conception of language; it is sufficient to demonstrate the implausibility of the assimilation of meaning to communicative validity to show the illegitimacy of the thesis that such conceptions depend upon or invoke a fully self-referential subject. What a dual-axis conception of language does demand is the acknowledge- ment that the needs and purposes of communication, for the sake of the coordination of action, say, must themselves be responsive to the *pull* of the world, with the further acknowledgement that that pull need not be commen- surable with what conduces to communicative agreement. This is not to deny that when interpretive claims are raised we desire or hope that others can and will agree, for the discovery that they cannot agree would turn what I find true or valuable or beautiful into something merely subjective or idiosyncratic. Agreement matters because what is agreed to matters, and matters independ- ently of finding agreement in it.

The reason why strong idealizing assumptions are inappropriate in raising interpretive claims is because in order to heed them, in order to find reasons and justifications open to everyone, I would have to discount my subjectivity, the quite particular alignment between me and the world that is staked in the interpretive claim. Aristotle knew he could not fully justify his ethical claims because he knew that in order to appreciate those claims a particular formation of the self into a virtuous character was necessary in order to hear them. What Stanley Cavell says about the task of the art critic seems to me to hold for all discourses except those concerned with logic and the natural sciences: 'The problem of the critic, as of the artist, is not to discount his subjectivity but to include it; not to overcome it in agreement but to master it in exemplary ways.'[11] Because subjectivity is not to be overcome, then the notion of 'force of better reasons' becomes equivocal. The point being not that I wish to deceive or coerce others into agreeing with me – if I did, their agreement would not matter; but rather, that the justification does not have the form of an argument as such. What I am attempting to do in bringing my responses to language is to make them exemplary for you, to allow the possibility of you 'turning around', being transfigured so that we might find ourselves sharing the same space.

When Taylor objected to Habermas on the ground that there was an internal connection between the requirement that we value reaching an understanding and world-disclosure, he was wanting to underwrite the thought that even morality, as Habermas conceives it, is unintelligible unless it lets us in as moral *subjects*. In order for this to be the case, there cannot be the radical distinction between what motivates through reason and what has 'the force of purely empirical motives' (*JA*, 41). The unconditionality of validity claims does require us to discount our subjectivity, which is to make whatever is agreed to as a consequence meaningless for us. Communicative rationality drives out subjectivity. When Habermas states that 'duties *bind (binden)* the will but do not *bend (beugen)* it' (p. 41), he is supposing that the order of reasons can be separated from what those reasons are about, and hence what we are responding to when we raise validity claims. They too are responses; that is the place of the pull of the world in claims of that kind. So even in the case of justifying a moral norm, I am responding to a perception of others that I cannot disavow without disavowing myself. To believe that I could begin to justify such norms without mastering my subjectivity, my responses to you and others, is to wrench the meaning of moral norms out of their actual embeddedness in lifeworld interactions. Part of the *reasons* why we hold moral norms to be *true* (and not just right) is that they express an intrinsic feature of how we conceive of ourselves in relation to others. But that response to others, including a response to the kinds of hurt and injury they can suffer, has a force that binds the will because it bends it. (I take sympathy, for example, to be an act of bending the will in Habermas's sense of the term.) Good reasons for keeping promises and truth-telling cannot be separated from the quite specific hurts that broken promises and deceit bring about; if our justifications cannot include mention of the agonies of betrayal and exclusion, then our reasons for accepting the norms go in the wrong direction, say in the direction of pragmatic self-interest. Forms of hurt and injury as *reasons* for accepting those norms only become available discursively, however, through my making my *subjective responses* exemplary. In responding to such an exemplary account you would not be giving reasons for or against it, but judging it in order to see if your responses tallied. If they did, that would be as much as to say that your will was bound and bent by the account. Further, because you found yourself in that account, then in acceding to it you would be acceding to a certain conception of your *self* – who you were and wanted to be. Justification, even for norms possessing universalistic scope, is hence necessarily provincial.

RATIONAL TRANSFIGURATIONS: A QUESTION OF JUDGMENT

Dual-axis conceptions of language, by counterpointing the pull of the world to the claims for intersubjective justification, undermine the idealizations that Habermas attributes to communicative rationality. For all that, it may still be objected that I have failed to show that we can locate rationality elsewhere than in normatively governed justificatory procedures. One might believe, for example, that only where justificatory procedures and the pull of the world can be fully aligned, as perhaps is the case in logic and the natural sciences, can we still speak of rationality in a non-metaphorical way.

At the very conclusion of the last section I began to suggest that Habermas's deontological approach to morals suffers two overlapping flaws. Firstly, moral norms should not be regarded as merely action coordinating; it is the presumption that they possess only that role that prohibits them from being a component of our self-interpretations and ethical identity. Secondly, in their expressive function, the reasons offered for taking a moral norm as valid are themselves solidaristic; and those reasons can only be elicited by means of the exemplary communication of subjective experience. By suppressing the world axis, the pull of the world in our reasoning about the validity of moral norms, Habermas drives out of consideration the deepest reasons we have for holding them. We do not think, for example, that promise-keeping is a valid norm *because* it could meet with the agreement of all, but rather, maybe, because it is an expression of our respect for others which if acted against would cause them harm incompatible with the other ideals of a person we already hold for them and ourselves. The search for impartiality in communicative reason forces us to take a stand outside the circle of reasons and experience that typically underwrites our allegiance to moral norms. Placing moral norms within the framework of communicative rationality would lead to them being accepted for the wrong reasons, reasons that would force us to discount what permits us to value, and so care about them. It is by that route that the ethical becomes separated from the moral, and the moral becomes separated from what

221

motivates us to act. Hence the procedure of rational vindication performs an act of self-estrangement that simultaneously estranges us from others.

One possible explanation of this is that Habermasian impartiality begins from and then models itself upon the position of the sceptic, the position of the individual who has already refused to recognize her habitation in an intersubjective world, a disclosed lifeworld. Instead of defusing the sceptic's denial of habitation, Habermas agrees with the sceptic that, under conditions of modernity, moral norms lack intersubjective content and thus can only be vindicated at a higher level as rules acceptable to everyone for action coordination. In Chapter 4, this movement was identified as one from a cognitive to a will-formation conception of the moral. Its evident premise is the acceptance of the generalized account of the disenchantment of nature. But the acceptance of the disenchantment of the social world is only possible on the basis of either the denial of linguistic world-disclosure or its assimilation to communicative speech. If Habermas's refusal of the dual-axis conception of language is false, then so must be his acceptance of disenchantment and his siding with the sceptic.

Typically, reasons for believing and affirming moral norms are quite distinct from the kinds of reasons communicative reason permits. In speaking of the 'exemplary communication of subjective experience' as well as in the references to Adorno in the previous two chapters, an alternative conception of rationality has been projected, one which includes an ineliminable moment of judgment. Judgment forms the bridge between the two phenomena which communicative reason and the discourse-theoretical interpretation of morality suppresses: in judgments we respond to worldly happenings, and through judgments we apply existing concepts and norms to novel states of affairs, thus extending and transfiguring the meaning of the original concept or norm. In fine, the art of judgment connects the worldly axis of language and the creative dimension of linguistic practice. What connects those two forms of judgment is that in both cases they form the interface between (the social and historical) world and language (as system). In order to substantiate the place of judgment, we can turn to the problem of the application of moral norms, since it is one to which Habermas has become increasingly sensitive.

In Chapter 5 I noted Seyla Benhabib's objection to Habermas's theory that it separates the justification of moral norms from their application, and that this is illicit because the meanings of moral norms alter, shift and are extended, as they are applied to new and different circumstances. Habermas has since acknowledged this difficulty by adopting Klaus Günther's suggestion that we supplement discourses of justification with discourses of application, and thus analytically in considering what is the right thing to do in given circumstances there is implied a two-stage process of argument consisting of justification followed by application (*JA*, 36).[12] This is an imaginative and engaging suggestion, picking up two standard objections simultaneously. By requiring that moral norms go through a second process of rational application to particular cases which has a distinct logic of its own, Habermas explicates how the determinate meanings that norms attain in particular situations feed back into the general or typical indeterminate meaning of the norm, its potentiality for application, and simultaneously translates Benhabib's perspective of the generalized and concrete other into the *logic* of moral reasoning and justification. The perspective of the generalized other now matches the logic of justification, while the perspective of the concrete other is realized in discourses of application. Habermas goes as far as to say that one of the requirements for justificatory discourses is ascertaining the suitability of moral norms for context-sensitive application (*JA*, 58). Discourses of application involve all the judgmental abilities, attention to particularity and the uniqueness of situations that his critics have called for; hence the idea of the two-stage process looks like the ideal synthesis of perspectives that Benhabib projected at the end of her book.

Pace Habermas and Günther, the revised theory does not salvage discourse ethics but dissolves it because once judgment-dependent considerations are permitted to have an ineliminable role in the constitution of the meaning of moral norms, then there is no way of protecting the original justificatory moment from its effects. What *independent* role or function can the discourse of justification have once its results have to be continually re-configured in accordance with the specifics of cases and the alteration of circumstances?

If moral norms are to be open to supplementation by the way in which they are applied in novel circumstances, then their status must alter: they must, if their exposure to historical alteration is to be meaningful, bear a time and knowledge index. Günther thus proposes the formula: 'A norm is valid if the consequences and side effects of its general observance for the interests of each individual *under unaltered circumstances* can be accepted by all.'[13] The reservation expressed in the new clause excludes the possibility of moral norms having unconditioned validity, offering to them instead the status of prima facie validity that, as such, is defeasible in the light of both the specific features of particular cases and altered circumstances. This notion of prima facie validity is equivocal between: valid but defeasible, and potentially valid if appropriately applicable to particular circumstances. Habermas cannot be sanguine about this equivocation: in order for moral duty to be binding on the will he requires the valid but defeasible formula; conversely, if there is a *necessary* step in which we determine if the proposed norm is to be applicable in a particular circumstance, then it is only potentially valid until the moment when it is discovered to to be appropriate to at least *one* actual case. This suggests the second conception of prima facie validity, eliminating the declared conception of moral duty. Habermas and Günther, although unaware of these two possibilities, must be construed as opting for the latter.

Discourses of application operate in accordance with the principle of appropriateness rather than the principle of universalization. When applying a specific norm to a case, questions concerning individual interests drop out of consideration; our concern is with the appropriateness of the norm in relation to the particular features of a concrete situation. In judging the appropriateness of a norm to a case we are judging if action in accordance with that norm is appropriate to the complexity of the case, and ideally more appropriate than any competing norm. Reasons that make acting in one way appropriate are of a different kind than reasons that make acting one way more appropriate than another, although the comparative reasoning of the latter kind can be an element in reasoning of the former kind. In determining appropriateness the first issue is *descriptive*: what are the salient features of the case and how are they best articulated? I interpret the descriptive requirement to presuppose the following: because description of cases would be impossible unless they had already appeared in some way with some aspects already demanding attention, then it follows that there are cases demanding attention and action only insofar as they appear as already partially disclosed and thereby interpreted. To say a situation appears as always already (partially) disclosed and interpreted means: the situation affects me in a manner demanding a response. There *is* a moral situation only insofar as I am already subjectively implicated in it, and only insofar as I am already implicated in it can the question of application arise. Application is thus not the subsumption of a case *under* a norm but a further interpretation and determination of what is already there.

Because subjective response (in the form of self-implication) is partially constitutive of a situation being the situation it is, the justification of an appropriateness claim, the further reinterpretation of the case, can never go further than the exemplary communication of subjective experience. Moral argumentation with respect to appropriateness claims is in this respect no different from the activity of the literary or art critic; in mastering your subjectivity in order to make it exemplary, you can but *offer* to your interlocutor the opportunity to holistically perceive the situation as you do. The perception is holistic because seeing it in one way rather than another is not fully objective, but means finding a perspective where moral self-implication and the claim about what is to be done match. That match is necessarily internal since without it there is no situation to which a response is called for. Bringing your interlocutor to find that match – by means of analogies or critical re-descriptions of features of the case – means offering her the opportunity of finding herself in a different moral space. That alternative moral space arises through the force of an exemplary moment which can only be sustained by surrendering existing self-world correlations and adopting a new one. Because there is no logical path from the old to the new, then justifying an appropriateness claim, finding agreement, occurs through one or another of the parties to the argument transfiguring their understanding of self and world through the force of the exemplary communication of subjective experience. The agreement reached is thus unlike agreeing to a factual truth claim where no self-alteration is called for; agreeing to a moral judgment is coming to share the same world, which is why moral disagreement can be so terrifying.

It would not be untoward to say here that what is here being called re-interpretation corresponds to what Kant calls reflective judgment in the third *Critique*, and that the logic attending what is here being described as the exemplary communication of subjective experience corresponds to what Kant, in the same text, analyses in terms of the logic of the work of genius – the production of exemplary items. Moral arguments work through the production of exemplary communications (which is equally what was claimed about ethical self-identities in Chapter 4). The production and reception of exemplary communications are both works of reflective judgment.

On this analysis of appropriateness claims there is no space for an analytically independent moment of justification because moral norms can only factitiously be described as being *applied* to the world. That we respond to and acknowledge moral claims does not mean that we recognize a moral norm as potentially valid, it means that the world appears as already 'coded' in moral terms. The moral norm is constitutive of the world being disclosed as calling for a certain type of response. The *illusion* that there is such a thing as a moral norm apart from how the world is derives from the fact that we have alternative interests that can lead us to want to deny the claims being lodged (as factually we might want to go on holiday without the funds to pay for it), and further that experience can be reinterpreted. On this analysis, because moral norms refer to certain ways in which the world appears that call for us to respond in particular ways, it follows that moral norms are not prima facie in either of the ways described above; they are unconditionally valid but fallible.[14]

For Habermas and Günther the terminus of an appropriateness argument is the same as the above: a prima facie moral norm (one having passed the universalization test) becomes valid if it is the one that best 'fits' the case described as exhaustively as possible. Since exhaustive description is idle independently of its moral import, then the notion of 'fit' cannot presume a neutral description for which one or another moral norm might best account. 'Fit' is equivalent to whatever best describes the situation, and defeated candidates, as in the case of conflict between norms, are equivalent to defeated descriptions. Vindicated appropriateness arguments reveal the world as having a particular normative shape.

Because Habermas is concerned to sustain a discourse of justification, and because he has agreed that the full justification of a moral norm just means that it is found actually applicable, then he must find a space for defeated candidates that does not entail them losing their prima facie validity. His response is the thought that eclipsed norms join all others 'to form a *coherent normative order*' (*JA*, 38). The structure and so meaning of the norms belonging to this order shift with each selection of an appropriate norm for each case. It is the order as a whole that first permits the possibility of a norm being selected, but it is the 'particular situation whose appropriate interpretation first confers the determinate shape of a coherent order on the unordered mass of valid norms' (p. 38). What is extraordinary in this account of the dialectic between the 'coherent normative order' and its re-formation and transfiguration with each application is that it is all but indistinguishable from the substantialist interpretive position of Taylor, where instead of a coherent normative order we find the complex language of strong evaluations.

The idea of a coherent normative order as used by Habermas and Günther has all the features of a neo-Aristotelian ethical theory that was originally to be pressed aside:

> If every valid norm is dependent on coherent supplementation by all others in situations in which norms are applicable, then their meaning changes in every situation. In this way we are dependent on history, since it first produces the unforeseeable situations that compel us in each instance to produce a new interpretation of all valid norms.[15]

The justification for the claim that every valid norm is dependent on all others depends on two thoughts. Firstly, the language of norms implies semantic clusters and chains which make the meaning of each norm dependent on others; so concepts like integrity, respect, vulnerability, probity, autonomy, etc. form a cluster in which the actual use of any one has implications for the meaning and potential use of any other. Without this thesis, the claim that the correct application of any one norm depends on all others would be idle; the language system of norms itself provides the constraints that make possible the selection of just one. Secondly, we can only have a recognizable moral world, to the degree we do, if normative discourse permits accounts of how things are and what is to be done to be commensurable with one another. From the other direction: unless a judgment of appropriateness had reverberations for how we must judge in other cases, there would not be rational constraints sufficient to make its claim to correctness now right or wrong. Together these two thoughts yield the conclusion that the idea of a coherent normative order is equivalent to an interpretive normative framework which discloses the normative order of the world.

If the meaning of moral norms is dependent on their place within a coherent normative order, and that normative order is dependent as a whole on its interpretive realization in the normative description of particular cases, then where could a separate analytic stage of justification find a place for itself? The dialectic between interpretive scheme and the interpretation of cases does all the work. More to the point, given the coherence requirements of the interpretive scheme, typically manifest in significant moral debates over difficult new cases, the attempt to offer prima facie validity to a putative norm apart from its fit in the interpretive scheme would be pointless. Conversely, all the reason we might have for thinking a norm valid is satisfied if it both fits into our interpretive scheme, its meaning meshing with existing semantic clusters and chains, and it is appropriate in some cases. Habermas's oddly sanguine conclusion to his argument almost says as much: 'Deontological ethical conceptions assume in the final analysis only that the moral point of view remains identical; but neither our understanding of this fundamental intuition, nor the interpretations we give morally valid rules in applying them to unforseeable cases, remain invariant' (*JA*, 39).

To argue that there is no space or point to there being an identical moral point of view in ethical life is equivalent to claiming that there is no space or point to an analytically separate step of justification apart from application. Even analytically, I cannot see from the position we have reached what function such a separate state of justification could have. The question posed by discourses of application is: which of the norms that are equally in the interests of all is appropriate in the given situation once all its determinate features are taken into consideration? It is the 'equally in the interests of all' clause that is to refer back to the stage of justification. But this reference back is necessarily opaque once the meaning of the norm has been doubly re-inscribed: first by its placement within a coherent normative order and secondly by its further reinterpretation in accordance with circumstances that necessarily take into account subjective experience. In other words, if appropriateness claims are to be more than formal and external, then context-sensitivity cannot abstract from all the affective bonds, desires, hopes, the concrete social location, personal histories and identities of the individuals concerned. Applications that ignored these phenomena would be just subsumptions of cases under norms. Once these phenomena are taken into account, however, then the distinction between the moral and the ethical collapses. If a coherent normative order appears in that form for *me* in virtue of the continual dialectic between it and my and your activities, then putative reference to any bit of it being equally in the interests of all construed procedurally and operationally becomes redundant. If the meaning of the norm is determined by its position within the coherent normative order, then abstraction from that order for the sake of testing would abstract from the semantic and empirical references the norm has in virtue of its place in the order. Either the constraints on meaning and rationality (with respect to application) are holistic or they are not; if they are, then the presumptive analytic step of justification would be meaning destroying if acted upon.

Again, I am tempted to say that the universalistic core of the interpretive scheme we actually employ is best captured by its central terms referring to abstract features and characteristics of persons (integrity, autonomy, vulnerability, etc.), and its rules of application barring scope restrictions on the basis of race, colour, creed and so on. Further, that those features of the scheme are now so prominent is best explained through just the kind of history of interaction between scheme and experience that Günther underlines. The communication theoretical interpretation of the moral point of view transforms a complex ethical achievement, how our coherent normative order has been formed, into a formal characteristic of linguistic action. We can and do hear the force of Habermas's claim that in communicative actions we must be willing to change perspectives and give everyone concerned the opportunity to voice their view; we can hear it because it is one application of the substantive universalism of our interpretive scheme – just the point that Hegel made against Kant's procedural interpretation of universalism.

In place of what would prove a futile effort to find some independent content for the idea of a moral point of view which remains identical in the context of ethical life, we might instead note that there is a domain of social life in which a two-stage process is plausible, namely, in the production of positive laws and social policies, and their judicial and administrative application. Indeed, all of Habermas's descriptions of the two-stage process, which appear so strained in the case of moral norms, look perfectly natural in the case of the legislation and application of laws and policies. While throughout I have argued that Habermas's attempt to keep the moral and the ethical separate is deeply misguided, there is an obvious formal distinction to be drawn between ethical life and the domain of positive law. In the latter domain the abstraction from the thick ethical identity of subjects is necessary. Further, the actual practice of producing positive laws and social policies is procedural and atomistic – distinct laws and policies each require normative legitimation – while not only is ordinary ethical life not atomistically productive in this way, applications being reinterpretations that impact on the scheme as a whole, but its coherence requirements must be stronger since the coherence of an ethical scheme, unlike a legal system, must be sufficient for the thick ethical identity of individuals. While even in the political sphere I would wish to deny that we can distinguish the right from the good – how could the ideal of democratic citizenship not be part of our conception of the good life? – it is nonetheless the case that in matters political both a certain type of proceduralism and the construction of a two-stage process of rational argumentation, corresponding, for example, to the distinct processes of legislation and judicial review, appear deeply plausible. To import this model into the ongoing praxis of everyday life, however, yields a politicization of the ethical that reduces the complex achievements of our coherent normative order to a mere consensus over rules that are to regulate personal interactions.

NEGATIVITY AND THE FUTURE OF CRITICAL THEORY

Habermas's critical theory is a creature of its place and time. Its recurrent search for a moment of unconditionality is unintelligible unless set against the background of recent German history: in a culture in which modern ethical life proved itself so fragile as to be incapable of withstanding the onslaught of a politics insensitive to the claims of universalism, what grounds might there be for perceiving the progressive elements in modernity as sustained only in that medium? Against the background of that terrible history, who could blame Habermas for searching out a claim to rightness not spatially and temporally bound? If who his fellow citizens once wanted to be was proud Aryans in an ethnically cleansed state, then separating questions of ethics and self-identity from moral questions becomes all but imperative. If the legacy of the achievements of modern universalism could not be identified with the concrete ethical life of twentieth-century Germany, then it must be lodged elsewhere, say in the pragmatic presuppositions of communicative actions oriented to reaching an understanding. Habermas's proceduralism is itself a profound ethical response to the history of the world surrounding him. Moreover, the increasingly Kantian thrust of his philosophy corresponds to what I regard as one of the deepest impulses of modern philosophical reflection: to salvage the claims of rational universalism while acknowledging the full force and import of contingency and history. Habermas's imaginative and unique proposal of giving the Hegelian turn to intersubjectivity a linguistic and procedural twist is one of the very few real philosophical inventions of recent times that demands, and repays, extended engagement. Finally, that Habermas has resolutely placed his philosophical programme in the setting of a critical theory that confronts both the injustices and meaning-destroying mechanisms of modern, western societies has offered us all a model of how philosophy and social theory can and must be joined. In all, Habermas has done all that could be asked in the way of keeping alive the project of a critical theory of society.

As scientific theories are born refuted, so philosophical programmes are born flawed and partial. But philosophical ideas are unlike theories in that they possess what Castoriadis might call imaginary cores, insights, which no theoretical elaboration ever exhausts. Hence, as Habermas has recently noted, his universalistic programme cannot be reduced to an elaboration of what has been theoretically worked out in developmental moral psychology (*JA*, 114–16); rather, the philosophical and the scientific/theoretical must each sustain their programmes separately and test them against one another. Philosophical ideas are deep interpretations of the human, exemplary figures of the nature of human experience; as such they belong to the practice of world-disclosive discourses more surely than they belong to natural scientific discourse. From this angle of vision, the kind of reconstructive sciences to which Habermas has aligned his thought are peculiar half-breeds: they are interpretations of human experience pursued in an empirical and theoretical manner.

This thought should be uncongenial to Habermas since its conception of philosophy's interpretive praxis cannot easily be situated within any one of his three validity spheres: if primarily philosophy is a form of world-disclosing discourse, it nonetheless reaches out, critically and reflectively, into the other domains in an unregulated but persistent manner. Unregulated and persistent because its imaginative core – for Habermas the linguistic reinscription of the Hegelian reformulation of Kant's moral theory in intersubjective terms – immediately outruns the notions of aesthetic harmony or evaluative cogency directly applicable to world-disclosive discourse without, for all that, being identifiable with any other validity sphere. When Habermas speaks about the process whose moments are communicative action, the raising of validity claims, a challenge to one of those claims, the movement into discourse, the rational, normative constraints on argumentation, and the telos of consensus he is after all etching a scenario whose archetype is found in Aristophanes's speech in the *Symposium* which tells of circle men, cut in half by Zeus, who continually seek their other half in order to restore themselves to wholeness. That this dialectic of union, separation and repair can be fleshed out in speech pragmatic terms cannot but find an echo in our self-understanding. Moreover, if we canvass the history of the reception of Habermas's theory we cannot fail to notice how the main lines of criticism relate, eventually, to the three central moments of the process it describes: what is the status and character of our original togetherness? how originally circular are we? how deep is, and what is the meaning of human separateness? is it contingent and accidental or more permanent than a temporary loss? what is the character and motive for seeking re-unification? and what would such reunion be like if achieved? In very broad terms, my arguments have attempted to show that the idea of consensus is too weak to explicate the character of our bonds with others with respect to where we begin and with respect to where we desire to end up; that human separateness is both more abiding and more intimate to our self-understanding than what is captured by the idea of disagreement over validity claims, which is but a symptom of separateness; and that the drive for reunion is more urgent and intimate than finding rules for the coordination of action, but it lacks formal guidelines and guarantees (the norms of argumentation).

In underlining the interpretive centre of Habermas's programme, I do not mean to suggest that it is incapable of argumentative defence and criticism. On the contrary, the question being pursued in this chapter has been to ascertain the character of rational argumentation. In his lucid reconstruction of Habermas's theory of language, for example, Allen Wood has suggested that in time the hope is that the pragmatics of speech could be rendered and vindicated in wholly naturalistic terms.[16] This hope, which equally has represented until recently a certain temptation for Habermas himself, is incompatible with the very specific problems over world-disclosure and discourses of application that have emerged. More to the point, Habermas's acceptance of Günther's account of discourses of application entails far-reaching changes to his general scheme. Let us follow this through for a moment.

In order to accommodate the ongoing dialectic between a coherent normative order and concrete applications as a distinctive form of interaction between a conceptual scheme and empirical reality which is quite unlike the relation between natural scientific truth claims with respect to 'their' empirical world, Habermas supplements the distinction among validity spheres with a further *ontological* distinction between the historical and the natural. Moral knowledge is not (only) cognitively provincial with respect to the future, it possesses as well an existential provinciality 'resulting from historical transformations in the objects themselves' (*JA*, 39). We can only construe this conception of transformations in the objects themselves as a concession to the notion of language having a distinct world-disclosing axis since the notion of substantive transformations depends on objects being really language dependent – their meaning and being becoming inseparable. This, of course, was Castoriadis's original suggestion. Now, having accepted some notion of an ontological distinction between the natural and the historical, shouldn't Habermas be prepared to accept that the idea of truth-only cognition belongs only to the natural sciences, and that historical life does not distinguish validity spheres in this way? In this respect, discourses of application are an embarrassment since in judging the appropriateness of a norm to a case we are judging holistically, which is to say aesthetically, for a match between rightness and truth. The very idea that cases are unique and not substitutable requires that we judge them holistically and so reflectively; again, because some of the predicates we require in order to describe fully particular cases are equally those which determine their moral character, then in interpreting a situation we cannot fully distinguish empirical truth from moral salience. That entails that in the feedback from application to a coherent moral universe, empirical characterizations of how the world is must figure in the meaning of moral terms, otherwise the idea of the moral salience of situations, what makes norms context-sensitive, would be absent. Since Habermas has already affirmed the ontological distinctiveness of moral-historical experience, then he must regard the transfigurative praxis projected by the idea of discourses of application to be equivalent to, so to speak, the practical/rational realization of that ontological specificity. And this entails that the logic of discourses of application in which the three validity spheres are non-metaphorically interwoven itself represents the grammar of rational historical praxis.

Against the background of the ontological specificity of historical action and meaning Habermas can no longer easily gesture toward the different spheres of validity as if lifeworld praxis simply and happily ignores their differentiations but that the pragmatics of speech reveals their constitutive separateness. On what grounds should the pragmatics of communicative action trump the claims of discourses of application when the latter seem to first reveal an ontological abyss between historical experience and the natural world as pictured by scientific practice? In his reply to Martin Seel, whose own position closely approximates the one being forwarded in these pages, Habermas notes that the different spheres of validity refer internally to one another, and that therefore we must be able to use our faculty of judgment for assessing when switching from one sphere to another is appropriate, and hence, equally, when those internal references are in balance or not in the context of everyday life (*R*, 226).[17] This presupposes that the internal connection between the validity spheres is practical, and that their discourse references to one another track only those moments when the assessment of a validity claim in one sphere can only be answered by claims in another sphere. Habermas wishes to keep separate world-disclosures, the presentation of factual matters, the creation of personal relationships and the expression of subjective experiences and expressive self-presentation. In the new category of discourses of application, which postdates his reply to Seel, these concerns are all interwoven. Since the logic of discourses of application is all but indistinguishable from how philosophers like Castoriadis and Taylor conceive of worldly interpretive praxis, then the a priori separation of the historical world into distinct domains of validity cannot be regarded as an innocent methodological manoeuvre.

What encourages Habermas to uphold his division of reason are everyday distinctions: that there were three cookies in the cookie jar is a different matter from your stealing them. Who would want to deny this separation? But this is misleading in that the fact of the three cookies is no more or less an independent fact of social experience than the fact that the colour of the woman's dress in this Matisse painting is red. What would justify a full distinction of spheres with their own forms of argumentation would be that the occurrence of any of the phenomena standing under the different spheres be *constitutively* distinct in the manner described by the different logics of the different spheres. Only the physical world of nature has this level of constitutive distinctiveness – a fact Habermas now accepts.

Once the constitutive or ontological unity of the social is acknowledged, Habermas's formal account of balancing validity spheres, as against the unbalanced present, itself begins to look like a reification. So, instead of seeing the fragmentation of validity spheres and their individual subjection to proceduralism as a mechanism for freezing interpretive praxis, Habermas continues to diagnose modernity in terms of a 'selective pattern of rationalization' which occurs when at least

> one of the three constitutive components of the cultural tradition is not systematically worked up, or when (at least) one cultural value sphere is insufficiently institutionalized, that is, is without any structure-forming effect on society as a whole, or when (at least) one sphere predominates to such an extent that it subjects life-orders to a form of rationality that is alien to them.
>
> (*TCA*, I, 240)

Are these analyses compelling? Is morality not systematically worked out, or is moral vision deformed by the separation of the moral from the truth-functional? When considering the problems of ecology and related green issues, it is difficult not to believe that it is the concept of nature as disenchanted that leads to its mastery by technology. At the very conclusion of 'Remarks on discourse ethics', Habermas himself proffers a vision that works only because it *fuses* moral, ethical and aesthetic categories:

> *aesthetic reasons* have here even greater force than ethical, for in the aesthetic experience of nature, things withdraw into an unapproachable autonomy and inaccessibility; they then exhibit their fragile integrity so

232

clearly that they strike us as inviolable in their own right and not merely as desirable elements of a preferred form of life.

$(JA, 111)$

If it is aesthetic reasons that allow things to exhibit their autonomy and fragile integrity, must there not be a distortion in our moral vision such that other people(s) cannot or do not appear in this way? And when they do, is it reasonable to believe that only procedural requirements are guiding our perception?

Is art insufficiently institutionalized or is the political sphere reified by disallowing interpretive praxis? The example of the new social movements, where again ethical, moral and aesthetic reasons are fused, makes the latter analysis more compelling. When the moral and political spheres lack both a moment of ethical identity and of disclosure then, arguably, they perpetuate the draining of meaning from the practices they govern. Habermas is not unaware of or insensitive to these problems, nor does he avoid attempting to offer analyses that tally with those being suggested here. The question is whether the best explanation for the problems of modernity are the three he notes or the combination of separation and proceduralism? And whether the resolution of those problems requires more systematic working out of the individual spheres, institutionalizing and balancing, or categorial fusion and a renewal of interpretive praxis? What is most 'alien' to interpretive praxis is its trisection; and the best analysis of the consequences of rationalization and fragmentation is not the inhibition of communicative relations or the lack of balance among the spheres, but the increasing unavailability for concrete praxis of ethical meanings and orientations which entwine the three registers. Which is, of course, just the picture of modernity originally offered by Nietzsche and Weber, and taken up by Adorno.

In saying this, I do not mean to refute or undervalue two fundamental theses that Habermas has been anxious to forward: (i) 'The concept of rationality includes the pragmatic roles of criticizable validity claims which are at the same time geared toward intersubjective recognition.' And (ii) 'The internal connection of the meaning, validity and justification of validity claims demonstrates . . . that naive everyday practice itself refers to the possibilities of argumentation' $(R, 223)$. I would argue, however, that these cannot be read off from the pragmatics of speech (as if it were itself a natural object), and that in particular the role of justification in (ii) is a component of the modern *ethical* experience of individuals and groups having to justify themselves before others. Justification belongs to the ethical arrival of individuation, autonomy and historical self-consciousness. With those three phenomena what is revealed is that despite the individual's subjectivity always being grounded in its relation to another, that intersubjectivity itself is a free or autonomous accomplishment, an active and free recognizing of the one by the other. Negativity, as the heart of autonomy, makes subjectivity aporetic: forever dependent on others from whom it nonetheless remains almost infinitely

233

distant, independence and dependence explicitly coming to form irreducible but unreconcilable moments of subjectivity. Once the moment of independence is recognized, the normative authority of the intersubjective whole becomes answerable to the individual, and the individual forever answerable to the whole which gives her a life and without whose allegiance it would disintegrate. The demand that validity claims find argumentative justification is the linguistic re-presentation of mutual dependency and answerability. The *force* of validity claims and the requirement for justification, all too frighteningly misrepresented by Rousseau in his *Confessions*, derives not from the formal pragmatics of speech but from the ethical constitution of the self as outlined in the aporetic dialectic of independence and dependence. The combination of the elements in this scenario is equally the mechanism through which the force of constitutive *negativity* in the form of the practice of meaning destruction and renewal, now hibernating in the sphere of art and aesthetics, finally appears in human history – the historicity of human experience coming to self-consciousness. This is the picture of modernity offered by Hegel and recounted in the opening lectures of *The Philosophical Discourse of Modernity*. In Chapter 4 I argued that the interpretation of civic citizenship and democracy offered by Rousseau represented the institutional embodiment of this ethical ideal.

This is not the place to attempt to vindicate Adorno's analysis of modernity, Hegel's account of intersubjectivity or the ethical ideals of democratic civic citizenship, the synthesis of which would provide a critical theory for the future. Instead, we should note how often and how closely the central arguments in these pages have rehearsed that strange ur-text of the aesthetic critique of modernity, the so-called 'Oldest System Programme of German Idealism' of 1796. Whether its two pages were penned by Hegel, Hölderlin or Schelling, or all three working together, remains undecided. What is unavoidable is its analysis of the ills of modernity as a consequence of the trisection of reason, with its optimistic belief that a unification of reason was possible without forsaking modernity's commitments to either reason or negativity. 'Before we make the ideas aesthetical, i.e., mythological, they have no interest for the people; on the other hand, before mythology is rational, the philosopher must be ashamed of it.' Clause one of this sentence fits too well the abstraction of the moral from the ethical that forms one of the grounds for the unlimited communication community (the disenchantment of nature being the other); clause two rehearses our collective shame at an autonomous art world that continually attempts to raise ethical matters but equally continually finds itself speaking only aesthetically, its creative and world-disclosing praxis forever locked in a world of semblance and illusion. Habermas simplifies this analysis too much in underlining the aesthetic critique of abstract reason and forgetting our shame before art's want of rationality.

NOTES

1 CRITICAL THEORY – THE VERY IDEA

1 See Max Horkheimer, *Critical Theory: Selected Essays*, trans. Matthew J. O'Connell and others (New York: Continuum, 1986), pp. 188–252.

2 Ibid., p. 200.

3 So, for example, begin with the first history of critical theory: Martin Jay, *The Dialectical Imagination: A History of the Frankfurt School and the Institute of Social Research, 1923–1950* (Boston, MA: Little, Brown and Co., 1973). Douglas Kellner in his review of Jay, 'The Frankfurt School revisited: a critique of Martin Jay's *The Dialectical Imagination*', *New German Critique* 4 (1973), pp. 131–52, convincingly argues that the original idea for critical theory was more Marxist than Jay allows. Rolf Wiggershaus, in his *The Frankfurt School: Its History, Theories and Political Significance*, trans. Michael Robertson (Cambridge: Polity Press, 1994; the original German edition appeared in 1986) offers an Adornoian construal of its history that works against Habermas's version; while Seyla Benhabib's *Critique, Norm, and Utopia: A Study of the Foundations of Critical Theory* (New York: Columbia University Press, 1986) makes Habermas's accession the inevitable outcome of the theoretical difficulties of both the tradition of critique (Marx and Hegel) and the original programme. I contest Benhabib's history in Chapter 5.

4 As a reminder: Habermas sets up his analysis in *KHI* against the background of Hegel's critique of Kant (Ch. 1) and Marx's critique of Hegel (Ch. 2); the core of the argument of the first volume of *TCA* turns on an analysis of Weber (pp. 143–272), which then permits a reconsideration of Adorno's and Horkheimer's views on the scope of instrumental reason in Chapter 4. These engagements with the tradition in his systematic writings leaves aside his numerous occasional essays. For a beauty on Horkheimer, see *JA*, pp. 133–46.

5 *Critical Theory*, op. cit. note 1, p. 227.

6 Ibid., p. 215.

7 Ibid., p. 3.

8 *Negations: Essays in Critical Theory*, trans. Jeremy J. Shapiro (Harmondsworth, Middlesex: Penguin Books, 1968), p. 135.

9 See *Critical Theory*, op. cit. note 1, p. 203.

10 Here I am agreeing with the astute analysis to be found in Axel Honneth's *The Critique of Power: Reflective Stages in a Critical Social Theory*, trans. Kenneth Baynes (London: MIT Press, 1991), Chapter 1.

11 In Stephen Bonner and Douglas Kellner (eds), *Critical Theory and Society* (London: Routledge, 1989), pp. 33–4.

12 Jürgen Habermas, 'Notes on the developmental history of Horkheimer's work', *Theory, Culture & Society* 10 (1993), p. 64.
13 Honneth, *The Critique of Power*, op. cit. note 10, pp. 26–7.
14 In this diagnosis I am agreeing with Habermas, *The Theory of Communicative Action (Volume II): The Critique of Functionalist Reason*, trans. Thomas McCarthy (Cambridge: Polity Press, 1987), pp. 374–85.
15 I am using Fred Jameson's translation, usefully included in Bonner and Kellner, op. cit. note 11. Page references are to this edition; here, p. 267.
16 Ibid., p. 271.
17 Ibid., p. 273.
18 Ibid., p. 275.
19 'Cultural criticism and society', in *Prisms*, trans. Samuel and Shierry Weber (London: Neville Spearman Ltd, 1967), p. 33.
20 These terms are central to Seyla Benhabib's reconstruction of critical theory, *Critique, Norm, and Utopia: A Study of the Foundations of Critical Theory*, op. cit. note 3.
21 For a precise reconstruction of the debate over 'reification' see Gillian Rose's *The Melancholy Science: An Introduction to the Thought of Theodor W. Adorno* (London: The Macmillan Press, 1978), Ch. 3.
22 The attempt to demonstrate that Kantian moral reason really is Hobbesian and instrumental in character is central to my defence of Adorno in *The Ethics of Non-identity* (forthcoming).
23 Kenneth Baines, 'Rational reconstruction and social criticism: Habermas's model of interpretive social science', *The Philosophical Forum* 21(1–2) (1989–90), p. 156. In the critical line that follows I ignore a further problem with Habermas's theory, namely, his assumption that systems (as relieved from communicative control by the 'media' of money and power) and lifeworld represent two distinct tiers of the social world. So:

> Via the media of money and power, the subsystems of economy and the state are differentiated out of an institutional complex set within the horizon of the lifeworld; *formally organized domains of action* emerge that – in the final analysis – are no longer integrated through the mechanism of mutual understanding, that shear off from the lifeworld contexts and congeal into a kind of norm-free sociality.
>
> (*TCA*, II, 307)

For astute criticisms of this view – how could economic exchanges not be lifeworld practices imbued with certain values? didn't Weber demonstrate that only a certain formation of the human 'soul' could explain the rise of capitalism? and how can lifeworld practices not be subject to deformations by structural displacements caused by relations of money and power (consider the role of money in marriage)? – see Honneth, op. cit. note 10, pp. 294–302, and Hugh Baxter, 'System and lifeworld in Habermas' *Theory of Communicative Action*', *Theory and Society* 16 (1987), pp. 39–86. In Chapter 6, below, I suggest that the right way to understand 'media' is in terms of a certain syntax dominating and reifying semantic implications and possibilities. Finally, with respect to my argument here about Hegel, which is elaborated in different, Rousseauian, terms in Chapter 4, I note the following complaint by Baxter (p. 71) about the 'uncoupling' of system from lifeworld:

> Habermas, after all, classifies societies as democratic or authoritarian, capitalist or socialist, and thus it seems that the nature of the economic and political/administrative systems define the identity of the society. In what sense, then, can Habermas also claim that these systems are 'uncoupled' from the identity-securing core of society seen as lifeworld?

It would be worthwhile interrogating to what extent Habermas's sociological formalism, as analysed by Honneth and Baxter, supports or licenses his philosophical formalism.

24 See the diagram in Habermas's 'A reply to my critics', in John Thompson and David Held (eds), *Habermas: Critical Debates* (London: Macmillan, 1982).

25 For a good conspectus on this debate see I. Lakatos and A. Musgrave (eds), *Criticism and the Growth of Knowledge* (Cambridge: Cambridge University Press, 1970). It is certainly worth reminding ourselves that anti-positivist philosophy of science depends in part on defending the idea that there are no formal criteria for scientific rationality. Why should morals be different?

2 LIBERTY AND THE IDEAL SPEECH SITUATION

1 *Four Essays on Liberty* (Oxford: Oxford University Press, 1969), p. 132.

2 Ibid., pp. 133–8.

3 'Does political theory still exist?', in P. Laslett and W.G. Runciman (eds), *Philosophy, Politics and Society*, Second Series (Oxford: Oxford University Press, 1962), p. 13. See also Berlin's discussion of science and human freedom in 'Historical inevitability', collected in *Four Essays on Liberty*, op. cit. note 1.

4 'Hannah Arendt's communications concept of power', *Social Research* 44 (1977), p. 15.

5 'The public sphere', *New German Critique* 3 (1974), p. 42. This essay summarizes the results of *Strukturwandel der Öffentlichkeit* (1962), which has only recently been translated: *The Structural Transformation of the Public Sphere*, trans. Thomas Burger (Cambridge: Polity Press, 1989).

6 Ibid., p. 49.

7 Ibid.

8 For a good discussion of this see Jean Cohen's 'Why more political theory?', *Telos* 42 (1979), p. 79.

9 'Technology and science as "ideology" ', in *Toward a Rational Society* (London: Heinemann, 1970), p. 103 (emphasis in original).

10 'The scientization of politics and public opinion', in *Toward a Rational Society*, op. cit. note 9, p. 75.

11 'Technology and science as "ideology" ', op. cit. note 9, p. 112.

12 By 'interests' Habermas means 'the basic orientations rooted in specific fundamental conditions of the possible reproduction and self-constitution of the human species, namely work and interaction' (*KHI*, 196).

13 'Technology and science as "ideology" ', op. cit. note 9, p. 92.

14 In English one finds a defence of this position in Peter Winch's *The Idea of a Social Science and Its Relation to Philosophy* (London: Routledge and Kegan Paul, 1958). Habermas's view of hermeneutics is indebted to H.-G. Gadamer's *Truth and Method* (New York: Seabury Press, 1975). On Gadamer see Habermas's 'A review of Gadamer's *Truth and Method*', in F. Dallmayr and T. McCarthy (eds), *Understanding and Social Inquiry* (Notre Dame, IN: Notre Dame University Press, 1977).

15 Ibid., p. 360.

16 Ibid., p. 341.

17 For an excellent account of this argument see T. McCarthy's 'A theory of communicative competence', *Philosophy of the Social Sciences* 3 (1973), esp. pp. 151–4.

18 'Wahrheitstheorien', in *Wirlichkeit und Reflexion: Walter Schulz zum 60 Geburstag* (Pfullingen: Nesk, 1973), pp. 251–2, quoted in T. McCarthy's *The Critical Theory of Jürgen Habermas* (London: Heinemann, 1978), p. 316.

19 'A postscript to *Knowledge and Human Interests*', *Philosophy of the Social Sciences* 2 (1972), p. 177. This essay is now available in the revised edition of *Knowledge and Human Interests*. I take up the suggestion about forming and discovering in the next chapter.

20 *Legitimation Crisis*, trans. T. McCarthy (London: Heinemann, 1975), p. 113.

21 'For rational beings all stand under the law that each of them should treat himself and all others, never merely as a means, but always at the same time as an end in himself. But by so doing there arises a systematic union of rational beings under common objective laws . . . [T]his can be called a kingdom of ends (which is admittedly only an Ideal).' *Groundwork of the Metaphysics of Morals* in Paton's translation: *The Moral Law* (London: Hutchinson, 1969), p. 95 (p. 433 of the Academy edition).

22 'On the Common Saying: "This may be true in theory, but it does not apply in practice" ', in H. Reiss (ed.), *Kant's Political Writings* (Cambridge: Cambridge University Press, 1970), p. 73.

23 For a good discussion of the relation between Kant and Habermas see *The Critical Theory of Jürgen Habermas*, op. cit. note 18, pp. 325–31.

24 Gadamer's 'Replik' in K.-O. Apel et al., *Hermeneutik und Ideologiekritik* (Frankfurt: Suhrkamp, 1971), p. 316.

3 SELF-KNOWLEDGE AS PRAXIS

1 All page references in the body of the text are to Jürgen Habermas, *Knowledge and Human Interests*, trans. Jeremy J. Shapiro (London: Heinemann, 1972) (*KHI* in Abbreviations). For a review of the inadequacies of psychoanalysis as a model for critical theory see Thomas McCarthy, *The Critical Theory of Jürgen Habermas* (London: Hutchinson, 1978), pp. 205–13. On Habermas's repression of sexuality in Freud, see Rainer Nägele, *Reading after Freud* (New York: Columbia University Press, 1987), pp. 67–90; and now, Joel Whitebook, 'Reason and happiness: some psychoanalytic themes in critical theory', in R.J. Bernstein (ed.), *Habermas and Modernity* (Cambridge: Polity Press, 1985), pp. 140–60. Although I here accept, for the purposes of argument, Habermas's linguistification of the id and the unconscious, there is nothing about the theory I am presenting, especially the use I want to make of avowal, which ties me to that construction.

2 McCarthy, op. cit. note 1, pp. 101–2, 182–92; and J.B. Thompson and D. Held (eds), *Habermas: Critical Debates* (London: Macmillan, 1982), essays 4, 7, 8. My contention will be that there is a uniform ground for these objections, i.e. in Habermas's refusal of a fully hermeneutic theory of self-consciousness; but that because that ontologized conception of self-consciousness is implicit in his reading of Freud, then the idea of a depth hermeneutic, of a science of self-reflection, in fact overcomes the conservatism of hermeneutic theory, thus releasing the radicality of its conception of history. We now cannot have self-knowledge without the mediation of theory; our ignorance, our unconscious individual and social, is profound.

3 On the relation between his reading of Freud and his critique of hermeneutics, see Jürgen Habermas, 'The hermeneutic claim to universality', in Josef Bleicher (ed.), *Contemporary Hermeneutics* (London: Routledge and Kegan Paul, 1982), pp. 181–211.

4 Paul Ricoeur, 'Narrative time', *Critical Inquiry* 7 (Autumn 1980), p. 174. For considerations of narrative in relation to questions of action and self-identity directly pertinent to what follows see my *The Philosophy of the Novel: Lukács, Marxism and the Dialectics of Form* (Minneapolis: University of Minnesota Press, 1984), Chs 1, 4. As

I acknowledge there, there is an overlap between the way I connect identity and reason and MacIntyre's theory. The reader might now want to consult Michael Kelly's 'MacIntyre, Habermas, and philosophical ethics', *Philosophical Forum* 21 (1989–90).

5 Hans-Georg Gadamer, *Truth and Method*, trans. Garrett Barden and John Cumming (New York: Seabury Press, 1975), pp. 273 ff.

6 Amelie Rorty, 'Explaining emotions', in her (ed.), *Explaining Emotions* (London: University of California Press, 1980), p. 110.

7 See 'The Hermeneutic claim to universality', op. cit. note 3, pp. 192–4.

8 See Hilary Putnam, 'Realism and reason', in his *Meaning and the Moral Sciences* (London: Routledge and Kegan Paul, 1978), pp. 123–37.

9 William Connolly, 'Appearance and reality in politics', *Political Theory* 7(4) (November 1979), p. 461.

10 Habermas reveals how the problem of narrative sentences entailing an ultimate end of history (a last historian) can be resolved if we move from a contemplative to practical comprehension of historical teleology in his 'A review of Gadamer's *Truth and Method*', in F.R. Dallmayr and T. McCarthy (eds), *Understanding and Social Inquiry* (London: University of Notre Dame Press, 1977), pp. 349–52. I am here, of course, accepting this idea and using it against Habermas. As we will see in the next chapter, Habermas has attempted to constrain the narrative productivity which is inseparable from self-identity, which he accepts, by drawing a categorial distinction between ethical self-identity and moral reason. Hence, he will want to argue that ethical reasoning and moral reasoning are wholly distinct forms of reasoning and rationality. This I will contest.

11 Philip Rieff (ed.), *Therapy and Technique* (New York: Collier Books, 1963), p. 93.

12 For two recent articles that present and defend this practical conception of self-knowledge as the one properly attributable to Freud, see Morris Eagle, 'Privileged access and the status of self-knowledge in Cartesian and Freudian conceptions of the mental', *Philosophy of the Social Sciences* 12 (1982), pp. 349–73; and Bela Szabados, 'Freud, self-knowledge and psychoanalysis', *Canadian Journal of Philosophy* 12(4) (1982).

13 See now Chapters 1–5 of Charles Taylor, *Philosophy and the Human Sciences* (Cambridge: Cambridge University Press, 1985), esp. Chapters 1 and 3 ('Interpretation and the sciences of man' and 'Social theory as practice'); and Kenneth Baines, 'Rational reconstruction and social criticism: Habermas' model of interpretative social science', *Philosophical Forum* 21(1–2) (1989–90).

14 'The spirit of Christianity and its fate', in *On Christianity: Early Theological Writings*, trans. T.M. Knox (New York: Harper and Brothers, 1961), p. 225.

15 Ibid., p. 229.

16 *Natural Law*, trans. T.M. Knox (Philadelphia, PA: Iniversity of Pennsylvania Press, 1975), p. 105.

4 MORAL NORMS AND ETHICAL IDENTITIES

1 I attempt an austere accounting of this in my 'Autonomy and solitude', in Keith Ansell-Pearson (ed.), *Nietzsche and Modern German Thought* (London: Routledge, 1991), pp. 192–215.

2 The best account of which, and the one I am presupposing here, remains Marx's 'On the Jewish question'.

3 *Sociology and Philosophy*, trans. D.F. Pocock (New York: The Free Press, 1974), p. 69.

4 Ibid., p. 43.

5 In this I agree with the analysis of Henry Allison, *Kant's Theory of Freedom* (Cambridge: Cambridge University Press, 1990), Chs 12 and 13.

6 *Religion within the Limits of Reason Alone*, trans. Theodore M. Greene and Hoyt H. Hudson (New York: Harper and Row, 1960), pp. 17–18n.

7 *Elementary Forms of Religious Life* (New York: The Free Press, 1965), p. 474.

8 *The Division of Labor in Society* (New York: The Free Press, 1933), p. 41.

9 In her 'The discourse ethics of Habermas: critique and appraisal', *Thesis Eleven* 10/11 (1984–5), pp. 11–15, Agnes Heller convincingly argues that Habermas's attempt to claim the cognitive high ground in opposition to Tugendhat's conception of will-formation fails precisely because of the cognitive deficits in Habermas's account. An easy way to see this is to ask: to what extent Habermas's principle U simply amounts to a sophisticated, procedurally oriented collective consequentialism? It is difficult to see how acceptability to all of 'consequences and side effects' can amount to more. Indeed, it is difficult to see that there is more to Habermas's deontological principle than a conjunction of consent theory and the calculation of consequences. And this, to my ear at least, no matter how universalized, does not sound as if it has much to do with *morals*, and restricting that notion of morals to questions of justice does not make it any more plausible. As we shall see in Chapter 6, in a sense Habermas knows this.

10 *The Division of Labor in Society*, op. cit. note 8, p. 240.

11 For Rousseau, without *pitié*, mimetic affinity or affective self-recognition in otherness, there is no morality, only prudential calculations. In the *Geneva Manuscript*, Rousseau responds to the wise man who explains the rational advantages of consent to general laws in these terms:

> I am aware that I bring horror and confusion to the human species, but either I must be unhappy or I must cause others to be so, and no one is dearer to me than myself. I would try in vain to reconcile my interest with that of another man. Everything you tell me about the advantages of the social law would be fine if while I were scrupulously observing it toward others, I were sure that all of them would observe it toward me. But what assurance of this can you give me, and could there be a worse situation for me than to be exposed to all the ills that stronger men would want to cause me without my daring to make up for it against the weak? Furthermore, it will be my business to get the strong on my side, sharing with them the spoils from the weak. This would be better than justice for my own advantage and my security.
>
> (*On the Social Contract: with Geneva Manuscript and Political Economy*, ed. Roger Masters and trans. Judith Masters [New York: St Martin's Press, 1978], p. 160)

12 I take this argument up in *The Ethics of Nonidentity* (forthcoming).

13 I begin a defence of this thesis in my 'Right, revolution and community: Marx's "On the Jewish question"', in Peter Osborne (ed.), *Socialism and the Limits of Liberalism* (London: Verso, 1991), pp. 91–120.

14 'On the Jewish question', in trans. Gregor Benton, *Early Writings* (Harmondsworth: Penguin, 1975), p. 231.

15 The phrase is, of course, Thomas Nagel's, *The View from Nowhere* (Oxford: Oxford University Press, 1986).

16 A rough version of this idea can be found in Albrecht Wellmer, *The Persistence of Modernity*, trans. David Midgley (Cambridge: Polity Press, 1991), p. 226.

NOTES

17 For elaboration see my *The Fate of Art: Aesthetic Alienation from Kant to Derrida and Adorno* (Cambridge: Polity Press, 1992), pp. 57–60.
18 The quoted sentence in this passage is from Andrew Reck (ed.), *George Herbert Mead: Selected Writings* (Chicago: University of Chicago Press, 1964), p. 404.
19 For an analogous account, see Wellmer, op. cit. note 16, pp. 216–21.
20 To my knowledge, the first person to argue convincingly for this way of construing *amour-propre* is N. J. Dent, *Rousseau* (Oxford: Basil Blackwell, 1988), Ch. 2.
21 See Axel Honneth, *Struggles for Recognition* (Cambridge: Polity Press, 1994).
22 Alan Gewirth, *Reason and Morality* (Chicago: University of Chicago Press, 1978).
23 *A Theory of Justice* (Cambridge, MA: Harvard University Press, 1971), §67. For the following quote, p. 441.
24 *Mind, Self, and Society* (Chicago: University of Chicago Press, 1962), p. 199.
25 For more on the logic of innovative performances, see Ch. 7.
26 Wellmer, op. cit. note 16, p. 224.
27 See Stanley Cavell, *Conditions Handsome and Unhandsome* (London: University of Chicago Press, 1990), pp. xxix–xxx, 28–9. I think that this is the way to read what Adorno is doing with his conception of concepts and the preponderance of the object.
28 I am putting aside here Habermas's ongoing debate with Dieter Henrich over whether or not fundamental features of the self are attributable to it independently of socialization.
29 Rawls, op. cit. note 23, p. 422 for this and the following quote.
30 *Being and Time*, trans. John Macquarrie and Edward Robinson (New York: Harper and Row, 1962), §§27, 38, 60; *On Liberty* (Harmondsworth: Penguin Books, 1982), Ch. 3; *Contingency, Irony, and Solidarity* (Cambridge: Cambridge University Press, 1989), Chs 2, 4–6.
31 Harold Bloom, *The Anxiety of Influence* (New York: Oxford University Press, 1973), p. 80.
32 Rorty, op. cit. note 30, pp. 24–5.
33 *Aesthetic Theory*, trans. C. Lenhardt (London: Routledge and Kegan Paul, 1984), pp. 30, 47, 246–7. I comment on this in my *The Fate of Art: Aesthetic Alienation from Kant to Derrida and Adorno* (Cambridge: Polity Press, 1992), pp. 191–2.
34 For this understanding of autonomy I am indebted to the late Deborah Fitzmaurice, 'Autonomy as a good: liberalism, autonomy and toleration', *The Journal of Political Philosophy* 1(1) (1993), pp. 1–16. In this piece she is developing an idea of Joseph Raz's; see note 35 below.
35 *The Morality of Freedom* (Oxford: Clarendon Press, 1986), p. 372.
36 Despite his bluff about an overlapping consensus, it is this idea, which he takes from Humboldt, that is doing the real work in *Political Liberalism* (New York: Columbia University Press, 1993), pp. 319–24. I defend this reading of Rawls in my 'Republican beauty, the democratic sublime', forthcoming.
37 My account here follows that of Deborah Fitzmaurice, 'Liberal neutrality, traditional minorities and education', in John Horton (ed.), *Liberalism, Multiculturalism and Toleration* (London: Macmillan, 1993), pp. 50–69. Part of my point in treating this example is to underwrite the significance and meaning of *free* religious belief in democratic polities, something which Rawls simply takes for granted in *Political Liberalism*.
38 In this I am siding with Thomas McCarthy, 'Practical discourse: on the relation of morality to politics', in *Ideals and Illusions: On Reconstruction and Deconstruction in Contemporary Critical Theory* (London: The MIT Press, 1991), against Habermas, *JA*, pp. 8–90. I disagree with McCarthy in thinking of this problem in terms of value pluralism.

39 See note 13.

5 THE GENERALIZED OTHER, CONCRETE OTHERS

1 Seyla Benhabib, *Critique, Norm, and Utopia* (New York: Columbia University Press, 1986). All unspecified page references in the text are to this book.
2 Habermas, 'Reply to my critics', in J.B. Thompson and D. Held (eds), *Habermas: Critical Debates* (London: The Macmillan Press, 1982), p. 262.
3 See Lionel Trilling's *Sincerity and Authenticity* (London: Oxford University Press, 1974).
4 See Donald Davidson, 'On the very idea of a conceptual scheme', *Proceedings of the American Philosophical Association* 17 (1973–4), pp. 5–20; Richard Rorty, 'The world well lost', in his *Consequences of Pragmatism* (Brighton: Harvester Press, 1982), pp. 3–18. Rorty's free-wheeling, pragmatist Hegelianism does suffer from the sorts of worries about contextualism that are routine in Habermas. In order to circumvent this pragmatist version of objective reason, whose institutional reply to Habermas seems right to me, one would need both something like Hegel's phenomenological narrative of *Geist* and a deeper concern for particular truths. I have had a start on the second half of this project in 'De-divinization and the vindication of everyday life: reply to Rorty', *Tijdschrift voor Filosofie* 54(4) (1992), pp. 668–92.
5 See the item in note 13 to Chapter 4.
6 'Subject and object', in A. Arato and E. Gebhardt (eds), *The Essential Frankfurt School Reader* (Oxford: Basil Blackwell, 1978), pp. 499–500.
7 I am here referring to Hegel's discussion of the 'spiritual animal kingdom'. For a helpful commentary on the issues here, that refers to Habermas along the way, see Robert Pippin, 'You can't get there from here: transition problems in Hegel's *Phenomenology of Spirit*', in Frederick C. Beiser (ed.), *The Cambridge Companion to Hegel* (Cambridge: Cambridge University Press, 1993), pp. 52–85, esp. pp. 72–7.
8 See Mary Hesse, 'Habermas' consensus theory of truth', in her *Revolutions and Reconstructions in the Philosophy of Science* (Brighton: Harvester Press, 1980), pp. 206–31; Alessandro Ferrara, 'A critique of Habermas' consensus theory of truth', *Philosophy & Social Criticism* 13(1) (1987), pp. 39–67.
9 See my *The Fate of Art: Aesthetic Alienation from Kant to Derrida and Adorno* (Cambridge: Polity Press, 1992), pp. 23–9, 55–63.
10 A transformational reading of principle U, along with a tough defence of it, is to be found in William Rehg, 'Discourse and the moral point of view: deriving a dialogical principle of universalization', *Inquiry* 34 (1991), pp. 27–48. Without addressing the details of Rehg's account, I will have to say simply: (i) that the theory is still tied to the problem of order (p. 32) in a way I found objectionable in Chapter 4; (ii) the transformational model Rehg generates cannot be equated with the problem of generalizable need interpretations *as* that would be constituted by the perspective of the concrete other; (iii) the theory still has as its object domain a society beset by real value pluralism (p. 38); (iv) but nonetheless presupposes deep conditions of trust and lifeworld mutualities (p. 42), and even more a deployment of empathy combined with a use of self-presentation in the forwarding of arguments (p. 44). Indeed, the way in which Rehg presents the practice of argumentation seems to me quite like the version of it offered by Kohlberg that Habermas has explicitly rejected in 'Justice and solidarity' (see notes 22 and 24 to the next chapter and the discussions preceding them). In brief, there is a contradiction between the emphasis on the problem of order and the claim for impartiality, the starting point of value pluralism and mutual disinterest, on the one hand, and a procedure that

presupposes lifeworld mutuality, empathy and shared value horizons on the other. But this is not surprising since Rehg wants to claim, I think, a deeper inseparability of justice and solidarity than is compatible with the idea of principle U being quasi-transcendental. After all, if justice and solidarity are *logically* inseparable, if, that is, solidarity provides more than empirical conditions which permit the operation of principle U, then that principle is bound to the ethical identity of its solidaristically bonded bearers. In which case, of course, the whole idea of the bonding occurring through the illocutionary force of speech acts drops out, and the distinction between the illocutionary and perlocutionary lapses, just as Allen Wood has argued that it lapses for the defence of the general theory of communicative rationality (see Chapter 7, note 15).

11 In his 'Truth, semblance, reconciliation: Adorno's aesthetic redemption of modernity', in *The Persistence of Modernity*, trans. David Midgley (Cambridge: Polity Press, 1991), pp. 3–7, Albrecht Wellmer presents a nuanced account of the relationship between art (music) and philosophy, only, without justification, to label their speculative unity elements of a negative theology (p. 7). If philosophy stands to art as concept to intuition, and if indeed concepts without intuitions are empty and intuitions without concepts blind, then our conceptual practices (philosophy) and intuitional practices (art) can only be dirempted if both are significantly deformed. Hence for Adorno the diremption of philosophy and art is equivalent to concrete practices behaving as if we could peel off our conceptual scheme from the world, and conversely what he means by utopia is not far from the thought of social practices that explicitly and fully acknowledge the mutual entwining of conceptual scheme and world, concept and intuition. I urge a version of this via the idea of world-disclosure in Chapter 7. The quasi-theological reading of Adorno blunts his materialism and skews what he means by the 'preponderance of the object'. To shift Adorno's thought from social epistemology, which is what he is always explicitly concerned with, to idiosyncratic utopianism makes nonsense of the bulk of his corpus. I press for an austere reading of Adorno in *The Ethics of Nonidentity* (forthcoming).

6 THE CAUSALITY OF FATE

1 *The Philosophical Discourse of Modernity* (Cambridge: Polity Press, 1987) [*PDM* in Abbreviations]. All unspecified page references in the text are to this work.

2 See, for example, Derrida's 'Signature event context', *Glyph*, Vol. 1 (Baltimore, MD: Johns Hopkins Press, 1977), pp. 172–97.

3 On this see Thomas McCarthy, 'Complexity and democracy, or the seducements of systems theory', *New German Critique* 35 (Spring/Summer 1985), pp. 27–33; and in the same place, Nancy Fraser's 'What is critical about critical theory? The case of Habermas and gender', esp. pp. 103–11.

4 For a summary of these objections see Thomas McCarthy, *The Critical Theory of Jürgen Habermas* (London: Hutcheson, 1978), pp. 101–2, 182–92; and J.B. Thompson and D. Held (eds), *Habermas: Critical Debates* (London: The Macmillan Press, 1982), essays 4, 7, 8.

5 See Foucault's 'What is Enlightenment?', in Paul Rabinow (ed.), *The Foucault Reader* (New York: Pantheon, 1984). Nowhere does Adorno disown the ideals of the Enlightenment.

6 See Thomas McCarthy, 'Reflections on rationalization in the Theory of Communicative Action', *Praxis International* 4(2) (1984), pp. 77–91; D. Ingram, 'Philosophy and the aesthetic mediation of life', *Philosophical Forum* 18(4) (Summer

1987), pp. 329–57; John McCumber, 'Philosophy as the heteronomous center of modern discourse: Jürgen Habermas', in Hugh Silverman (ed.), *Philosophy and Non-Philosophy since Merleau-Ponty* (New York and London: Routledge, 1988), pp. 211–31.

7   On this see my *The Fate of Art: Aesthetic Alienation from Kant to Derrida and Adorno* (Cambridge: Polity Press, 1992), pp. 44–55; and Howard Caygill's indispensable *The Art of Judgement* (Oxford: Blackwell, 1989), Chs 4–5.

8   Habermas takes himself to be arguing against J. Culler here; which leaves the relation between Culler's position and Derrida's moot.

9   This is nearly the central theme of Rudolphe Gasché's *The Tain of the Mirror* (Cambridge, MA and London: Harvard University Press, 1986).

10 On Foucault's trajectory see John Rajchman's 'Foucault, or the ends of modernism', *October* 24 (Spring) 1983, pp. 37–62. My quote is from p. 51.

11 Kai Nielsen, 'Rationality and relativism', *Philosophy of the Social Sciences* 4 (1974), p. 320.

12 I. Kant, *The Critique of Judgement*, trans. J.C. Meredith (Oxford: Clarendon Press, 1952), p. 314.

13 For a comparable account of Foucault's practice of writing see Charles Scott's *The Language of Difference* (Atlantic Highlands, NJ: Humanities Press, 1987), pp. 89–119.

14 Or immortality. The point at issue here is the relation between traditional philosophical ambitions and human finitude. How are we to keep doing philosophy, whose project has depended upon its departure (either directly as in Plato, or analytically as in Kantianism) from the empirical, from the world of life and death, and keep our inquiry immanent? Fallibilism is indeed a 'trivial' acknowledgement of finitude and mortality.

15 See, for example, 'Philosophy as stand-in and interpreter', in K. Baynes, J. Bohman and T. McCarthy (eds), *After Philosophy* (Cambridge, MA and London: The MIT Press, 1987), pp. 298–9; and *The Theory of Communicative Action*, Vol. I, pp. 140–1, 233–42. My *The Philosophy of the Novel: Lukács, Marxism and the Dialectics of Form* (Minneapolis, MN: University of Minnesota Press, 1984), attempts an indirect demonstration of this thesis.

16 'Questions and counterquestions', in R.J. Bernstein (ed.), *Habermas and Modernity* (Cambridge: Polity Press, 1985), pp. 202–3.

17 'Philosophy as stand-in and interpreter', op. cit. note 15, pp. 312–13.

18 Nancy Fraser, 'What is critical about critical theory?', op. cit. note 3, pp. 102–3.

19 Habermas is quoting from K. Heinrich, *Versuch über die Schwierigkeit nein zu sagen* (Frankfurt: Suhrkamp, 1964), p. 20.

20 'Normatively grounding "critical theory" through recourse to the lifeworld?', in Axel Honneth, et al. (eds), *Philosophical Interventions in the Unfinished Project of Enlightenment* (London and Cambridge, MA: The MIT Press, 1992), p. 132.

21 For this objection to Apel see Albrecht Wellmer, *The Persistence of Modernity*, trans. David Midgley (Cambridge: Polity Press, 1991), pp. 174–82.

22 'Justice and solidarity: on the discussion concerning "Stage 6" ', in Michael Kelly (ed.), *Hermeneutics and Critical Theory in Ethics and Politics* (London and Cambridge, MA: The MIT Press, 1990), p. 48.

23 Seyla Benhabib, *Situating the Self* (Cambridge: Polity Press, 1992), pp. 36–7.

24 Although I agree with Habermas that Kohlberg's revision of the theory in which justice and benevolence are conceived of, quite Kantianly, as the two fundamental expressions of the principle of equal respect fails, Habermas is too hasty in damning Kohlberg's considerations of dialogue as psychological. It is the austerity of communicative rationality itself which transforms Kohlberg's account into group dynamics, and as a consequence finds nothing in his attempt to make benevolence

co-equal with justice. See 'Justice and solidarity', op. cit. note 22, pp. 38–40, 44–5.

25 The theory of substantive universals employed here is Marcuse's: *One-Dimensional Man* (Boston, MA: Beacon Press, 1964), pp. 105–6. For an elaboration see Andrew Feenberg, 'The bias of technology', in R. Pippin, A. Feenberg, C.D. Webel and contributors, *Marcuse: Critical Theory and the Promise of Utopia* (London: Macmillan, 1988), pp. 244–8.

26 Again, see Nancy Fraser, op. cit. note 18, pp. 128–9.

27 *Strukturwandel der Öffentlichkeit* (Neuwied: Luchterhand Verlag, 1962).

7 LANGUAGE, WORLD-DISCLOSURE AND JUDGMENT

1 See also Habermas's engagement with the Budapest version of the philosophy of praxis in the 'Excursus' following Lecture III.

2 For a clear account of a liberal Marxism inspired by Rawls, see R.G. Peffer's *Marxism, Morality and Social Justice* (Princeton, NJ: Princeton University Press, 1990).

3 'Modernity as project and field of tensions', in Axel Honneth and Hans Joas (eds), *Communicative Action* (Cambridge: Polity Press, 1991), p. 210.

4 Habermas's final criticism of Castoriadis (*PDM*, 333–5) concerns his analysis of the mediation between individual and society.

5 See Thomas McCarthy, 'Reflections on rationalization in the *Theory of Communicative Action*', in R.J. Bernstein (ed.), *Habermas and Modernity* (Cambridge: Polity Press, 1985), p. 188.

6 See, for example, D. Ingram, 'Philosophy and the aesthetic mediation of life', *Philosophic Forum* 18(4) (Summer 1987), pp. 329–57; and John McCumber, 'Philosophy as the heteronomous center of modern discourse: Jürgen Habermas', in Hugh Silverman (ed.), *Philosophy and Non-Philosophy since Merleau-Ponty* (New York and London: Routledge, 1988), pp. 211–31.

7 See Habermas's 'Questions and counterquestions', in R.J. Berstein (ed.), op. cit. note 5, p. 203.

8 *Critique of Judgment*, trans. James Meredith (Oxford: Clarendon Press, 1952), §. 46, p. 308.

9 'Language and society', in Honneth and Joas (eds), op. cit. note 3, p. 31.

10 For a fuller account of what lies behind these brief thoughts see Stanley Cavell, *Must We Mean What We Say?* (Cambridge: Cambridge University Press, 1976), pp. 18–21. For a somewhat different account of the question of meaning and validity offered here see Rudi Visker, 'Habermas on Heidegger and Foucault: meaning and validity in *The Philosophical Discourse of Modernity*', *Radical Philosophy* 61 (1992), pp. 15–22.

11 Ibid., p. 94. See also Stephen Mulhall's telling elaboration of this point in his *Stanley Cavell: Philosophy's Recounting of the Ordinary* (Oxford: Oxford University Press, 1993), pp. 26–30.

12 Klaus Günther, *Der Sinn für Angemessenheit* (Frankfurt: Suhrkamp, 1988), pp. 23–100. Throughout I will follow Habermas's appropriation of Günther. For an earlier account criticizing Habermas for lacking an adequate appreciation of the problem of judgment see Herbert Schnädelbach's illuminating 'Remarks about rationality and language', in Seyla Benhabib and Fred Dallmayr (eds), *The Communicative Ethics Controversy* (London: The MIT Press, 1990), pp. 270–92.

13 Ibid., p. 53; quoted in *JA*, p. 37.

14 This is, in fact, a distortion. In *The Ethics of Nonidentity* (forthcoming) I argue that

moral norms as such are neither valid nor invalid; rather, moral judgments are true or false. The point of the comment in the text is to press against the quite wrong-headed notion of prima facie validity, which begs all the deep questions without obligation. The way around the matter is to suggest that obligations are absolute but indexed to situations.

15 'Ein normativer Begriff der Kohärenz für eine Theorie der juristischen Argumentation', *Rechtstheorie* 20 (1989), p. 182; quoted in *JA*, p. 39.

16 Klaus Günther, 'Habermas' defense of rationalism', *New German Critique* 35 (1985), pp. 145–64.

17 For Seel see his 'The two meanings of "communicative" rationality: remarks on Habermas's critique of a plural concept of reason', in Honneth and Joas (eds), op. cit. note 3, pp. 36–48.

INDEX